AF823062

Women's Reproductive and Sexual Health

Edited by
Kristina S. Brown

Routledge
Taylor & Francis Group
LONDON AND NEW YORK

First published 2024
by Routledge
4 Park Square, Milton Park, Abingdon, Oxon, OX14 4RN

and by Routledge
605 Third Avenue, New York, NY 10158

Routledge is an imprint of the Taylor & Francis Group, an informa business

© 2025 Taylor & Francis

All rights reserved. No part of this book may be reprinted or reproduced or utilised in any form or by any electronic, mechanical, or other means, now known or hereafter invented, including photocopying and recording, or in any information storage or retrieval system, without permission in writing from the publishers.

Trademark notice: Product or corporate names may be trademarks or registered trademarks, and are used only for identification and explanation without intent to infringe.

British Library Cataloguing-in-Publication Data
A catalogue record for this book is available from the British Library

ISBN13: 978-1-032-71848-4 (hbk)
ISBN13: 978-1-032-71851-4 (pbk)
ISBN13: 978-1-032-71853-8 (ebk)

DOI: 10.4324/9781032718538

Typeset in Minion Pro
by codeMantra

Publisher's Note
The publisher accepts responsibility for any inconsistencies that may have arisen during the conversion of this book from journal articles to book chapters, namely the inclusion of journal terminology.

Disclaimer
Every effort has been made to contact copyright holders for their permission to reprint material in this book. The publishers would be grateful to hear from any copyright holder who is not here acknowledged and will undertake to rectify any errors or omissions in future editions of this book.

Women's Reproductive and Sexual Health

Edited by
Kristina S. Brown

Routledge
Taylor & Francis Group
LONDON AND NEW YORK

First published 2024
by Routledge
4 Park Square, Milton Park, Abingdon, Oxon, OX14 4RN

and by Routledge
605 Third Avenue, New York, NY 10158

Routledge is an imprint of the Taylor & Francis Group, an informa business

© 2025 Taylor & Francis

All rights reserved. No part of this book may be reprinted or reproduced or utilised in any form or by any electronic, mechanical, or other means, now known or hereafter invented, including photocopying and recording, or in any information storage or retrieval system, without permission in writing from the publishers.

Trademark notice: Product or corporate names may be trademarks or registered trademarks, and are used only for identification and explanation without intent to infringe.

British Library Cataloguing-in-Publication Data
A catalogue record for this book is available from the British Library

ISBN13: 978-1-032-71848-4 (hbk)
ISBN13: 978-1-032-71851-4 (pbk)
ISBN13: 978-1-032-71853-8 (ebk)

DOI: 10.4324/9781032718538

Typeset in Minion Pro
by codeMantra

Publisher's Note
The publisher accepts responsibility for any inconsistencies that may have arisen during the conversion of this book from journal articles to book chapters, namely the inclusion of journal terminology.

Disclaimer
Every effort has been made to contact copyright holders for their permission to reprint material in this book. The publishers would be grateful to hear from any copyright holder who is not here acknowledged and will undertake to rectify any errors or omissions in future editions of this book.

Women's Reproductive and Sexual Health

This book offers a groundbreaking exploration of women's health through a feminist lens, challenging the status quo for both clinicians and medical providers, highlighting the critical need for a more inclusive and empathetic approach to clinical practice and mental health research.

Addressing a spectrum of health concerns—from prevalent issues such as heart disease, cancer, and stroke as leading causes of death for women to conditions uniquely affecting biological women such as pregnancy, menopause, miscarriage, abortion, polycystic ovary syndrome, and endometriosis—the chapters in this volume examine how these challenges intersect with gendered experiences. It critically assesses the gaps in current healthcare practices, including the often-overlooked impact on couples and families, and exposes the disparities faced by transgender women, non-binary, and gender non-conforming individuals. By incorporating the latest literature and research on reproductive and sexual health, this volume challenges traditional paradigms and gives voice to experiences that are often silenced.

This book will serve as a crucial resource for students, clinicians, researchers, and advocates committed to advancing women's health through a more equitable and intersectional framework.

The chapters in this book were originally published in the *Journal of Feminist Family Therapy.*

Kristina S. Brown, PhD, LMFT, is Professor and Chair of the Couple and Family Therapy at Adler University, Chicago, USA. She is Editor-in-Chief of the *Journal of Feminist Family Therapy* and Editor of the new *AAMFT Systemic Ethics Textbook.* Dr Brown is a feminist qualitative researcher with a broad focus on the experiences of women across identities as represented in her scholarly work. She lives in her "empty nest" in the Chicago Loop with her husband of 30 years and their two polydactyl cats, Cameron and Ferris.

Feminist Family Therapy

The books in this series delve into the intersections of gender, power, and culture, providing innovative therapeutic approaches that challenge traditional narratives. The *Feminist Family Therapy* book series contains a wide range of the journal's special issues and features contributions from leading experts in the field. The series addresses diverse family structures and experiences, promoting empowerment and social justice. The books in this series are ideal for practitioners, scholars, and students and they serve as essential resources for anyone seeking to understand and transform the complexities of family life in modern society.

Recent books in the series include

Women's Reproductive and Sexual Health
Edited by Kristina Brown

Women's Health
Gender and Pain
Edited by Kristina Brown

Contents

Citation Information

The following chapters in this book were originally published in the *Journal of Feminist Family Therapy*, volume 32, issue 1–2 (2020). When citing this material, please use the original page numbering for each article, as follows:

Introduction
Women's Health: Reproductive Health and Sexual Health
Kristina S. Brown
Journal of Feminist Family Therapy, volume 32, issue 1–2 (2020), pp. 1–4

Chapter 1
Fatness and Fertility: A Feminist Therapist Perspective
Heidi L. Henry and Sarah E. Walters
Journal of Feminist Family Therapy, volume 32, issue 1–2 (2020), pp. 5–18

Chapter 2
Female Partner Family Formation: Cultivating Love and Healing Disconnection
Jessica Danielson, Jodi Tangen and Jill Nelson
Journal of Feminist Family Therapy, volume 32, issue 1–2 (2020), pp. 19–37

Chapter 3
Use of the VeedaMom Electronic App as a Pregnancy Treatment Companion
Adriana Dyurich and Marvarene Oliver
Journal of Feminist Family Therapy, volume 32, issue 1–2 (2020), pp. 38–56

Chapter 4
"A Silent Battle": Using a Feminist Approach to Support Couples after Miscarriage
Angela R. Hiefner
Journal of Feminist Family Therapy, volume 32, issue 1–2 (2020), pp. 57–75

Chapter 5
Latina Sexual Health Care (IN) the US: Community-based Participatory Research and Her Lived Experience
Angela L. Lamson, Rebekah J. Clark, Roberta W. Bellamy, Jennifer Hodgson, Sharon M. Knight, Eboni J. Baugh and Jasmine Flores
Journal of Feminist Family Therapy, volume 32, issue 1–2 (2020), pp. 76–96

Chapter 6

Sexual Health of Women with Obesity: A Review of the Literature
Özlem Köse, Jennifer Hodgson and Karlene Cunningham
Journal of Feminist Family Therapy, volume 32, issue 1–2 (2020), pp. 97–114

Chapter 7

Impact of Sexual and Interpersonal Violence and Trauma on Women: Trauma-Informed Practice and Feminist Theory
Jennifer V. Pemberton and Tamra B. Loeb
Journal of Feminist Family Therapy, volume 32, issue 1–2 (2020), pp. 115–131

Chapter 8

Exploring the Link between Autoimmune Disorders and Pain with Sexual Activity in Ova-Having Individuals
Karen Washington and Helen Wyatt
Journal of Feminist Family Therapy, volume 32, issue 1–2 (2020), pp. 135–151

Chapter 9

Invisible Loss: A Delphi Approach to Develop a Term for Individuals Who Experienced Perinatal Loss
Rachel Diamond, Jessica L. Chou and Susan Bonis
Journal of Feminist Family Therapy, volume 33, issue 1 (2021), pp. 81–100

For any permission-related enquiries please visit:
http://www.tandfonline.com/page/help/permissions

Notes on Contributors

Eboni J. Baugh, College of Health and Human Performance, East Carolina University, Greenville, USA.

Roberta W. Bellamy, Medical Family Therapist, East Carolina University, Greenville, USA.

Susan Bonis, College of Nursing, University of Wisconsin-Milwaukee, Chicago, IL, USA

Kristina S. Brown, Couple and Family Therapy, Adler University, Chicago, USA.

Jessica L. Chou, Department of Counseling and Family Therapy, Drexel University, Philadelphia, PA, USA

Rebekah J. Clark, College of Health and Human Performance, East Carolina University, Greenville, USA.

Karlene Cunningham, Department of Psychiatry and Behavioral Medicine, East Carolina University, Greenville, USA.

Jessica Danielson, Psychology and Counselor Education, North Dakota State University, Fargo, USA.

Rachel Diamond, Couple and Family Therapy, Adler University, Chicago, IL, USA

Adriana Dyurich, Long School of Medicine, University of Texas Health San Antonio, USA.

Jasmine Flores, East Carolina University, Greenville, USA.

Heidi L. Henry, St. Bonaventure University, USA.

Angela R. Hiefner, Family and Community Medicine, University of Texas Southwestern Medical Center, Dallas, USA.

Jennifer Hodgson, College of Health and Human Performance, East Carolina University, Greenville, USA.

Sharon M. Knight, College of Health and Human Performance, East Carolina University, Greenville, USA.

Özlem Köse, Couple and Family Therapy Montreal, Canada.

Angela L. Lamson, College of Health and Human Performance, East Carolina University, Greenville, USA.

Tamra B. Loeb, Department of Psychiatry and Biobehavioral Sciences, University of California, Los Angeles, USA.

Jill Nelson, Counselor Education, North Dakota State University, Fargo, USA.

Marvarene Oliver, Department of Counseling and Educational Psychology, Texas A&M Corpus Christi, USA.

Jennifer V. Pemberton, Department of Educational Psychology and Counseling, California State University Northridge, USA.

Jodi Tangen, Counselor Education, North Dakota State University, Fargo, USA.

Sarah E. Walters, Department of Counselor Education, Robert Morris University, USA.

Karen Washington, Couple and Family Therapy, Adler University, Chicago, IL, USA

Helen Wyatt, Couple and Family Therapy, Adler University, Chicago, IL, USA

Introduction: Women's Health: Reproductive Health and Sexual Health

Kristina S. Brown

The Centers for Disease Control and Prevention (2017) estimates that 13.4% of women over the age of 18 are in "fair or poor health" according to the Summary Health Statistics: National Health Interview Survey (https://www.cdc.gov/nchs/fastats/womens-health.htm). Drug and alcohol use, lack of physical activity, smoking, obesity, and hypertension were some of the cited issues of specific concern with leading causes of death for women being heart disease, cancer, and stroke. In addition to these general issues of health, there are diseases and conditions that predominantly (or only) present in biological women. The US Department of Health and Human Services describes gendered issues such as pregnancy and menopause to gynecological conditions including, for example, menstrual irregularities, urinary tract health, miscarriage, abortion, and breastfeeding as well as disorders related to infertility including polycystic ovary syndrome and endometriosis. The medical care provided for these varieties of health issues – both common and unique to women – often does not address the impact on the couple and family. Additionally, sexual and gender identity often exacerbate obstacles to care. Research on women's health issues frequently exclude experiences of transgender women, non-binary, or gender non-conforming identities. Access issues to both health insurance and actual care are rampant including access to mental health care.

This special call for submissions focused on all women's health presentations including physiological and mental changes across the lifespan highlighting the mental health perspective and experience of the patient/client and the systems in which they exist including clinical application that applies feminist approaches for treatment. In response to the call, we received an abundance of manuscripts – so many voices who have something to say. As a result, we were able create a full volume including four separate issues gathering articles around different areas of women's health. This first double issue is on reproductive health and sexual health.

Reproductive health

The first two articles – "Fatness and Fertility: A Feminist Therapist Perspective" by Heidi L. Henry and Sarah E. Walters and "Female Partner Family Formation: A Rollercoaster Ride of Cultivating Love and Healing Disconnection" by Jessica Danielson, Jodi Tagen, and Jill Nelson – focus on different perspectives around fertility. Henry and Walters explore the discriminatory experiences of fat women around their fertility finding that it is often more stigma-based then due to health status. Providing the reader with information on stigma in the media and healthcare as well as the intersecting impact of fatness and infertility on self and relationships, the authors lay the groundwork for the fit of the feminist family therapist to work with this population. Henry and Walters highlight the feminist tenet of empowerment to combat the shame, guilt, and stigma while also acknowledging the importance of advocacy within the healthcare system. In the second article, Danielson et al. describes the experiences of female partners receiving third-party fertility treatments utilizing interpretative phenomenological analysis. Through a feminist informed used of relational-cultural theory, superordinate themes around love and disconnection emerged driving the focus of findings. Couple participants provided their firsthand experiences of the impact of disconnection, e.g., minority stress, and love confirming the literature. The authors utilized their unique approach to provide implications for feminist therapists to support family formation with female partners.

During pregnancy, women seek and receive support in multiple ways attending to their physical and emotional needs. In the article, "Use of The Veedamom Electronic App as a Pregnancy Treatment Companion," Adriana Dyurich and Marvarene Oliver share their phenomenological findings on firsthand experiences of a new electronic intervention specifically designed (and co-created by the first author) to monitor risk factors for perinatal depression. Included in the app are features to both help screen for depression including the Edinburgh Depression Scale, and interventions to manage symptoms with psychoeducational videos and audio mindfulness exercises as well as an in-app journal.

Finally, we would be remiss in an issue on reproductive health, if we did not address miscarriage. Angela Hiefner in her article, "'A silent battle': Using a feminist approach to support couples after Miscarriage," focuses on the emerged themes of disenfranchisement and the norm of silence surrounding early pregnancy loss in her interviews. Though this article is for the feminist family therapist and the ways in which they are called to collaborate with the couple and deconstruct dominant discourse around miscarriage, Hiefner also highlights the need for shifts in the way medical providers intervene. This is especially important as they may unintentionally minimize the couple's loss.

Sexual health

Though specific exploration around sexual health (issues) in women often prioritizes reproduction and ignores risk factors to pleasure and sexual well-being, this double issue also focuses on the sexual health of (biological) women. In the first article, Angela L. Lamson and Rebekah J. Clark and colleagues looked at "Latina Sexual Healthcare in The Us: Community-Based Participatory Research and Her Lived Experience." From Latina immigrants' perspectives, the authors explore their experiences of seeking sexual health care from US providers in the face of common health disparities including lack of access and language barriers. Themes such as communication and stigma are highlighted to provide a recommended framework of healthcare incorporating *peronsalismo, familismo*, and the feminist lens.

Comorbid health issues can intersect the sexual health of biological women as presented in the following two articles, "Sexual Health of Women with Obesity: A Review of the Literature" by Özlem Köse, Jennifer Hodgson, and S. Karlene Cunningham and "Exploring the Link Between Autoimmune Disorders and Pain with Sexual Activity in Ova-Having Individuals" by Karen Washington and Helen Wyatt. Köse and colleagues reviewed 63 studies that met inclusion criteria of intersections between sexual functioning and obesity in women, determining that biological and psychological factors were two main themes that emerged across the literature. Their review provides recommendations utilizing a biopsychosocial health perspective both for clinical implications as well as for recommendations regarding the gaps in the literature. For ova-having individuals, a more inclusive term, Washington and Wyatt propose a link between sexual dysfunction and autoimmune disorders. Supported by the literature, the authors recommend clinicians to focus on the comorbidity especially attending to sexual pain as these presenting complaints are often ignored or not prioritized in treatment. Medical family therapists utilizing a feminist lens are positioned to best support ova-having individuals presenting with these overlapping complaints.

The next article in this double issue is "The Impact of Sexual and Interpersonal Violence and Trauma on Women's Health: Trauma-Informed Practice and Feminist Theory" by Jennifer V. Pemberton and Tamra B. Loeb. Using parallels between Substance Abuse and Mental Health Services Information (SAMSHA) principles for trauma-informed care and feminist theory, the authors present the physical, sexual, and mental health impact of violence and trauma for women. Comprehensive care is recommended in consideration of both health disparities of gender and the intersectionality of race. Pemberton and Loeb highlight the necessity for future research specifically on the disproportionate lack of diversity in the literature to positively impact the therapeutic relationship bringing victim to survivor status.

Two additional chapters round out this collection. The first, "Exploring the Link between Autoimmune Disorders and Pain with Sexual Activity in Ova-Having Individuals" by Karen Washington and Helen Wyatt, describes the connection of these two diagnoses providing clinical implication to improve care. Research across medical and sexual health fields are brought together to better understand the bidirectionality of the mind-body connection. Rachel Diamond, Jessica Chou, and Susan Bonis did a Delphi pilot study, "Invisible Loss: A Delphi Approach to Develop a Term for Individuals Who Experienced Perinatal" seeking the expertise from perinatal loss professionals and perinatally bereaved parents to determine a shared term to describe the experience. Both parents and professionals agreed not only on the importance to developing terminology, but also on the term, "bereaved parent."

We invite you to look forward to future issues, which will include additional articles focused on a variety of intersections of gender and health and on women's experiences of cancer. By viewing women's health through a feminist lens, these articles give voice to experiences that are often silenced challenging the status quo in both clinicians and medical providers, as well as a charge to the field to carry-on with inclusive research.

Fatness and Fertility: A Feminist Therapist Perspective

Heidi L. Henry and Sarah E. Walters

ABSTRACT

Fat women experiencing infertility are often stigmatized; they are told by doctors that their fatness is to blame for their trouble conceiving and are refused medical treatment. However, researchers are finding that the evidence for refusing such treatments may be based more on stigma than science. Because fat women experiencing infertility often feel disempowered, using feminist family therapy to help fat women and their partners is explored as a beneficial approach for treatment. This paper will address the many issues fat women with infertility face and the resulting implications for feminist family therapists.

Fat women experience a variety of issues in White European society where thinness is viewed as ideal and attractive. They are viewed as an epidemic and as unhealthy, lazy, and unattractive (e.g., Johnstone & Grant, 2019). These perceptions are intensified through stigmatizing images in the media (Fraser et al., 2010) which impacts the way fat women are treated by doctors (Davis & Bowman, 2015). Doctors may possess negative attitudes toward fatness and this can potentially impact the quality of care that fat women receive (American Psychological Association [APA], 2017; Lee & Pausé, 2016). For fat women experiencing infertility issues, this stigma is intensified and they may either be refused treatment, such as in vitro fertilization (IVF), or told to lose weight before anything can be done to help them with their fertility issues (Sole-Smith, 2019).

Infertility, i.e. the inability to get pregnant in sexually active couples who are not using contraception and are trying to get pregnant for at least one year (Cedars & Jaffe, 2005), not only impacts the woman, but can also impact a couple's sexual satisfaction, levels of stress, and mental health (Berger et al., 2013; Bhat & Byatt, 2016; Greil et al., 2010). Treating fat women dealing with fertility issues and their partners from a feminist family therapy perspective can help empower women coping with infertility (Parry, 2005). The purpose of this article is to address the issues fat women dealing with infertility experience and to discuss the implications for feminist family therapists when treating this population.

Obesity in Women

Obesity is defined as having an excessive amount of body fat that may negatively affect an individual's health, and it is often classified according to body mass index (BMI) as recommended by the World Health Organization (WHO; Haththotuwa et al., 2013). An individual with a BMI greater than or equal to 25 km/m2 is considered overweight, an individual with a BMI greater than or equal to 30 km/m2 is considered obese, and at 40 km/m2 individuals are considered morbidly obese. If co-morbid disorders are present at 35 km/m2, such as hypertension or diabetes, then those individuals are also considered morbidly obese (Yazdani et al., 2019).

In 2016, approximately 1.9 billion adults were overweight, 40% of which were women, i.e. female sex assigned at birth (World Health Organization [WHO], 2018). From 2013 to 2016, Hales et al. (2018) found that 40.8% of women aged 18 and older in the United States were obese. More women (40.8%) than men, i.e. male sex assigned at birth, (36.5%) were obese and more women (9.8%) than men (5.5%) were morbidly obese (Hales et al., 2018). Additionally, many racial and ethnic minority groups experience disproportionately higher rates of being overweight and obese than White individuals in the United States, including Hispanic individuals and non-Hispanic Black individuals (Ogden et al., 2006).

Although obesity in men can negatively affect men's health, women experience comorbid conditions specific to their sex, including infertility, ammenhoria, urinary incontinence, and an increased risk for endometrial, cervical, breast, and ovarian cancer (e.g., Frisco & Weden, 2013). Clinical research also shows that obesity can lead to disease-induced sterility, further impacting a woman's fertility by way of an increased risk of ovulation failure and other medical conditions such as polycystic ovary syndrome (PCOS; Frisco & Weden, 2013). PCOS is one of the most common endocrine system disorders in women, causing both insulin resistance and hypoandrogenism (Joham et al., 2015). Additionally, women who are diagnosed with PCOS are also more likely to struggle with obesity and infertility (Joham et al., 2015).

Weight stigma, bias, and discrimination of fat women

In addition to the medical conditions experienced, obese women face many social and cultural issues. To begin, the word obesity is often paired with the word epidemic, which leads to an association between the words (Monaghan, 2005). Analyzing the discourse surrounding obesity as an epidemic, Fraser et al. (2010) argued that the word epidemic is associated with an emotional response, and those emotions may be hindering the subjectivity of how researchers and medical professionals approach the study of obesity. In turn, the medical community and media who equate fatness with obesity and epidemic are further contributing to the stigmatization of fat women (e.g., Gailey & Harjunen, 2019).

Because there are many negative connotations related to the words obesity and epidemic, we will elect to use the words and phrases fat, fatness, or women of size in replace of the word obese. In this article, we will use obese only when referring to medically related literature or definitions such as BMI. In recent years, many women of size are reclaiming the word fat because it is simply an adjective describing one's physicality, similar to the reclaiming of the word queer for those identifying as LGBT (Corner, 2019). Reclaiming the word and referring to oneself as fat is being viewed as a way to liberate fat women from what has become a pejorative term (Corner, 2019).

Being viewed as an epidemic has led women of size to experience many social and cultural issues, including but not limited to weight stigma, weight bias, and discrimination (Olson et al., 2019). Weight stigma, or weight bias, further impacts fat persons because of the negative experiences or discrimination received because they are fat. Fat women may be simultaneously dismissed because of their size while also being subjects of intense scrutiny, a term referred to by Gailey and Harjunen (2019) as hyper(in)visibility. This hyper(in)visibility means that fat women's needs and desires are ignored, yet their bodies are continuously and publicly judged. "Fat presents an apparent paradox because it is both visible and dissected publicly – it is hypervisible – and it is marginalized, neglected, and erased – it is hyperinvisible" (Gailey & Harjunen, 2019, p. 379).

Weight stigma can be internalized, producing significant physical and emotional consequences for people of size. Internalized weight stigma has been associated with higher levels of physical pain and increased food consumption (Olson et al., 2019; Puhl et al., 2018). Depression, low self-esteem, and body dissatisfaction have also been linked to internalized weight stigma and discrimination (e.g., Puhl et al., 2018). Gailey and Harjunen (2019) analyzed in-depth interviews and autobiographical accounts of fat women and found that participants had internalized feelings of self-hatred because they were fat. Additionally, Himmelstein et al. (2017) found that women were more likely than men to internalize weight stigma, and White men and women reported higher levels of internalized weight bias than Black men and women.

Stigma and the media

Hypervisibility, the public scrutiny that fat women experience, and internalized weight stigma are exacerbated by media in a variety of ways. The media perpetuates the stigmatizing discourse surrounding fatness (Fraser et al., 2010). The media's social and political commentary on obesity has created moral panic (Campos et al., 2006). Campos et al. (2006) argue that this commentary has led to an exaggeration of health risks related to obesity and an increase in stigmatization by treating weight gain as an imminent disaster.

In addition to the negative discourse displayed in the media, the stigmatization of people of size is perpetuated by the images used in antiobesity campaigns (Johnstone & Grant, 2019) and weight-biased media (Savoy & Boxer, 2020). Fat individuals are often portrayed as lazy, unattractive, unhealthy, and stupid in antiobesity campaigns (e.g., Johnstone & Grant, 2019). Davis and Bowman (2015) conducted a qualitative study and found that participants reported that the media often sends messages that "thin is good and fat is bad," further increasing the stigmatization experienced by people of size (p. 277).

Media also impacts opinions regarding infertility treatment for fat women. Women and men in the general public were asked in a survey to rate their support for denying obese women infertility treatment (Brochu et al., 2014). They were provided with the same report about denying fertility treatment to fat women but some of the reports were accompanied by stigmatizing, nonstigmatizing, or no images. Participants who read the report that was accompanied by a stigmatizing image were more likely to support the denial of fertility treatment for obese women (Brochu et al., 2014).

Stigma in healthcare

Stigma of fat persons has permeated healthcare. When seeking medical treatment, individuals have reported that doctors focused primarily on weight rather than the presenting issues, even stating that doctors were "unsupportive and unhelpful" (Davis & Bowman, 2015, p. 277). Gina Balzano, a self-identified fat woman struggling to conceive, shared her story regarding this experience with the New York Times (Sole-Smith, 2019). Balzano (as cited in Sole-Smith, 2019) told the New York Times that even though she did not have any weight-related health conditions, such as high blood pressure, cholesterol, or diabetes, her doctor automatically blamed her inability to get pregnant on her weight. Balzano stated that her doctor told her, "I would never give you I.V.F. You're too fat. Have more sex and lose the weight" (Sole-Smith, 2019, para. 5).

Black women, Latina women, American Indian/Alaskan Native women, sexual minorities, and transgender and gender non-conforming (GNC) individuals are even more likely to experience adverse healthcare treatment, especially when it comes to using medical assistance to conceive (Blanchfield & Patterson, 2015; Eichelberger et al., 2016; Gonzales & Henning-Smith, 2017; Janitz et al., 2019). Specifically related to infertility treatment, many minority populations are less likely to seek medical treatment for infertility issues. Blanchfield and Patterson (2015) found that White women were twice as likely to receive medical assistance to become pregnant than nonwhite and sexual minority women. In another study, American Indian/Alaskan Native and Black women were less likely to use medical assistance to get pregnant than White and Hispanic women (Janitz et al., 2019).

Overall, Black, American Indian/Alaskan Native, lesbian, and bisexual women and transgender individuals are less likely to seek medical assistance to get pregnant than White and Hispanic women, and this is partially due to insurance coverage. Blanchfield and Patterson (2015) found that insurance coverage partially mediated the discrepancy between nonwhite and sexual minority (lesbian and bisexual) women when seeking medical assistance for infertility. Additionally, Gonzales and Henning-Smith (2017) found that transgender women were less likely to have health insurance coverage than cisgender women, and transgender men were less likely to have health insurance coverage than cisgender men (Gonzales & Henning-Smith, 2017). Regarding infertility, Eichelberger et al. (2016) reported that Black women were twice as likely to experience infertility as White women when controlling for SES, pregnancy intentions, and infertility risk factors. Eichelberger et al. (2016) also reported that Black women are less likely to get pregnant than White women even when given equal access to IVF.

Fatness' and infertility's impact on self and relationships

Fat women and women dealing with infertility issues experience a variety of emotional and psychological issues. Being fat or unable to conceive can also impact relationships. The research is mixed on how fatness impacts relationship satisfaction, sexual behaviors, and sexual satisfaction. Some researchers have found that being fat is associated with less sexual functioning (Costa & Brody, 2014), while other researchers have found that BMI has no relationship to sexual behavior (e.g., Satinsky et al., 2012). Costa and Brody (2014) found that sexual and relationship satisfaction were directly related to penile-vaginal intercourse, making the argument that fat women experience less frequencies of orgasms from vaginal intercourse; therefore, their relationship and sexual satisfaction will be less than thinner women who experience vaginal orgasms more frequently. Additionally, findings were similar in a Canadian sample of women, where fatter women had less positive affective body image and poorer body image related to sexual encounters (Milhausen et al., 2015). Milhausen et al. (2015) also found that as body fat increased, sexual functioning decreased.

One critique of Brody and Costa's (2009) hypothesis is that fatter women are seen as less attractive in European-dominated societies and attractiveness has been linked to more frequent sexual experience (Perilloux et al., 2013). Thinner women are viewed as more attractive and therefore, may be more sexually experienced. Having more experience may teach thinner women what they prefer in the bedroom, and they can then inform their partners about their sexual preferences, which would increase sexual frequency and satisfaction.

Another critique is that fat women may internalize the stigma and negative views of their bodies and these negative views, rather than body fat, are what impact sexual behavior. Being fat has been associated with lower affective and sexual-encounter body image (Milhausen et al., 2015). Having less appreciation for one's own body has been shown to result in less arousal, orgasms, and sexual satisfaction, rather than BMI alone (Satinsky et al., 2012). Women who demonstrated more body appreciation reported greater satisfying sexual experiences (Gailey, 2015). Based on these findings, body appreciation and body image seem to have a greater impact on sexual satisfaction than body fat.

Feminist perspective on fatness and fertility

The issues faced by fat women and those dealing with infertility may be best approached from a feminist perspective. Fatness is a feminist issue because "fat stigma is recognised as having an impact on the lives of all women and is symptomatic of the unequal burden placed on women to accrue 'erotic capital' in patriarchal, capitalist societies" (Simic, 2015, p. 30). The injustices that fat women encounter are based in oppressive, cultural roots and power imbalances. Additionally, the negative impact of fat stigma is experienced more greatly by women than by men. The injustices encountered by fat women when being treated for infertility further substantiate the rationale to view this issue from a feminist perspective (Brown, 2019).

Simic (2015) argues that feminist activism has much left to accomplish in terms of fat activism. Diet culture and fatphobia remain most prevalent in societies where feminism has been most influential, and this demonstrates the progress that still needs to be made within the feminist movement (Simic, 2015). Fat activism arose from the feminist movement of the 1970s mainly through the formation of The Fat Underground (e.g., Simic, 2015). The Fat Underground consisted of radical therapy and feminist individuals, including Sara Fishman (also known as Aldebaran) and Judy Freespirit, and it first emerged in southern California (e.g., Simic, 2015). Aldebaran and Freespirit were the first feminists to advocate against fat oppression (e.g., Simic, 2015). Around the same time, fat feminist activists emerged on the east coast, and Karen Stimson joined with the Fat Underground and penned essays on fat feminism. In April of 1980, the first national conference of fat feminist activists was held (Simic, 2015).

Fat women are treated unfairly when seeking infertility treatment, and this injustice is perpetuated by medical policy. This unfair treatment provides further justification for viewing fatness as a feminist issue. In many regions of the world, women who meet the medical definition of being obese are denied treatment for infertility using Assisted Reproductive Technologies (ART), primarily in vitro fertilization (IVF; Brown, 2019). They are usually denied treatment because these technologies are publicly funded and national organizations use various arguments for denying obese women (defined as being at or above a BMI of 30 km/m2 or 35 km/m2) fertility treatment. There are many arguments justifying the denial of IVF for obese women. These include that IVF has poor success rates for obese women, it is not cost effective, and fat women have increased rates of miscarriage (e.g., Brown, 2019).

However, there are numerous researchers that have refuted the medical justifications denying obese women fertility treatment (Brown, 2019; Maheshwari et al., 2009; Tremellen et al., 2017). Brown (2019) refutes some of these arguments and suggests that denying obese women IVF is because of the pervasive implications of the stigmatization of fatness as described in this article. Tremellen et al. (2017) found that live birth rates in North America did not differ much between morbidly obese women and those who were neither obese nor underweight. Additionally, a recent study found that there were no significant differences in costs of ART between fat women and those of a normal weight (Maheshwari et al., 2009). Fat women seeking infertility treatment can be educated about the risks, but also be given the autonomy, control, and power to make a choice regarding fertility treatment (Tremellen et al., 2017).

Implications for feminist family therapists

Because fatness and its relationship with infertility are both feminist issues impacting women and couples, there are many implications for feminist family therapists. In order to fully grasp the implications, feminist family therapists must understand the experiences of fat women, specifically those seeking infertility treatment. Fat women suffer from internalized stigma affecting their body appreciation. This stigma is in part because of the media's portrayal of fat women. This lack of body appreciation can affect body image, sexual satisfaction, and relationship satisfaction. Fat women dealing with infertility experience shame and blame, and this is exacerbated by the way they are treated by medical professionals which is culturally influenced. Feminist family therapists can intervene on a microlevel, e.g., therapy, and a macro-level, e.g., advocacy, to address these issues.

Understanding and addressing the power distribution in a system is at the core of feminist family therapy (Goodrich, 2003). Understanding the gendered distribution of power in the family system will be integral when treating a heterosexual couple, and understanding the power dynamics between partners will be important when working with same-sex couples. Fat women have less power in society than thinner women because of weight stigma and cultural ideals of beauty. When in a relationship, add the dynamic of the inability to get pregnant, and power differentials widen. Strengthening the couple bond amidst infertility issues will be a therapeutic goal for feminist family therapists (Luk & Loke, 2015). Helping fat women cope with the shame and blame they may be feeling for issues with infertility will be necessary in understanding their own sense of power and agency. Additionally, assessing and addressing any potential blame their partner is directing toward them for infertility issues will be necessary in order to strengthen the couple's bond. Advocating against systemic issues that further oppress fat women will be another implication discussed for feminist family therapists.

Therapeutic implications

Feminist family therapists must first assess their own biases, values, attitudes, and opinions about fatness, fat women, and their relationship to infertility before working with fat women experiencing fertility issues. Carneiro et al. (2013) assert that therapists have their own views about how self and others should look and those views may impact the therapeutic relationship. To begin to assess one's beliefs about fat women and fertility, feminist family therapists can take inventory of their attitudes by asking themselves the following questions: What are your beliefs about how women should look? How have you internalized standards of beauty? What are your initial thoughts whenever you see a fat woman walk into your office? When a couple with fertility issues enters your office, what are your initial thoughts and assumptions? How are your thoughts impacted whenever one or both of the partners is fat? Is your office conducive to doing therapy with a fat person, i.e. comfortable chairs, etc.? It is essential to consider your thoughts and assumptions related to blame, sexual performance and satisfaction, and overall relationship quality when working with fat women. Assessing one's attitudes and considering how they might impact the therapeutic relationship is necessary before providing therapy to fat women and couples experiencing fertility issues.

Empowerment

One tenet of feminist family therapy is empowerment, and helping empower women is an essential therapeutic goal when working with clients who are experiencing infertility (Parry, 2005). If a woman is unable to get pregnant because of infertility issues, this can further intensify the power differential in the couple's relationship. Women experiencing fertility issues or those who using ART to get pregnant may feel disempowered by needing to use medical assistance to reproduce (Parry, 2005). Fat women who may not be eligible for reproductive assistance because of the medical guidelines for IVF and obesity are further disempowered through this process. Providing couples with psychoeducation, strengthening their individual and family identities, and discovering and capitalizing on the family system's strengths are all techniques to help empower couples experiencing fertility issues (McDaniel & Cole-Kelly, 2003). In a qualitative research study interviewing 32 women who experienced infertility and decided to seek medical assistance to reproduce, Parry (2005) found that women were active in the decision-making process and were able to take ownership of the medical interventions that they were experiencing. Encouraging women to not just be the receivers of psychoeducation, but also to be active in finding and reviewing information related to infertility is one way feminist family therapists can empower their clients.

Additionally, helping the couple balance agency and communion is essential whenever one partner is dealing with any kind of illness (McDaniel & Cole-Kelly, 2003). Bolstering the couple to strengthen their connection in the midst of dealing with the stress of trying to conceive and the grief that accompanies failed attempts is an integral goal of feminist family therapists. Interventions that focus on the quality of the marital relationship and the support of each partner have been proven to lessen the negative impact of infertility challenges (Luk & Loke, 2015). Jaffe (2017) suggests that couples focus on their reproductive story in counseling. This will help couples to process grief and loss, further understand that this part of their reproductive story is just one component of their identity, and to ultimately control their story's narrative and rewrite a positive ending (Jaffe, 2017).

Shame, blame, and guilt

Guilt, shame, and blame plague fat women dealing with fertility issues for a variety of reasons. One of these reasons includes the public stigma dealing with weight and infertility, with public opinion supporting a BMI cut off level for treating fat individuals with ART (Shah et al., 2013). Also, many fat women receive messages from family, friends, and doctors that losing weight is the answer to their infertility problems. Fat women then internalize this stigma and believe if they were simply thinner, then they would not deal with issues of infertility. They may blame themselves solely for this issue; however the reality is that over 50 million couples are plagued with infertility issues (Mascarenhas et al., 2012). Although some studies have demonstrated that infertility is associated with weight (Frisco & Weden, 2013), there are a variety of issues and causes complicating the ability to become pregnant (e.g., Joham et al., 2015).

Self-blame is associated with higher levels of depression and anxiety in both men and women; however, women are more likely than men to blame themselves for issues of infertility (Péloquin et al., 2018). Fat women have the added stigmatization of associating their fatness with the reason for their inability to conceive. This is further exacerbated by medical professionals informing women that they must lose weight to get pregnant or even to receive treatment, such as IVF, for their infertility (Sole-Smith, 2019).

Advocacy implications

In addition to therapeutic interventions, feminist family therapists can engage in advocacy to help fat women dealing with fertility issues. Feminist family therapists working with fat women who are experiencing fertility issues must be willing to engage in advocacy as a way to empower their clients. Braithwaite (2000) states, "philosophically and pragmatically, to embrace empowerment means that one refrains from 'blaming the victim' for his or her disadvantaged status and focuses attention on the structural impediments and systemic reasons for the presence of negative forces in the environment" (p. 194). Two areas for advocacy include the media's representation of fat women and the oppression that fat women experience in healthcare.

Because sexual satisfaction seems to be more related to body image and acceptance than actual body size, it would be helpful for therapists to advocate for media promoting positive body image in fat women than promoting the need to lose weight (Satinsky et al., 2012). Brochu et al. (2014) found that viewing a stigmatizing image of a fat couple increased the likelihood that participants would deny fat women treatment for infertility issues. Because images can shape public opinion, Brochu et al. (2014) argued that non-stigmatizing images need to be used in the media's portrayal of fat people and may even reduce support for discriminatory medical policies.

Discriminatory policies toward fat women receiving infertility treatment may be intensified by the use of stigmatizing images, yet very little scholarly research exists regarding fat women's experiences of seeking treatment for infertility. Examining fat women's experiences of infertility treatment and doctors' attitudes toward treating fat women for infertility are both implications for future research, and this research can pave the way for advocacy efforts.

Although little scholarly research exists regarding this direct topic, researchers have begun studying how fat women are treated by doctors for other general medical conditions. The American Psychological Association (APA, 2017) argues that sizeism exists in research studies by excluding fat people from medical studies. Additionally, individuals identified as obese were 1.65 times more likely to have undiagnosed medical conditions (APA, 2017). Lee and Pausé (2016) also reviewed the literature regarding anti-fat attitudes and doctor practices and found that doctors spent less time with fat patients, offered fewer tests, and showed less respect toward fat patients. Fat women experience injustices when seeking medical treatment, including seeking treatment for fertility issues (Sole-Smith, 2019).

In addition to researching fat women's experiences when seeking fertility treatment, advocating for a change in policy is another implication for feminist family therapists. Currently, many medical policies prohibit women with a BMI of 30 km/m2 or 35 km/m2 from receiving ART, specifically IVF (Brown, 2019). Although researchers have shown that there are little differences in birth rates and cost for obese women using IVF, discriminatory policies persist (Maheshwari et al., 2009; Tremellen et al., 2017). Advocacy and research efforts directed toward the culturally sensitive and nondiscriminatory development of medical policies for treating fat women experiencing infertility is recommended.

Conclusion

Fat women face a variety of issues in White, European culture. The stigmatization they receive may be internalized, especially when dealing with infertility and gender expectations around reproduction. The media and medical community only further intensify this stigmatization, leading many fat women to blame themselves for their trouble conceiving. Infertility affects women, their partners, and their relationships. Empowering fat women experiencing infertility and advocating against the policies and systems that discriminate against size can have positive impacts including improving self-image, body appreciation, access to medical care, relationships, and fertility.

ORCID

Heidi L. Henry http://orcid.org/0000-0001-5511-0352

References

American Psychological Association. (2017, August 3). *Fat shaming in the doctor's office can be mentally and physically harmful: Health care providers may offer weight loss advice in place of medical treatment, researchers say. ScienceDaily*. www.sciencedaily.com/releases/2017/08/170803092015.htm

Berger, R., Paul, M. S., & Henshaw, L. A. (2013). Women's experience of infertility: A multisystemic perspective. *Journal of International Women's Studies*, *14*(1), 54–68.

Bhat, A., & Byatt, N. (2016). Infertility and perinatal loss: When the bough breaks. *Current Psychiatry Reports*, *18*(3), 1–18. https://doi.org/10.1007/s11920-016-0663-8

Blanchfield, B. V., & Patterson, C. J. (2015). Racial and sexual minority women's receipt of medical assistance to become pregnant. *Health Psychology*, *34*(6), 571–579. https://doi.org/10.1037/hea0000124

Braithwaite, R. L. (2000). Empowerment. In A. E. Kazdin (Ed.), *Encyclopedia of psychology* (pp. 193–194). Oxford University Press.

Brochu, P. M., Pearl, R. L., Puhl, R. M., & Brownell, K. D. (2014). Do media portrayals of obesity influence support for weight-related medical policy? *Health Psychology*, *33*(2), 197–200. https://doi.org/10.1037/a0032592

Brown, R. C. H. (2019). Irresponsibly infertile? Obesity, efficiency, and exclusion from treatment. *Health Care Analysis*, *27*(2), 61–76. https://doi.org/10.1007/s10728-019-00366-w

Campos, P., Saguy, A., Ernsberger, P., Oliver, E., & Gaesser, G. (2006). The epidemiology of overweight and obesity: Public health crisis or moral panic? *International Journal of Epidemiology*, *35*(2), 41–60. https://doi.org/10.1093/ije/dyi254

Carneiro, R., Zeytinoglu, S., Hort, F., & Wilkins, E. (2013). Culture, beauty, and therapeutic alliance. *Journal of Feminist Family Therapy*, *25*(2), 80–92. https://doi.org/10.1080/08952833.2013.777873

Cedars, M, & Jaffe, R. B. (2005). Infertility and women. *The Journal Of Clinical Endocrinology & Metabolism*, *90*(4), E2. doi: 10.1210/jcem.90.4.9997

Corner, L. (2019, February). Reclaiming the word queer: What does it mean in 2019? *Gay Times*, *492*, 16–19. https://www.gaytimes.co.uk/community/117642/reclaiming-the-word-queer-what-does-it-mean-in-2019/

Costa, R. M, & Brody, S. (2014). Orgasm and women's waist circumference. *European Journal Of Obstetrics & Gynecology and Reproductive Biology*, *182*(1), 118-122. doi: 10.1016/j.ejogrb.2014.09.007

Davis, H. A., & Bowman, S. L. (2015). Examining experiences of weight-related oppression in a bariatric sample: A qualitative exploration. *Translational Issues in Psychological Science*, *1* (3), 271–286. https://doi.org/10.1037/tps0000036

Eichelberger, K. Y., Doll, K., Ekpo, G. E., & Zerden, M. L. (2016). Black lives matter: Claiming a space for evidence-based outrage in obstetrics and gynecology. *American Journal of Public Health*, *106*(10), 1771–1772. https://doi.org/10.2105/AJPH.2016.303313

Fraser, S., Maher, J., & Wright, J. (2010). Between bodies and collectivities: Articulating the action of emotion in obesity epidemic discourse. *Social Theory & Health*, *8*(2), 192–209. https://doi.org/10.1057/sth.2009.28

Frisco, M. L., & Weden, M. (2013). Early adult obesity and U.S. women's lifetime childbearing experiences. *Journal of Marriage & Family*, *75*(4), 920–932. https://doi.org/10.1111/jomf.12049

Gailey, J. A. (2015). Transforming the looking-glass: Fat women's sexual empowerment through body acceptance. In H. Hester & C. Walters (Eds.), *Fat sex: New directions in theory and activism* (pp. 51–66). Ashgate.

Gailey, J. A., & Harjunen, H. (2019). A cross-cultural examination of fat women's experiences: Stigma and gender in North American and Finnish culture. *Feminism & Psychology*, *29*(3), 374–390. https://doi.org/10.1177/0959353518819582

Gonzales, G., & Henning-Smith, C. (2017). Barriers to care among transgender and gender nonconforming adults. *The Milbank Quarterly*, *95*(4), 726–748. https://doi.org/10.1111/1468-0009.12297

Goodrich, T. J. (2003). A feminist family therapist's work is never done. In L. B. Silverstein & T. J. Goodrich (Eds.), *Feminist family therapy: Empowerment in social context* (pp. 3–15). American Psychological Association.

Greil, A. L., Slauson, B. K., & McQuillan, J. (2010). The experience of infertility: A review of recent literature. *Sociology of Health & Illness*, *32*(1), 140–162. https://doi.org/10.1111/j.1467-9566.2009.01213.x

Hales, C. M., Fryar, C. D., Carroll, M. D., Freedman, D. S., Aoki, Y., & Ogden, C. L. (2018). Differences in obesity prevalence by demographic characteristics and urbanization level among adults in the United States, 2013–2016. *Journal of the American Medical Association*, *319*(23), 2419–2429. https://doi.org/10.1001/jama.2018.7270

Haththotuwa, R., Wijeyaratne, C. N., & Senarath, U. (2013). Worldwide epidemic of obesity. In T. Mahmood & S. Arulkumaran (Eds.), *Obesity* (pp. 3–11). Elsevier.

Himmelstein, M. S., Puhl, R. M., & Quinn, D. M. (2017). Intersectionality: An understudied framework for addressing weight stigma. *American Journal of Preventive Medicine*, *53*(4), 421–431. https://doi.org/10.1016/j.amepre.2017.04.003

Jaffe, J. (2017). Reproductive trauma: Psychotherapy for pregnancy loss and infertility clients from a reproductive story perspective. *Psychotherapy*, *54*(4), 380–385. https://doi.org/10.1037/pst0000125

Janitz, A. E., Peck, J. D., & Craig, L. B. (2019). Racial/ethnic differences in the utilization of infertility services: A focus on American Indian/Alaska natives. *Maternal & Child Health Journal*, *23*(1), 10–18. https://doi.org/10.1007/s10995-018-2586-y

Joham, A. E., Teede, H. J., Ranasinha, S., Zoungas, S., & Boyle, J. (2015). Prevalence of infertility and use of fertility treatment in women with polycystic ovary syndrome: Data from a large community-based cohort study. *Journal of Women's Health*, *24*(4), 299–307. https://doi.org/10.1089/jwh.2014.5000

Johnstone, G., & Grant, S. L. (2019). Weight stigmatization in antiobesity campaigns: The role of images. *Health Promotion Journal of Australia*, *30*(1), 37–46. https://doi.org/10.1002/hpja.183

Lee, J. A., & Pausé, C. J. (2016). Stigma in practice: Barriers to health for fat women. *Hypothesis and Theory*, *7*(2063), 1–15. https://doi.org/10.3389/fpsyg.2016.02063

Luk, B. H.-K., & Loke, A. Y. (2015). The impact of infertility on the psychological well-being, marital relationships, sexual relationships, and quality of life of couples: A systematic review. *Journal of Sex & Marital Therapy*, *41*(6), 610–625. https://doi.org/10.1080/0092623X.2014.958789

Maheshwari, A., Scotland, G., Bell, J., McTavish, A., Hamilton, M., & Bhattacharya, S. (2009). The direct health services costs of providing assisted reproduction services in overweight or obese women: A retrospective cross-sectional analysis. *Human Reproduction*, *24*(3), 633–639. https://doi.org/10.1093/humrep/den424

Mascarenhas, M. N., Flaxman, S. R., Boerma, T., Vanderpoel, S., & Stevens, G. A. (2012). National, regional, and global trends in infertility prevalence since 1990: A systematic analysis of 277 health surveys. *PLOS Medicine*, *9*(12), 12. https://doi.org/10.1371/journal.pmed.1001356

McDaniel, S. H., & Cole-Kelly, K. (2003). Gender, couples, and illness: A feminist analysis of medical family therapy. In L. B. Silverstein & T. J. Goodrich (Eds.), *Feminist family therapy: Empowerment in social context* (pp. 267–280). American Psychological Association.

Milhausen, R. R., Buchholz, A. C., Opperman, E. A., & Benson, L. E. (2015). Relationships between body image, body composition, sexual functioning, and sexual satisfaction among heterosexual young adults. *Archives of Sexual Behavior*, *44*(6), 1621–1633. https://doi.org/10.1007/s10508-014-0328-9

Monaghan, L. (2005). Discussion piece: A critical take on the obesity debate. *Social Theory & Health*, *3*(4), 302–314. https://doi.org/10.1057/palgrave.sth.8700058

Ogden, C. L., Carroll, M. D., Curtin, L. R., McDowell, M. A., Tabak, C. J., & Flegal, K. M. (2006). Prevalence of overweight and obesity in the United States, 1999–2004. *JAMA*, *295*(13), 1549–1555. https://doi.org/10.1001/jama.295.13.1549

Olson, K. L., Landers, J. D., Thaxton, T. T., & Emery, C. F. (2019). The pain of weight-related stigma among women with overweight or obesity. *Stigma and Health*, *4*(3), 243–246. https://doi.org/10.1037/sah0000137

Parry, D. C. (2005). Women's experiences with infertility: Exploring the outcome of empowerment. *Women's Studies*, *34*(2), 191–211. https://doi.org/10.1080/00497870590923890

Péloquin, K., Brassard, A., Arpin, V., Sabourin, S., & Wright, J. (2018). Whose fault is it? Blame predicting psychological adjustment and couple satisfaction in couples seeking fertility treatment. *Journal of Psychosomatic Obstetrics & Gynecology*, *39*(1), 64–72. https://doi.org/10.1080/0167482X.2017.1289369

Perilloux, C., Cloud, J. M., & Buss, D. M. (2013). Women's physical attractiveness and short-term mating strategies. *Personality and Individual Differences*, *54*(4), 490–495. https://doi.org/10.1016/j.paid.2012.10.028

Puhl, R. M., Himmelstein, M. S., & Quinn, D. M. (2018). Internalizing weight stigma: Prevalence and sociodemographic considerations in US adults. *Obesity*, *26*(1), 167–175. https://doi.org/10.1002/oby.22029

Satinsky, S., Reece, M., Dennis, B., Sanders, S., & Bardzell, S. (2012). An assessment of the relationship between body appreciation and sexual function in women. *Body Image*, *9*(1), 137–144. https://doi.org/10.1016/j.bodyim.2011.09.007

Savoy, S., & Boxer, P. (2020). The impact of weight-biased media on weight attitudes, self-attitudes, and weight-biased behavior. *Psychology of Popular Media Culture, 9*(1), 31–44. https://doi.org/10.1037/ppm0000232

Shah, D. K., Ginsburg, E. S., Correia, K. F., Barton, S. E., & Missmer, S. A. (2013). Public opinion regarding utilization of assisted reproductive technology (ART) in obese women. *Journal of Women's Health, 22*(11), 978–982. https://doi.org/10.1089/jwh.2013.4399

Simic, Z. (2015). Fat as a feminist issue: A history. In H. Hester & C. Walters (Eds.), *Fat sex: New directions in theory and activism* (pp. 15–35). Ashgate.

Sole-Smith, V. (2019, June). When you're told you're too fat to get pregnant. *The New York Times Magazine.* https://www.nytimes.com/2019/06/18/magazine/fertility-weight-obesity-ivf.html

Tremellen, K., Wilkinson, D., & Savulescu, J. (2017). Should obese women's access to assisted fertility treatment be limited? A scientific and ethical analysis. *Australian and New Zealand Journal of Obstetrics and Gynaecology, 57*(5), 569–574. https://doi.org/10.1111/ajo.12600

World Health Organization. (2018). *Obesity and overweight.* https://www.who.int/news-room/fact-sheets/detail/obesity-and-overweight

Yazdani, N., Sharif, F., Elahi, N., Hosseini, S. V., & Ebadi, A. (2019). Exploration of the quality of life in Iranian morbid obese people: A qualitative study. *International Journal of Community Based Nursing and Midwifery, 7*(2), 138–149.

Female Partner Family Formation: Cultivating Love and Healing Disconnection

Jessica Danielson, Jodi Tangen and Jill Nelson

ABSTRACT
Female partners continue to experience homophobia when creating families. In this study, we utilized Interpretative Phenomenological Analysis (IPA) and Relational-Cultural Theory (RCT) to explore the experiences of female partners receiving third-party fertility treatments and to investigate the counseling profession's potential role in the family formation process. Two themes emerged: love and disconnection. Therapists are encouraged to employ RCT when working with female partners engaging in family formation. Application of RCT emphasizes enhancing love by addressing relational images and integrity and healing disconnection by addressing autonomy and belonging. Recommendations for future research are discussed.

As social and institutional shifts toward lesbian, gay, bisexual, queer, questioning, and asexual/ally (LGBQQA) human rights continue in the United States, females identifying as members of the LGBQQA community are increasingly more visible (Lavner, 2016; Wojnar & Katzenmeyer, 2013). This increased visibility challenges the heteronormative nature of mainstream culture surrounding relationships, marriage, and families and encourages the examination of existing heterosexism and homophobia experienced in these contexts. Specifically, more females are deciding to have children in the context of their queer relationships (Dionisius, 2015) and redefining the traditional concept of family (Wall, 2011).

Though counseling research is scarce in this area, research conducted in the field of nursing suggests sufficient evidence that the healthcare system provides heteronormative services and that female partners experience multiple forms of homophobia when seeking fertility services (Cherguit et al., 2012; B. Hayman, Wilkes, Halcomb et al., 2013; Wall, 2011; Wojnar & Katzenmeyer, 2013). Specifically, this homophobia presents in the form of heterosexism, which is present at macro, meso, and micro-levels in the healthcare system. There is a significant gap in the literature between the healthcare services and mental health services related to female partners' fertility services. Due to this significant gap in research, it is difficult to identify the role the counseling profession has in female partners' family formation including their specific needs and experiences.

The purpose of this study is to explore the experience of female partners receiving third-party fertility treatments, to identify the perceived implications of counseling services during the family formation process, and to develop implications for counseling practices (perhaps creating a foundation for future empirically-supported systemic counseling practices) specific to female partners during family formation. Researchers have outlined many issues female partners face when engaging in the process of family formation: (a) navigating heterosexist stigmatization and marginalization, (b) negotiating the fertility process, and (c) redefining the family within a heteronormative society.

Heterosexist stigmatization and marginalization

Female partners face heterosexist stigmatization and marginalization both in the larger context of life in society and in the more narrow context of the family formation process. From incorrect labeling to discrimination, female partners must continually navigate the prevalence of of this stigmatization and marginalization. In terms of labeling, researchers (Diamond, 2016) have historically described a romantic relationship between two females as a "lesbian relationship," which is problematic in that females may not identify as lesbian or place their sexual or affectional orientation within the heterosexual/homosexual dichotomy. The lack of consistent language (e.g., co-mothers, same sex co-parents) magnifies issues around identity and role development (Miller, 2012), which are all part of the family formation process.

Female partners also experience sexual minority stress, which is the stress resulting from heterosexist societal stigmatization and marginalization (Cherguit, Pettle, Burns, & Tasker, 2012; Holley, 2016; Lewis et al., 2012). Female partners considering parenthood are moving against heterosexism and marginalization by continuing to challenge societal norms defining relationships and family. With this endeavor comes additional barriers and challenges that are unique to female partners' experiences of family formation. In fact, raising children in a heterosexist society is one of the most prominent fears of female partners considering parenthood (Hayman & Wilkes, 2016; Wall, 2011). Common examples of heterosexism include confined legal protection from discrimination based on affectional orientation in employment, housing, and services (Wall, 2011); legal and social recognition of relationship and family; discrimination from family, friends, and strangers; invisibility in society; and rejection and social exclusion (Hayman et al., 2013; Holley, 2016). Furthermore, the stress associated with the intersectionality of sexism and heterosexism is unique (Hayman et al., 2013; Hayman & Wilkes, 2016; Lewis et al., 2012).

Fertility process

Female partners engaging in family formation experience unique barriers including consideration of a multitude of questions before, during, and after engaging in family formation that is not typical of heterosexual partners. Female partners describe their journey toward parenthood as a "rollercoaster ride" due to the multitude of decisions, limited social support, financial stress, and additional barriers experienced in the process of family formation (Rausch & Wikoff, 2017; Somers et al., 2017). When female partners decide not to pursue or continue to pursue family formation, it is often fraught with limited access to health insurance coverage, financial concerns, and medical concerns potentially impacting the fertility process (Carpinello et al., 2016; Fields & Scout, 2015). Furthermore, female partners must discuss and decide who will conceive, how they will conceive, how they will finance conception, determine the type of donor, explore their roles in the conception process, and define their roles as parents, their family dynamics and structure, and legal and societal legitimacy for their family. Each of these decisions can have unforeseen complications, yet the main challenge female partners experience during the conception process is homophobia (Ryan & Berkowitz, 2009).

When seeking fertility services, female partners can experience homophobia through exclusion, heterosexual assumption, inappropriate questioning, and refusal of services (Hayman et al., 2013). When providers (i.e. physicians, nurses, therapists, staff) do not provide equal treatment, care, or services to female partners compared to their heterosexual counterparts, this is considered exclusion (Pelka, 2009). Examples of exclusion include not providing female partners appropriate and adequate educational fertility materials that are specific to their needs as two females, not allowing the social mother (the nonbiological mother) to participate in services, or using inappropriate labels to refer to the social mother (i.e., sister, cousin, friend) (Hayman et al., 2013).

Furthermore, when providers assume that the social mother is a sister, cousin, or friend they are also assuming that the birth mother is heterosexual (Wojnar & Katzenmeyer, 2013). Additional examples of heterosexual assumptions include providers asking questions about husbands or fathers and asking about infertility concerns when infertility services are not currently being sought (Hayman et al., 2013). This can lead to additional inappropriate questions by providers such as asking about male role models, parenting concerns, and justifications and explanations for the chosen conception method (Pelka, 2009). Lastly, providers can engage in homophobia when working with female partners during family formation by refusing to provide services either partially or fully and based on their own bias or due to legislation at-large (Hayman et al., 2013).

Redefining family

Female partners are continually required to justify their family structure and the legitimacy of their family (Hayman & Wilkes, 2016; Miller, 2012; Nordqvist, 2012). Before deciding to pursue family formation, female partners engage in lengthy discussions, often over a duration of years (Hayman & Wilkes, 2016). Prior to parenthood, female partners negotiate the way they would each like to be identified, the choice of surname, the names that will appear on the birth certificate, their roles within the context of their family, choosing who will birth and how to conceive, the involvement of each partner in the process of family formation, and the amount of donor involvement (Hayman et al., 2013; Hayman & Wilkes, 2016; Nordqvist, 2012; Somers et al., 2017).

An additional stress for female partners choosing parenthood is the absence of role models in society to help construct the definitions of relationships and family, specifically the expectations of roles and how to cope with various unique situations (Cherguit et al., 2012; Hayman & Wilkes, 2016). With the lack of societal recognition and the limited availability of role models, female partners are in a unique position that requires them to create their own definition of family and, more specifically, parenthood (Hayman & Wilkes, 2016). Thus, female partners are redefining parenthood and the traditional meaning of motherhood (Hayman & Wilkes, 2016; Nordqvist, 2012), which is complicated by social constructs of motherhood in relation to fatherhood (Patterson & Riskind, 2010; Pelka, 2009; Rausch & Wikoff, 2017). In the United States, females are socialized to be caretakers of others – nurturing and warm. Females are also socialized to believe that motherhood is their biological destiny (Hayman & Wilkes, 2016; Patterson & Riskind, 2010), whereas males are socialized to be hyper masculine, provide for their family, and be emotionally strong. These social constructs of motherhood and fatherhood complicate female partners' family formation process (Patterson & Riskind, 2010; Pelka, 2009; Rausch & Wikoff, 2017), as they can create further role confusion and conflict in female partners' relationships during family formation (Pelka, 2009).

As female partners engage in the family formation process, their roles and responsibilities begin to shift, especially after the birth of their first child (Rausch & Wikoff, 2017; Somers et al., 2017; Wojnar & Katzenmeyer, 2013). At this time, female partners tend to move toward a hierarchical way of operating, as compared to previous functioning as equal partners, due to the differences between the biological mother and social mother status (Rausch & Wikoff, 2017; Somers et al., 2017; Wojnar & Katzenmeyer, 2013). Female partners do not necessarily anticipate the differences in parental roles and initially expect equality in maternal roles (Pelka, 2009). Specifically, parental roles can trigger feelings of jealousy between female partners (Nordqvist, 2012; Pelka, 2009; Wojnar & Katzenmeyer, 2013).

Furthermore, social mothers are often more at risk of marginalization due to their other position (Hayman et al., 2013; Hayman & Wilkes, 2016; Pelka, 2009). Social mothers are outside of the typical heterosexual family construct excluding them from a legitimate position in the family due to not conceiving a child (Hayman et al., 2013). In addition to social invisibility, social mothers are often legally disenfranchised; this exclusion increases feelings of powerlessness and vulnerability within the family structure (Cherguit et al., 2012; Hayman et al., 2013; Hayman & Wilkes, 2016). To cultivate legitimacy for the social mother, the family establishes ceremonies, names, and methods of formal recognition which may be integrating heterosexual norms (Hayman et al., 2013; Kimberly & Williams, 2017; Miller, 2012). For example, choosing a surname that connects the social mother to their child(ren) (Hayman et al., 2013).

In addition, legal considerations for female partners during family formation exist. Legal considerations include the legal status of the female partners' relationship, the legal status between the social mother and the child(ren), and the legal status and rights of the donor (Miller, 2012; Patterson & Riskind, 2010; Wojnar & Katzenmeyer, 2013). The legal status between the social mother and the child(ren) and the legal status and rights of the donor depend largely on individual state laws and healthcare system policy (Patterson & Riskind, 2010; Rausch & Wikoff, 2017).

As female partners engage in the family formation process, there is a plethora of considerations which are impacted by homophobic healthcare systems, heterosexist society, and marginalization of female partners' intersectional identities. Yet, female partners are choosing to move forward in their decision to create a family. This research will explore female partners' experiences during family formation, specifically examining the discrepancies in creating a family built on love while homophobia, heteronormativity, and marginalization generate disconnection.

Method

This study is grounded in feminist theory, as it aligns with our focus on female partners as a marginalized population and addresses the principles of relationship, power differentials, resistance and transformation, and intersectionality. More specifically, Relational-cultural theory (RCT) was used as the framework for organizing, clarifying, and understanding the data. RCT is a feminist theory of human development that centralizes connection and emphasizes healing through growth fostering relationships (Jordan, 2010). It also maintains that systemic, societal, and cultural contexts affect individuals' ability to engage in authentic connections with others (Singh & Moss, 2016). Furthermore, RCT assumes that disconnections are caused by relational violations and traumas such as experiences of isolation, shame, humiliation, oppression, marginalization, and microaggressions (Singh & Moss, 2016). These central tendanciece of RCT were esstential in addressing the significant implications of homophobia and heterosexism on female partners engaging in family formation.

Relational-cultural theory outlines eight key concepts: growth fostering relationships, empathy, mutual empathy, authenticity, strategies for disconnection, central relational paradox, relational images, relational resilience, and relational competency (Duffey & Somody, 2011). These key concepts will be explored in more depth in the implications section; however, strategies for disconnection and central relational paradox will be discussed here to enhance understanding of the findings. Minority groups are more likely to experience disconnections, as they are marginalized and discounted by people in power (i.e., female partners) (Duffey & Somody, 2011). Disconnections occur in interactions when someone does not feel heard, understood, or responded to by someone else (Jordan, 2010). Disconnection decreases energy, ability to act, clarity of self and others, self-worth, and social contact; while chronic disconnection can lead to shame, isolation, self-blame, a sense of defectiveness, and immobilization (Duffey & Somody, 2011).

Oppression and marginalization can disconnect female partners from each other, friends, family, providers, and society at-large and female partners can use disconnection as a means of survival in a heteronormative society (Russell, 2009). When female partners engage in disconnection as a survival strategy, it enacts the central relational paradox. The central relational paradox outlines the yearning for connection, belonging, and inclusion when disconnection is occurring (Jordan, 2010). The individual engaging in the strategies of disconnection begins to alter themselves to the expectations of the other person, in an attempt to protect themselves, and results in the loss of authenticity and mutuality in the relationship (Jordan, 2010). This endeavor results in another disconnection (Jordan, 2010).

Interpretative Phenomenological Analysis (IPA) design was chosen to focus on female partners' lived experiences of family formation. IPA emphasizes the in-depth exploration of a particular lived experience which is expressed in its own terms, rather than being expressed in predetermined categories (Smith et al., 2012). Both Feminist Theory and IPA empower individuals, encourage equality in the researcher-participant relationship, and allow for the researcher and participant to make meaning of the experiences being shared.

As the methodology of choice, IPA aims to explore, in-depth, the lived experiences of individuals in particular circumstances or events (Smith et al., 2012). Researchers are concerned with eliciting rich, detailed, first-person accounts of the experiences under investigation (Pietkieqiez & Smith, 2012). In order to elicit the depth required for IPA, researchers typically recommend between three and eight participants (Smith et al., 2012). In addition, IPA researchers strive for homogenous samples (Pietkieqiez & Smith, 2012), which allow for greater immersion and analysis into the experiences of the participants (Pietkieqiez & Smith, 2012). The individual lived experience is central to IPA research and the goal is not to identify generalizations but rather particulars of individuals' experiences. Therefore, there is a specific rigor to analyzing individual cases prior to analyzing similarities and differences between individuals.

Due to the nature of this study and the depth of the findings, the findings of this study have been separated into two distinct manuscripts, study one and study two. Study one focuses on the emergent super-ordinate themes of the overall study, exploreing the experience of female partners engage in third-party family formation. More specifically, on how female partners experience homophobia and heteronormativity during family formation and the role Relational-Cultural Theory (RCT) has when counseling female partners during family formation. While study two discusses super-ordinate themes addressing therapist's competency when working with female partner family formation. Study two focuses on female partners' experiences with counseling services, which can help inform therapist competency when working with female partners during family formation.

Reflexivity statement

All three authors identify as feminists and have experience implementing RCT. The first author took a doctoral RCT course, which included history, theorectical prinicples, and practice and application. The first author is a White, queer, cisgender female married to her female partner. She is at the level of complete disclosure of her affectional orientation within her personal and professional lives and participates in activities hosted by queer community organizations. The first author and her partner have periodically discussed the potential of creating a family throughout the past four years and at this time they are not considering family formation. The first author identifies concerns with becoming a parent for personal reasons and due to concerns of homophobia and heterosexism in the rural community she currently lives. The second and third authors are both White, cisgender, heterosexual females that identify as feminists working in academia. The second author has experienced third-party fertility treatments as a cisgender, heterosexual, single female. The third author identifies as a cisgender, heterosexual, female. The second and third authors worked as mentors and auditors during the research process.

Participants

To be included in the study, participants met the following criteria; (a) self-identify as female; (b) identify as queer, including but not limited to, lesbian, bisexual, pansexual, or demisexual; (c) be coupled and both partners agreed to participate in interviews; and (d) have had received third-party fertility services to conceive at least one child together as a couple. Upon IRB approval, participant recruitment began by contacting statewide and national therapists via counseling listservs, colleagues, and queer support organizations via verbal communication, e-mail, and flyer. Three couples, or six individuals, agreed to participate. Three additional couples, or six additional participants, contacted the first author to participate in the study and were not included in the study. One of the additional couples, or two participants, were not included due to not meeting inclusion criteria, while the other two additional couples, or four participants, were not included due to contacting the first author after data collection and analysis were completed. To ensure confidentiality, specific demographic information was not obtained. Rather, the first author allowed participants to naturally share demographic information during the interview process. This allowed participants power in sharing information they felt comfortable sharing and believed was pertinent to their family formation experience.

Procedure

Participants were asked to participate in a 60–90-minute semi structured face-to-face or video/phone interview. The semi structured interview included questions pertaining to their experiences of services received during family formation, their perceptions of the services they received, their satisfaction with the services they received, their suggestions for therapists working with female partners during family formation, and the themes they identify in their experiences of counseling during family formation. The interviews were audio recorded and field notes were taken during and at the end of each interview. The interviews were then transcribed and analyzed.

Data analysis

The data were analyzed two separate times using a double analysis process. The first analysis yielded individual participant themes and the second analysis revealed data across participants as a whole; these themes were then explored for similarities and differences.

After the themes were categorized into possible overarching themes, the first author continued analysis to ensure that the themes were capturing the data within the context of the transcripts. The first author reviewed themes to ensure they were representative and were then organized into possible subthemes. Finally, the first author defined and named the themes. The second and third authors reviewed the themes and subthemes for accuracy as internal auditors.

Findings

Three couples, or six participants, were interviewed for this study, no demographic information was collected other than to confirm inclusion criteria were met. The three couples, or six participants, identified as female, in a relationship with another female, and have engaged in family formation in the context of their current female partner relationship. Participants have been given pseudonyms to protect their identities. Two super-ordinate themes emergered from the interviews: love and disconnection. Each theme will be defined and explored to elucidate the research question: What are the experience of female partners engaging in family formation?

Couple one, Merilou and Jessie, live in Midwest United States and conceived one child (age 20 months) via intrauterine insemination (IUI) using an unknown donor outside of the United States. Merilou and Jessie reported experiencing one miscarriage prior to the birth of their child. Furthermore, Merilou disclosed that she had attempted to conceive a child in a previous relationship that was unsuccessful using IUI and was unable to attempt conception again due to a medically necessary hysterectomy. Both Merilou and Jessie have completed graduate education. They have been coupled for five years.

Couple two, Terra and Dani, lived in Southwest United States and conceived one child (five years-old) via IUI using an unknown donor in the United States. Terra and Dani reported that pregnancy occurred on the first IUI attempt. However, they indicated that approximately a year and a half ago, they attempted IUI once again and were unsuccessful. Both Terra and Dani have completed graduate education and have been coupled for over a decade. In addition, Terra and Dani identified as Latina.

Couple three, Teagan and Sara, lived in Northeast United States and conceived one child (currently six weeks pregnant) via Frozen Embryo Transplant (FET). Teagan and Sara reported experiencing six unsuccessful IUIs and an unsuccessful IVF prior to conception. Both Teagan and Sara completed graduate education and they have been coupled for over a decade.

All six participants self-identified as queer females, completed at least one graduate degree, are married, and have conceived at least one child together in the context of their relationship. In addition, all participants were in a relatively similar age range, ranging from age 32-to-48, and represented differing regions of the United States.

Super-ordinate themes

After analyzing the data, two overarching super-ordinate themes emerged: love and disconnection. Love was the reason female partners were engaging in family formation; it was the foundation of family formation. Whereas, disconnection represented times love was disrupted by misunderstanding, invalidation, and exclusion. The two themes are described in detail here.

Love

Love was generally the concept that motivated the couples to engage in family formation; children were viewed as a product of love between two people. However, love was complicated in female partner family formation because of the physical constraints on their ability to create a product of love without intervention. All participants described love during their interviews. For example, Sara posed the question "Wouldn't it be nice to have a kid, you know, start making a family and memories?" While Terra outlined the pain associated with wanting to create a family out of love in the context of a queer relationship, "you fall in love with somebody and then you want your child to have a piece of that person, but you can't do that." Furthermore, Merilou described how the love created within a family is priceless, "It's tough, it's a tough thing in a lot of ways but at the end, if you get a child out of it, it's worth every, every second, every moment, every pain, every financial burden, everything. It's worth it." Love was further characterized by two subthemes: relational imaging and integrity.

Relational imaging

Relational images are our learned expectations of relationships, which are developed in childhood based on modeling and societal influences that impact our understanding of relationships including meaning and function (Jordan, 2010). Relational imaging accounted for individual role confusion and development and the transition from couple to family. More specifically, how the participants made sense of their position and their partner's position within the context of their relationship when transitioning from couple to family. This may be further complicated by heteronormative culture for female partners (e.g., gender roles or the concept of marriage). Jessie provided an example of how her relational image of a parent was being prepared and established in life:

> I always knew I wanted to have kids, um, so it was just a matter of time and waiting and being able to, you know, wait until I was "ready" ... I always thought that I needed to, you know, be done with my education and have a job and I'll have all the ducks in a row.

While Dani indicated concern for becoming a parent because she did not perceive herself as mother based on her relational image of motherhood, "I didn't have that motherly intuition." Merilou and Sara also identified parental relational image, specific to age, although Merilou identified additional physical abilities associated with a parent:

> Merilou: It was just a matter of, you know, me trying to convince myself that even though I'm older, I can still be a good parent ... I have to adapt and do things differently because of my joint issues ... I still wonder, am I missing out because I can't get down in [child's] world?

> Sara: When our second nephew was born, we started kind of getting the "awe, do you want to do this?" We're not getting any younger.

Integrity

In addition to relational images, integrity was a subtheme of love. Integrity was the intention of empowerment, values, and authenticity, including actions to promote the intention. Integrity accounted for individual navigation of the process (i.e., expanding individual knowledge or asking for help). For example, Merilou voiced self-empowerment regarding her personal understanding of her identity regardless of others' assumptions, "Do I call them out on it or do I not call them out on it? ... I know I'm a parent. I know I'm [Jessie's] partner, spouse."In addition to empowerment, Terra discussed the importance of incorporating values into family formation decisions. Specifically, Terra discussed how values influenced donor selection:

> It was important to us that he was, like, a good person ... kind of like, wanting to be environmentally friendly and seem to care about people ... we tried to get an idea of their personality and what they would bring to the table.

Sara echoed the importance of making decisions that align with personal values. She described how values impacted the process of selecting a provider, "We had to have an all-woman team ... we wanted all women. We wanted a woman doctor ... we kind of pride ourselves in this being an all-woman process ... we firmly believe in empowering women in their careers." Lastly, Teagan stated that challenges and complexities of family formation can diminish quality of life and that in order to navigate the family formation process, there needed to be boundaries to protect quality of life:

> We both decided that we weren't going to financially run ourselves into the ground for this because that would cause extra stress, um, quality of life issues that we weren't interested in, so we decided we would give it a good shot for maybe a year, year-and-a-half and then we would walk away with whatever we would walk away with.

Disconnection

The second overarching super-ordinate theme was disconnection. Disconnection was the crack in the foundation; it was the distance between cultures such as queer and heterosexual. Disconnection was the conflict between love being an emotional process and love existing as a medical process for female partners engaging in family formation. Heteronormative culture, heterosexism, homophobia, and marginalization contributed to disconnection by cultivating hopelessness and isolation (Jordan, 2010). Merilou described the conflictual emotional disconnection she experienced during the family formation process, "It was a whole bunch of different emotions. It was joyful, trepidation, nervous, fear, uh, all these things and I was worried about what happens." Similarly, Sara described an array of emotions during the family formation process; she also described how disconnecting those emotions can be due to the logistics of the conception process:

> I would describe it was as kind of a rollercoaster because, like we were not prepared for a lot of it . . . because, you know, you get your hopes up, and each cycle is kind of this rollercoaster . . . you're excited but you're exhausted with trying to manage all the moving parts and pieces . . . legitimately pushed me to my breaking point.

Furthermore, disconnection was enhanced by the medicalization of the conception process. Female partners required third-party assistance to conceive a child and in the participants' process, that meant services from fertility specialists. Jessie described being ready to start a family but having to wait because of the inclusion of fertility services:

> We just call and tell them we're ready and show up and do it . . . I was actually a little bit disappointed by the [Human Chorionic Gonadotropin], like, dang it, like we have to do something before we can even get started, so like, that whole hurdle was a little bit of a disappointment.

Teagan expressed feeling responsible for barriers of conception due her stress levels related to the medicalized conception process:

> Is that cause I'm freaked out and I'm just not relaxed, and am I stressed? Is that why I can't get, is that why my period isn't right? So, it's all about how do I relax and all this to happen, and then it should happen.

Terra also reported experiencing disconnection during the family formation process. She described her experience with receiving fertility services as a show for everyone to watch because of multiple medical tests and visits to providers. She indicated, "not only is it expensive but it's intrusive and uncomfortable and just ugly." Conversely, Merilou shared her excitement about choosing a donor and identified that disconnection played a role in selecting potential hereditary characteristics:

> I want *this* qualification, I want *this* qualification, I want *this* qualification, now who meets that? And it's like being able to pick your perfect spouse, in a way, but in this case a perfect parent who doesn't have to be a parent.

Disconnection was further defined by two subthemes: autonomy and belonging. Autonomy and belonging represented disconnections, struggles, and challenges that impacted various areas of the family formation process and the individual lives of the participants.

Autonomy

Autonomy was personal power and freedom (or a lack thereof) as described by the couples. It was present when female partners were confronted with decisions, during the family formation process such as donor selection, biological mother selection, conception method selection, etc. Autonomy was also the personal power and freedom to choose how to manage resources such as time and money. Autonomy was comprised of the conflict between personal power and freedom, and homophobia and discrimination, as homophobia and discrimination created an absence of autonomy.

Participants described experiencing barriers to autonomy; more specifically, they discussed how resources confined their ability to make decisions. For example, Terra indicated the role finances had on family formation, "we had to pay cash for all of our appointments, um, and I got pregnant the first time, with the first insemination. So, we were lucky because it was very expensive." Teagan also described how finances, specifically insurance coverage, impacted conception decisions, "well, insurance says we only need to do two, so why don't we save a few bucks because frozen sperm and IUI only has a like 2% success rate anyway."

In addition to finances, participants described the role time had in limiting their autonomy during family formation. Jessie described the pressure to plan and work around cycles in order to promote a smooth process and avoid additional financial burdens.

> You need to keep track of your cycle, you know, a good couple months so, to, you know, exactly when you ovulate. If you send out the wrong time because if you're, you're going to send at the wrong time you're going to have a problem. You're going to waste a lot of money.

Sara emphasized the lack of freedom available to individuals engaging in fertility services and how easily the process can become inconvenient and chaotic:

> You can't plan your life more than two weeks an advance . . . like they literally tell you day to day because they're doing this testing and the medication didn't show-up because of an issue with the truck and we needed it because it was one that prevented ovulation . . . we had to drive in the middle of the night to [city] to the emergency pharmacy, it was just a shit show.

Furthermore, legislation and policy can impact female partners' family formation process. Specifically, legal considerations and navigating the rights of each person involved in the process can limit autonomy. Merilou described donor considerations and possible concerns to address.

> Whether we were going to use a known donor or unknown donor and if we're going to use a known donor, how do we protect ourselves but how do we protect the known donor as well ... who gets to name, to name the baby, what are his financial responsibilities, if any, how is he going to be referred to when the kid is born.

Belonging

Belonging (or the lack thereof) was the second subtheme of disconnection. Belonging was the existence and acceptance in a culture. It encompassed the conflict between feeling supported and unsupported at the intersections of their lives (i.e., being daughter, partner, mother, colleague). Participants shared their struggles to live between identities and endorsed feeling unsupported at various times of their conception process. For example, Sara recalled an experience with a colleague that questioned her need to miss work to be present for the conception procedure at the fertility clinic:

> I was saying to [colleague], of all the times it looks like we're going to be going the second day of classes and in my world that is not the day to take off... and [colleague] said "why do you need to go?" and I'm like, that was the only, and I'm like, typically both parents are there for conception, just saying.

Also, Teagan expressed how having a child can change people's perceptions of your relationship and potentially further out female partners. Having children can impact relationships and further create isolation for female partners.

> Cause now we're, we're outing ourselves even more as a couple by having a child for all the people who thought we were, you know, good friends or roommates now suddenly, this baby makes it a little bit more real. We're forcing people to confront that we are a couple.

Discussion

The purpose of this study was to explore the experiences of female partners receiving third-party fertility treatments from an RCT lens. The superordinate themes that emerged reflect both RCT and the extant literature on female partner family formation. First, it was apparent throughout the superordinate theme of disconnection (including subthemes of autonomy and belonging) that female partners experience sexual minority stress, which according to researchers (Cherguit, Pettle, & Tasker; 2012; Holley, 2016; Lewis et al., 2012), results from heterosexist societal stigmatization and marginalization. Due to minority stress, sexual minority females have a higher risk of experiencing a variety of emotional, behavioral, and health problems (Rausch & Wikoff, 2017). All participants identified experiencing emotional, behavioral, or health problems during the family formation process including suicidal ideation and suicide attempts, postpartum anxiety, symptomology related to past trauma, German Measles, and pregnancy induced hypothyroidism. Furthermore, the vast decisions that participants had to consider reflect the authors' descriptions of the process as a "rollercoaster ride," characterized by a multitude of decisions, limited social support, financial stress, and additional barriers experienced in the process of family formation (Rausch & Wikoff, 2017; Somers et al., 2017; Wojnar & Katzenmeyer, 2013).

The super-ordinate theme of connection (including subthemes of love and integrity) are also prevalent in the current literature. As previously mentioned, female partners engage in lengthy discussions, often over a duration of years, before deciding to pursue family formation (Hayman et al., 2013; Hayman & Wilkes, 2016; B. Hayman et al., 2014; Wojnar & Katzenmeyer, 2013). Although this process may exemplify the struggles that female partners face in a heteronormative society, it also speaks to the love and commitment partners have toward each other and their future child. Furthermore, it is evident that the multitude of decisions that they make are not taken lightly, thus exemplifying our subtheme of integrity. Though this study did not elicit new findings from the participants but further confirmation of the current literature, the authors would like to uniquely apply the implications for therapists through the relational-cultural theory in working with female partners in family formation.

Implications for therapists

Based on the two super-ordinate themes discussed, we believe therapists could utilize a Relational-Cultural Theory (RCT) approach, which focuses specifically on connection, when working with female partners engaging in family formation. Because RCT emphasizes the relationship between the partners, repairing it where needed, and using it to overcome challenges during their journey (Rausch & Wikoff, 2017), it is an apt theoretical foundation for therapists to use in these situations. More specifically, RCT provides a framework to explore, identify, and process challenges related to disconnections caused by societal heteronormativity as confirmed in the experiences of female partner family formation. RCT acknowledges that although oppression is often systemic in society, is it ratified in the context of interpersonal relationships (Comstock, Hammer, Strentzsch, Cannon, Parsons & Salazar II, 2008). For female partners, this can include their relationship with each other, friends, family, and providers during their family formation journey. The relational trauma experienced in this context can only be healed by new and healing relationships (Comstock et al., 2008).

RCT can help therapists explore female partners' experiences related to oppression, such as role socialization, power, stigmatization, marginalization, and dominance and subordination, their impact on individual mental health and relational development (Comstock et al., 2008). Therapists can explore and address more specific forms of oppression such as homophobia, heterosexism, and sexism, which impact the intersectional identities of female partners (Singh & Moss, 2016). As confirmed by this study, these experiences are exacerbate for female partners in the experience of family formation.

Heteronormative culture does not provide female partners a sense of belonging (Russell, 2009). When female partners feel isolated, excluded, ostracized, or inferior because of their queer identity, it cultivates disconnection from heteronormative culture (Russell, 2009). To avoid these feelings and situations, female partners can utilize strategies of disconnection as protective factors (Russell, 2009). These strategies inhibit their ability to create and maintain growth fostering relationships, as they are unable to be vulnerable and authentic (Russell, 2009). It is crucial that counslors take time to explore and understand the development and purpose of female partners' self-protective strategies of disconnection in response to these societal conditions (Comstock et al., 2008) as it impacts the couple's decisions around family formation. Furthermore, this supports counselor efforts to also identify oppression and resilence in the context of the therapeutic relationship with female partners, which increases the ability to develop growth fostering relationships that promote healing (Singh & Moss, 2016).

Healing takes place in the context of mutually empathic, growth-fostering relationships (Comstock et al., 2008). Developing a therapeutic growth fostering relationship can evolve into empowerment, healing and transformation for the client, specifically for female partners as this relationship counters heteronormative culture (Singh & Moss, 2016). A growth fostering therapeutic relationship allows their voices to be heard and validated by becoming the center of dialogue (Singh & Moss, 2016). By creating a sense of belonging through growth fostering therapeutic relationships, therapists begin to heal disconnection (Russell, 2009) helping to create a conducive space to consider family formation. Moving toward connection, and away from disconnection, promotes relational development including healing, resilience, and resistance (Russell, 2009).

Therapists can address relational images with female partners, which means therapists will aid in the exploration of expectations and meaning in relationships. Relational images are learned expectations of relationships, which are developed in childhood based on modeling and societal influences (Jordan, 2010). Relational images impact our understanding of relationships including meaning and function (Jordan, 2010) which can cause self-doubt for female couples considering family formation. Relational imaging includes the associations given to specific roles within the context of relationship such as parent, spouse, partner, mother, child, etc. They often include negative stereotypes that increase individuals' self-doubt and feelings of shame (i.e., unworthy, unloveable, inadequate), as a result these images limit individuals' relational development (Comstock et al., 2008). Facilitating dialogue surrounding relational images will enhance the understanding of each individual's interpersonal worldview and potentially help shift negative relational images; for example, therapists can address potential heteronormative culture around motherhood and fatherhood through processing relational images.

Taken together, RCT provides a framework for therapists to work with female partners during family formation. Therapists can work with and process disconnection, including feelings of shame and loneliness, to increase female partners' ability to engage in vulnerable and authentic relationships while identifying strategies to develop these relationships. This encourages female partners to cultivate love (connection) and heal disconnection.

Limitations

To increase trustworthiness in this study reflective journals, field notes, researcher triangulation, thick description, and an audit trail were utilized. However, there are still a number of limitations that are important to acknowledge, including the theorectical framework, inclusion criteria, language constraints, sample size, and cultural considerations. Though one of the three couples identified as Latina, the study did not explore their unique cultural experiences as female partners engaging in family formation. Utilizing RCT as the framework for the study, may limit themes identified as outside the scope of the theory. Cultural considerations (such as ethnicity, socioeconomic status, age, geographic location, individual relationship dynamics) provide a potential limitation to the study, as female partners have intersectional identities that influence their experiences. Taken together, it is important that when reporting these results therapists and researchers carefully consider the inherent limitations of the study.

Future research

Future research is needed as female partner family formation continues to increase. This study focused on female partners engaging in third-party family formation, meaning the findings of the study are not theoretically transferrable to other targeted populations such as female partner adoption or surrogacy, male partner family formation, or heterosexual infertility counseling. These represent gaps in research that could be further explored. In addition, researchers could explore the impacts of shame on fertility success, couple relationship, and provider services. Exploration of shame resilience of female partners engaging in family formation in a heteronormative culture could also be explored. Application of RCT when working with female partners engaging in family formation to address disconnection and shame is an additional area for exploration. These findings could further inform affirmative counseling interventions and practices when with female partners engaging in family formation.

Funding

This work was supported by the North Central Association for Counselor Education and Supervision [2017 Research Award].

ORCID

Jill Nelson http://orcid.org/0000-0001-9695-5204

References

Carpinello, O. J., Jacob, M. C., Nulsen, J., & Benadiva, C. (2016). Utilization of fertility treatment and reproductive choices by lesbian couples. *Fertility and Sterility*, *106*(7), 1709. https://doi.org/10.1016/j.fertnstert.2016.08.050

Cherguit, J., Burns, J., Pettle, S., & Tasker, F. (2012). Lesbian co-mothers' experiences of maternity healthcare services. *Journal of Advanced Nursing*, *69*(6), 1269–1278. https://doi.org/10.1111/j.1365-2648.2012.06115.x

Comstock, D. L., Hammer, T. T., Strentzsch, J., Cannon, K., Parsons, J., & Salazar, G., II. (2008). Relational-Cultural Theory: A framework for bridging relational, multicultural, and social justice competencies. *Journal of Counsleing and Development*, *86*(3), 279–285. https://doi.org/10.1002/j.1556-6678.2008.tb00510.x

Diamond, L. M. (2016). Three critical questions for future research on lesbian relationships. *Journal of Lesbian Studies*, *21*(1), 106–119. https://doi.org/10.1080/10894160.2016.1143756

Dionisius, S. (2015). Queer matters: Family-building processes of lesbian couples using donor insemination. *Scandinavian Journal of Social Theory*, *16*(3), 283–301. https://doi.org/10.1080/1600910X.2015.1091781

Duffey, T., & Somody, C. (2011). The role of Relational-Cultural Theory in mental health counseling. *Journal of Mental Health Counseling*, *33*(3), 223–242. https://doi.org/10.17744/mehc.33.3.c10410226u275647

Fields, C. B., & Scout. (2015). Addressing the needs of lesbian patients. Journal of Sex Education and Therapy, 26 (3), 182–188. doi:doi: 10.1080/01614576.2001.11074412

Hayman, B., & Wilkes, L. (2016). De novo families: Lesbian motherhood. *Journal of Homosexuality*, *64*(5), 577–591. https://doi.org/10.1080/00918369.2016.1194119

Hayman, B., Wilkes, L., Halcomb, E., & Jackson, D. (2014). Lesbian women choosing motherhood: The journey to conception. *Journal of GLBT Family Studies*, *11*(4), 395–409. https://doi.org/10.1080/1550428X.2014.921801

Hayman, B., Wilkes, L., Halcomb, E. J., & Jackson, D. (2013). Marginalised mothers: Lesbian women negotiating heteronormative healthcare services. *Contemporary Nurse*, *44*(1), 120–127. https://doi.org/10.5172/conu.2013.44.1.120

Holley, S. R. (2016). Perspectives on contemporary lesbian relationships. *Journal of Lesbian Studies, 21*(1), 1–6. https://doi.org/10.1080/10894160.2016.1150733

Jordan, J. V. (2010). *Relational-cultural therapy*. American Psychological Association.

Kimberly, C., & Williams, A. (2017). Decade review of research on lesbian romantic relationship satisfaction. *Journal of LGBT Issues in Counseling, 11*(2), 119–135. https://doi.org/10.1080/15538605.2017.1310009

Lavner, J. A. (2016). Relationship satisfaction in lesbian couples: Review, methodological critique, and research agenda. *Journal of Lesbian Studies, 21*(1), 7–29. https://doi.org/10.1080/10894160.2016.1142348

Lewis, R. J., Kholodkov, T., & Derlega, J. D. (2012). Still stressful after all these years: A review of lesbians' and bisexual women's minority stress. *Journal of Lesbian Studies, 16*(1), 30–44. https://doi.org/10.1080/10894160.2011.557641

Miller, K. L. (2012). What will they call you? Rhetorically listening to lesbian maternal narratives. *International Journal of Listening, 26*(3), 134–145. https://doi.org/10.1080/10904018.2012.712471

Nordqvist, P. (2012). Origins and originators: Lesbian couples negotiating parental identities and sperm donor conception. *Culture, Health, & Sexuality: An International Journal for Research, Intervention and Care, 14*(3), 297–311. https://doi.org/10.1080/13691058.2011.639392

Patterson, C. J., & Riskind, R. G. (2010). To be a parent: Issues in family formation among gay and lesbian adults. *Journal of GLBT Family Studies, 6*(3), 326–340. https://doi.org/10.1080/1550428X.2010.490902

Pelka, S. (2009). Sharing motherhood: Maternal jealousy among lesbian co-mothers. *Journal of Homosexuality, 56*(2), 195–217. https://doi.org/10.1080/00918360802623164

Pietkieqiez, I., & Smith, J. A. (2012). A practical guide to using phenomenological analysis in qualitative research psychology. *Psychological Journal, 18*(2), 361–369. https://doi.org/10.14691/CPPJ.20.1.7

Rausch, M. A., & Wikoff, H. D. (2017). Addressing concerns with lesbian couples experiencing fertility treatment: Using Relational Cultural Theory. *Journal of LGBT Issues in Counseling, 11*(3), 142–155. https://doi.org/10.1080/15538605.2017.1346494

Russell, A. (2009). Lesbians surviving culture: Relational-cultural theory applied to lesbian connection. *Journal of Women and Social Work, 24*(4), 406–416. https://doi.org/10.1177/0886109909344059

Ryan, M., & Berkowitz, D. (2009). Constucting gay and lesbian parent families "beyond the clost.". *Qualitative Sociaology, 32*(2), 153–172. https://doi.org/10.1007/s11133-009-9124-6

Singh, A. A., & Moss, L. (2016). Using Relational-Cultural Theory in LGBTQQ counseling: Addressing heterosexism and enhancing relational competencies. *Jouranl of Counseling and Development, 94*(4), 398–404. https://doi.org/10.1002/jcad.12098

Smith, J. A., Flowers, P., & Larkin, M. (2012). *Interpretative phenomenological analysis: Theory, method, and research*. SAGE Publishers, Inc.

Somers, S., Van Parys, H., Provoost, V., Buysse, A., Pennings, G., & De Sutter, P. (2017). How to create a family? Decision making in lesbian couples using donor sperm. *Sexual & Reproductive Healthcare, 11*, 13–18. https://doi.org/10.1016/j.srhc.2016.08.005

Wall, M. (2011). Hearing the voices of lesbian women having children. *Journal of GLBT Family Studies, 7*(1–2), 93–108. https://doi.org/10.1080/1550428X.2011.537231

Wojnar, D. M., & Katzenmeyer, A. (2013). Experiences of preconception, pregnancy, and new motherhood for lesbian nonbiological mothers. *JOGNN, 43*(1), 50–60. https://doi.org/10.1111/1552-6909.12270

Use of the VeedaMom Electronic App as a Pregnancy Treatment Companion

Adriana Dyurich and Marvarene Oliver

ABSTRACT

This phenomenological study explored the lived experiences of pregnant women using VeedaMom, a mobile app created to screen for and manage symptoms of perinatal depression. Participants were required to complete the in-app Edinburgh Postnatal Depression Scale weekly, watch psycho-educational videos featured in the app, and practice mindfulness exercises offered through the app as audio recordings. Individual interviews were conducted with six pregnant women attending a maternal-fetal clinic in South Texas. Three of these participants also took part in a focus group. The findings of this study provide a deeper understanding of pregnant women's experiences while using the VeedaMom app. Some interesting findings refer to the role social media and social pressure play in their motherhood experience, and how an electronic intervention can help as treatment companion.

Use of the VeedaMom electronic app as treatment companion

This article presents the results of a phenomenological study exploring the use of a mobile app as a companion to help pregnant women screen and manage depression. Despite generally accepted beliefs and expectations that pregnancy is a happy and blissful time, pregnancy may be accompanied by feelings of anxiety, fear, insecurity, and sadness (Knudson-Martin & Silverstein, 2009; Puryear, 2007, 2014). Traditionally, the term postpartum depression has been used to identify these feelings. However, studies indicate depression often occurs during pregnancy (Bunevicius et al., 2009; Stowe et al., 2005). Hence the more appropriate term perinatal depression (PND) comprises a broad range of mood and anxiety disorders that can affect women from the beginning of pregnancy until up to one year after the birth of her child (New York State Department of Health, 2012). The DSM-5 (American Psychiatric Association, 2013) is the first edition to include a Major Depressive Disorder (MDD) specifier to read "with peripartum onset" noting, "fifty percent of 'postpartum' major depressive episodes actually begin prior to delivery" (American Psychiatric Association, 2013, p. 186).

Perinatal depression is a pervasive and serious issue. Researchers (Robertson et al., 2004; Thurgood et al., 2009) and renowned organizations such as March of Dimes (2016) and the World Health Organization (2012) recognize postpartum nonpsychotic depression as the most common complication of childbearing. In 2016, the U.S. Preventive Services Task Force issued a recommendation to screen pregnant and postpartum mothers for depression (Siu et al., 2016). The task force also cited the possibility of accurate diagnosis and successful treatment after screening and the harmful effects of untreated depression extending to the child.

Despite the number of women suffering from perinatal depression in the USA and around the world, treatment remains significantly low (Shivakumar et al., 2014). Access to mental health services by pregnant women is limited by factors including the ability of care professionals to explore the issue of perinatal depression, the willingness of the patient to self-report, and the accessibility to adequate mental health care (Shivakumar et al., 2014). Perinatal depression is more prevalent in rural and impoverished areas, and especially in developing countries (Fisher et al., 2012; Shidhaye & Giri, 2014). Risk factors for depression during pregnancy include teenage pregnancy, low income, lower educational attainment, history of depression, and history of abuse (Leigh & Milgrom, 2008). Researchers also suggest that some issues with seeking services relate to stigmatization and clients' negative beliefs surrounding mental health disorders (Shivakumar et al., 2014; Smith et al., 2009).

Use of technology in mental health treatment interventions

The advent of technology provides the opportunity to breach distances and connect providers to clients who otherwise have limited access to professionals and services. The use of health-related mobile interventions can be especially valuable for pregnant women. Derbyshire and Dancey (2013) conducted a review of clinical trials with health-related mobile interventions (n = 1,603 females) finding that smartphones are an excellent way to support women's health, especially in low-income areas. The authors also determined the usage of app technology increases during pregnancy.

Mobile applications (apps) can be an excellent platform to improve access to mental health care, especially in low-income areas, thanks to their ease of use, availability, financial accessibility, and the ability to rate mood/anxiety levels (Goodwin et al., 2016; Schlosser et al., 2017). They have the potential to offer support and promote the achievement of goals when most needed (Turvey & Roberts, 2015). Considering perinatal depression is commonly under-detected and under-treated, in part due to stigmatization and lack of access to services, the rationale for the use of mobile technology in mental health care becomes abundantly clear (Woody et al., 2017).

Few studies conducted on the adequate application and the effectiveness of app technology in mental health have been promising. Schlosser et al. (2017) found that participants using PRIME-D, a mobile app intervention to improve functioning and treat symptoms in adults with depression, showed a significant improvement on PHQ-9 scores over time (>50% reduction). Mood-related disability decreased significantly, and the benefits related to mood and functioning were prolonged over a 4-week follow-up (Schlosser et al., 2017).

Researchers have scarcely addressed the use of app technology during the perinatal period. Osma et al. (2016) conducting a cross-sectional online survey concluded there is "preliminary evidence to suggest the need to design, develop, and test apps that aim to disseminate prevention programs for perinatal depression" (p. 412). Fjeldsoe et al. (2010) conducted a randomized controlled trial on the efficacy of MobileMums, a text message based mobile intervention, to promote physical activity in postpartum women. They found a statistically significant increase in physical activity in the intervention group. Though these two studies are promising, available data about the effectiveness of using technology to improve pregnant women's mental health and access to mental health services is limited.

Purpose of the study

The purpose of this phenomenological study was to explore the lived experiences of pregnant women using *VeedaMom*, an electronic intervention to screen for and manage symptoms of perinatal depression and promote wellness during pregnancy. This study asked the following research questions: (1) What are the lived experiences of pregnant women using an electronic intervention as a companion during their pregnancies? and (2) what are the experiences of pregnant women in regard to anxiety, depression, and wellness while using an electronic intervention?

Method

We utilized the descriptive phenomenological psychological research method proposed by Amadeo Giorgi using Husserlian phenomenology as its philosophical underpinning (Broomé, 2011). Giorgi proposed formal procedures for studying person-in-context with scientific rigor, treating the person studied in a holistic rather than reductionistic manner (Broomé, 2011; Wertz et al., 2016). Only very few studies have concentrated on the use of app technology in the perinatal period. Because of its exploratory nature, phenomenological research was an appropriate approach to study this topic.

Participants

Six pregnant women agreed to take part in the study and completed the individual interviews; three of them participated in the focus group. Five were between 25–34 years old and one was between 35–44 years old. Two participants identified as white, one as Asian/white, and three as Hispanic or Latino origin. Five were married or in a domestic partnership, and one was single/never married. One was pregnant for the first time and five for the second time or more. There were no established eligibility criteria for previous experiences with mental health care or depression. The setting for inviting participants to the study was a maternal-fetal clinic attending to women with high-risk pregnancies located in South Texas. The nurses referred patients who owned an iPhone. The Principal Investigator (PI) was on site to explain the study and obtain informed consent.

Procedure

Participants were required to use the VeedaMom app for a minimum of six weeks and answer the in-app Edinburgh Postnatal Depression Scale (EPDS) on a regular basis, preferably once a week. They were also instructed to watch the psycho-educational videos, practice the provided mindfulness exercises, and use the in-app journal.

VeedaMom App

VeedaMom is a mobile application designed as a companion tool to educate women about PND, help screen for PND, and manage depressive and anxiety symptoms during the perinatal period. For the screening aspect of the app, users assessed their emotional wellbeing using the EPDS. The app sends weekly reminders for users to complete the questionnaire and creates a graph to visually track their progress or change in mood. Based on the results obtained, the app presents users with recommendations or comments such as directing users to the psycho-educational videos and mindfulness exercises; prompting users to call their emergency contact; or, if a mother responds positively to suicidal ideation, prompting her to immediately call her physician, emergency contact, or a suicide hotline, the number for which appears on the screen.

In terms of preventing and managing depressive symptoms and promoting wellness, the app presents users with six psycho-educational videos and six audio mindfulness exercises for stress and anxiety adapted to the perinatal period. The app also includes an in-app journal and other features for the purpose of facilitating social interaction or making the app fun to use.

Data collection

The raw data for this study consisted of the direct descriptions and accounts of the experience using the VeedaMom app while being pregnant, as lived by each participant in her natural way of understanding everyday life. An in-app journal allowed participants to record their thoughts, feelings, or reactions at any given time. Participants were requested to use the journaling feature, but no prompts or reminders were offered. All the entries were considered raw data and analyzed according to Giorgi's descriptive phenomenological method (Giorgi, 2009.) An external IRB-approved interviewer and the PI conducted semi-structured individual interviews lasting between 30 minutes and an hour. The interviews were conducted over the phone or face-to-face in a secure room in the maternal-fetal clinic. All the participants were invited to take part in a focus group and three participants accepted the invitation. The focus group was conducted through a conference phone call that was recorded and transcribed. The first author presented preliminary themes to the group obtained after an analysis of the data to generate feedback and participant check-in.

Trustworthiness

Giorgi (2009) argued that the clearly defined process of phenomenological inquiry offers trustworthiness to qualitative research. Phenomenology methods utilize bracketing to suspend personal biases and assumptions, separate previous knowledge from the participants' description, and ensure rigor in research (Wertz, 1984). The PI kept a journal as an instrument to record and brackets her experiences and reactions as she conducted the research study. A focus group was conducted as consultation with *critical others* to explore with participants the preliminary findings (Giorgi, 2009). Data was obtained from personal interviews, participant journals, and the focus group, achieving triangulation of different data sources. The population and setting offered revelatory descriptions with abundant instances in which the phenomenon investigated was contained in the descriptions (Giorgi, 2009).

Lens of the researcher

My (first author) interest in perinatal depression derived from my personal experiences during two pregnancies and the stories of important women in my life who have experienced perinatal depression. Conversations with respected colleagues and experts in the field informed my point of view on the phenomenon. In addition, I co-created the app, including design and content, used in this study. I am also featured in the videos and audios delivered as interventions.

Data analysis

I (first author and PI) intentionally bracketed any assumptions I might have had based on previous knowledge and scientific understanding of the phenomenon. I transcribed the recordings of each individual interview. The transcriptions became the revelatory descriptions Wertz (1983) called the *individual phenomenal descriptions*. I then read these descriptions to get the holistic awareness necessary to achieve a complete sense of each unit of meaning (Giorgi, 2009). I then re-read each individual description discriminating the intentional psychological objects provided by the participants and breaking them into parts to establish units of meaning (Giorgi, 2009). I highlighted whole phrases and sentences that carried the same fundamental meaning and marked each time the meaning shifted in the data.

I arrived at nine themes and two subthemes, encompassing all the revelatory data across the interviews, journals, and focus group. The main themes were of two types: related to the experience of motherhood and related to the experience of using an app during pregnancy (see Figure 1) I conducted a focus group with three of the six participants who participated in individual interviews. The group participants served as critical others to obtain validation, comments, and corrections on the themes as well as the two categories in which they seemed to fit. I then analyzed the new data from the focus group and compared it to the previously obtained themes. The group validated the

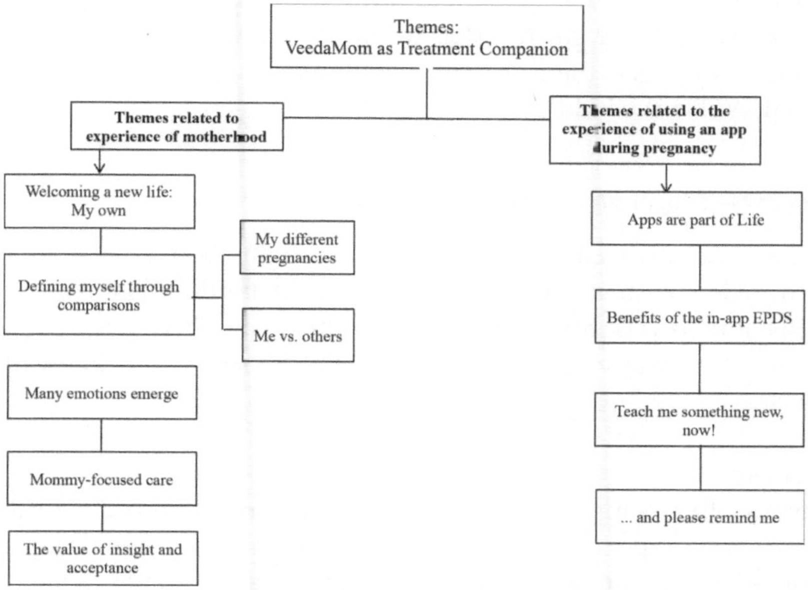

Figure 1. Interrelations among the essential constituents of the experience of using VeedaMom as a companion tool for PND during pregnancy.

previous analysis and offered a deeper understanding of some constituents, including interrelations and influences among themes.

Findings

Figure 1 provides a visual depiction of the resulting psychological structure of the experience as a representation of the nine themes organized within the context of two categories.

Welcoming a new life: my own

The first theme, *welcoming a new life: my own*, reflects the deep changes experienced by women once they become pregnant and have children. Ms. White said it bluntly, "Life changes when you are a mom. You feel different changes that you never even thought of, that worry and concern you . . . my life is *momming*." In many instances, participants expressed no longer having time for themselves, and how much it takes to be a mom. Ms. Rose said, "I think the hardest part for any new mom is finding the balance of still being you, being yourself, and taking care of the baby to the extent that you want to take care of the baby."

Having children emerged as the biggest influence in their experience of life and the main originator of these changes. Some participants described their challenges and difficulties while others its joys and rewards. Ms. White explained how the ability to do activities for her own sake is intrinsically connected to the activities she does with her children. About practicing meditation, she said, "I got to listen to one . . . while I was in the restroom. But I don't always get [the restroom] for myself (laughs). But I am thinking, I can do it WITH the kids."

Defining myself through comparisons

The changes experienced with motherhood brought about a need for participants to redefine their identities. This new definition happened mostly through comparisons between self and others and between pregnancies, further grouping it into two subthemes: (1) *me vs. others* and (2) *my different pregnancies*.

Me vs. others

Participants often compared themselves to other moms in order to describe their own lived experience. Ms. Rose frequently explained her experiences based on what she thought others might think, saying for example, "others would probably say I have let go of myself." Ms. White described a similar experienced when she said, "And then you see moms like breezing through, and you say, 'that must be a bottle-fed baby!'" in contrast with her experience of breastfeeding. Ms. Rose added "It's also the pressure from society, and I think social media plays a big part," and concluded "There's a lot of pressure from the family ... There's definitely a lot of comparison everywhere!" (Ms. Rose).

My different pregnancies

Although there were no questions about previous experiences, the most common comparisons were those among pregnancies for the five participants with older children. In some instances, phrases such as *this time* or *my last* gave away the psychological dimension of the experience while in other instances, participants offered an explicit description. For Ms. Green, the current pregnancy was difficult, and she expressed it as a comparison: "I never had to see a specialist, and with this pregnancy I see a specialist ... " Ms. White shared that her heightened worry happens solely during pregnancies and said, "For sure this one [third pregnancy] has confirmed that, but for my second one my husband was like, 'you got like this last time [first pregnancy]'." Ms. Rose offered a more explicit description of the experience when she said, "I kind of kept comparing what happened with this pregnancy to my previous pregnancy ... it made me more worried to make that comparison."

Need to address many emotions

Participants wanted to expand on the discussion of emotions instead of concentrating on depression. Some participants expressed the app helped them discover and identify these emotions, while others wished the app had more comprehensively addressed other feelings. The most evident emotions described in their experiences were anxiety, guilt, doubt, fear, worry, frustration, and anger. When faced with difficult news about her pregnancy, Ms. Rose's first thought was, "What could I have done differently?" Very similar was the case for Ms. Green, who wondered "What did I do wrong? ... Self blame." Ms. White was very eloquent in expressing, "Those are the things that I think my mind goes away with, like what am I doing wrong? There's almost like guilt."

Some experiences in pregnancy were also frustrating. Ms. Green offered, "I get frustrated, really frustrated with the doctors." Ms. Mustard said, "I felt uncomfortable emotions, and I don't think it has to do with depression, a moment would happen, and you get frustrated or you get mad." Ms. Rose never felt she had emotional issues during her pregnancy, especially not depression. She talked about being very happy to be pregnant, hence becoming one of only two participants discussing pleasant feelings surrounding pregnancy. Nevertheless, she expressed, "I don't know if it was frustration or sadness that I didn't have the time to enjoy the pregnancy."

Some participants experienced anger. Ms. White said after her first pregnancy she "was mad because nobody told me that you might poop when you have a baby." For Ms. Green anger derived from the lack of control she was experiencing over her pregnancy. She was frustrated with both the app and EPDS' focus on depression saying, "I am not sad! I'm probably more angry."

Participants described worry and fear among the emotions most commonly experienced. Ms. White described her fear and worry during pregnancy as paranoia, "I get paranoid [about] everything, kind of like my mind goes Final Destination. My worry is heightened to an extreme." Ms. Blue described experiencing "a lot of anxiety issues." During the focus group they added there is more "worry about the balancing act, than actually being depressed" (Ms. White).

There was also a fear of experiencing depression, especially among those participants with a history of mental health issues. Ms. White explained, "I had depression in the past, so there is always that fear in the back of my head." She added, "One of my fears is postpartum [depression], because I know you are more likely [to have it] when you've had depression before."

Mommy-focused care

The theme of *mommy-focused care* was further divided into two different categories based on the recipient of help and support: help for themselves or others. There was an explicit concern among participants to offer support to other moms. Ms. White explained she made sure other pregnant women in her family were checking on each other. Most participants thought the app could be a good resource to support others, saying "I did share it with some other pregnant people, so they know it's out there" (Ms. Mustard). Participants discussed wanting to feel taken care of in a more implicit manner. Ms. White eloquently explained how "as far as wellbeing" she obtained support from VeedaMom that was not provided by other apps. Other apps are "baby focused, not so much mommy focused. But it's important!"

The high value of insight and acceptance

All participants discussed *the high value of insight and acceptance* and related this self-awareness to the app. Ms. White described her reaction to the first time the EPDS yielded a higher score: "So I had to kind of take a step back and think what am I doing? What's going on?" She described the adverse effects of lack of insight and stated, "[depression] happens without you knowing it" and indicated the app was helping her achieve self-awareness because "you are keeping an eye on yourself." Other participants also valued the benefit of obtaining results immediately. Ms. Mustard described insight as a crucial first step to "wellness and healing."

During data analysis, it became apparent that increased acceptance of their feelings, condition, and reality surrounding them was helpful in dealing with their emotions. Ms. Green indicated, "I kind of accepted the fact that this pregnancy just is what it is; now I am becoming ok". Ms. Rose addressed acceptance after watching one specific video in the app, saying it helped her "focus on this one [pregnancy]. Things are different." Ms. White ended her interview alluding to acceptance: "It's ok to feel like I am not doing this right or I'm so exhausted. And it is something that I think with the app you get to gauge." The importance of acceptance became more obvious during the focus group, with participants agreeing that just "accepting what it is keeps me sane" (Ms. Rose).

Apps are part of life

There were few comments in relation to the use of apps in general, which was a telling sign of the ubiquitous manner in which apps have entered everyday life. Some disclosed having "a couple of baby apps" (Ms. Green). Mrs. Rose corroborated in the focus group that "apps are everywhere, I don't even think much about it, just use them."

Benefits of the in-app EPDS

All participants discussed the EPDS questions extensively. Some described it as their favorite feature in the app, as illustrated by Ms. Green: " ... for my personal use the best thing were the questions." Mostly, they described the benefit of answering the in-app EPDS because it was faster, private, and yielded results. "On the app it is quicker to get it done ... you actually have a physical result" (Ms. Blue). Ms. Green "liked the fact that it would tell me how I was doing fast," and was respectful of their privacy, "without it being intrusive or anything like that, because you know with the app it is very comfortable."

Participants described how accurately "the app has been reflecting my feelings" (Ms. Mustard), and two described instances in which the EPDS identified a risk for depression. As Ms. White noted, "I've been more overwhelmed, so I took it ... it gave me a sad face." For some, there was also a greater chance of them watching a psycho-educational video right after they had obtained results from the EPDS. Ms. Green explained, "There was a week that I was more sad than usual, and that's when [the app] recommended I watch a video ... it did help me."

Teach me something new, now!

Participants expected the app to offer new information or promote behavioral change, and they wanted it to be an immediate response to their needs. Ms.

Rose said the "thing that stuck with me" was the video introducing a new understanding of thoughts and emotions. Ms. Green thought she was learning nothing new until one week when she felt sadder than usual. Because she "was in the app I went ahead and did the video right away." As a result of that positive experience, she wished the app would incorporate other emotions "to provide more resources like it did the week that I was sad."

Participants appreciated mindfulness as a beneficial tool to have during pregnancy. However, they seemed to particularly value the fact that it was new information as helpful with pregnancy experiences. Ms. Rose indicated that "the most useful was the meditation thing because it is not something I would have thought of without the app." Ms. Mustard added, "I was really excited when she was talking about meditation ... It was kind of like something different"

... And please remind me

This last constituent made its way to revelatory descriptions as a stroke of luck after a glitch caused the app to stop sending reminders. Participants agreed the reminders are necessary to be able to keep track of their mood using the EPDS or to develop a mindfulness practice. Ms. Green explained, "If the reminders had been more constant, I would have keep up with it better." And Ms. Blue said this technical issue bothered her. "It needs to be set to send push notifications."

Discussion

Existing research about the use of app technology to promote maternal mental health is limited. Because the VeedaMom app was new, there was no existing research about it. Thus, this study served as an exploratory inquiry into the phenomenon of using the VeedaMom app through descriptive phenomenological methodology. The findings from this study expanded the understanding of the experience of pregnancy while using an app as a companion and the understanding of the experienced thoughts and emotions related to the app itself.

Welcoming a new life: my own

The theme *welcoming a new life: my own* emerged from the profound, life-altering, and ubiquitous changes experienced by women after they become pregnant and have children. These changes are so impactful that the need arises to redefine their identities. Participants agreed most of the changes come from a drastic difference in routine and the fact they are now caring for others first. They also described the influence motherhood had in their relationships with partners, friends, and other family members. Some participants expressed the challenges and difficulties of life with children and others, its joys and rewards. In every case, they referred to their children as one of if not the biggest influences in their experience of life.

Existing research into PND during pregnancy and postpartum makes little explicit reference to efforts in promoting healthy adjustment to this significant life change. But there is an implicit understanding of the need for interventions that promote healthy adjustment observed in the treatment modalities used when addressing perinatal depression.

Redefining myself through comparisons: me vs. others and my different pregnancies

Participants in this study compared themselves to other mothers and compared their own experiences across pregnancies to redefine a new identity and uncover a new understanding of self. Explicitly, the comparisons between self and others were meant to validate their own actions or the feeling of being good mothers. There was also an underlying sense of judgment in their descriptions, with attached nervousness and negative meaning. Participants in the focus group traced the source of these judgmental comparisons to others: close family members, friends, and societal pressure in general. The use of social media might have made it easier, and more pervasive, for mothers to experience these judgments and assessments about themselves.

This finding correlates to previous propositions that disclosing challenges and seeking mental health services is negatively affected by the stigmatization surrounding mental health disorders (Shivakumar et al., 2014; Smith et al., 2009). Women often feel inadequate or ashamed for experiencing negative feelings toward themselves, their babies, or their pregnancies, and hesitate to seek support (Barrera & Nichols, 2015; Megnin-Viggars et al., 2015). Another way in which participants used comparisons to define their experience was by exploring differences and similarities of the current pregnancy versus previous ones.

Need to address many emotions

Women in this study discussed experiencing multiple emotions including anxiety, guilt, doubt, fear, worry, frustration, and anger. A generally accepted definition of perinatal depression includes a wide range of mood and anxiety disorders characterized by feelings of anxiety, fear, insecurity, and sadness surrounding pregnancy (Knudson-Martin & Silverstein, 2009; New York State Department of Health, 2012; Puryear, 2007, 2014). Authors of the DSM-5 acknowledged anxiety and the 'baby blues' might increase the risk for postpartum MDD and included anxiety and panic attacks among the common co-existing symptoms of perinatal depression (American Psychiatric Association, 2013). Heightened fear, anxiety, worry, self-doubt, and an intensified concerned about *everything* during the pregnancy period were described across participants.

Participants in this study made a clear distinction between the emotions they felt and being depressed, thus defining their own experience. Previous findings have clarified that some of the symptoms of depression (e.g., fatigue, weight issues, and insomnia or hypersomnia) can naturally occur during pregnancy (Choate & Gintner, 2011; Marcus, 2009). Yet the participants' determination to differentiate the wide range of emotions they felt from perinatal depression is a unique finding of this study.

Mommy-focused care

Pregnant mothers seek support and information related to their own personal experience, and not just about their baby's growth and care. Participants uncovered the connection between self-care and caring for their babies and their families, and yet disclosed it was difficult to take care of themselves. *Mommy-focused care* also denotes the participants' concern about helping and supporting other moms. Other research findings have confirmed that pregnant women are more likely to seek peer-to-peer support (Shivakumar et al., 2014). Fjeldsoe et al. (2010) also found that mothers placed a high value on mother-centered care.

The high value of insight and acceptance

A noteworthy finding of this study was the value placed by mothers on insight and acceptance. The EPDS was perceived as a valuable tool to promote insight and self-reflection. Women approached answering the questions with intentionality in order to obtain meaningful results and appreciated the ability to see understandable scores immediately. Previous researchers had established the promotion of insight as valuable for maternal and mental health care professionals (Howard et al., 2014; Underwood et al., 2016), and noted the use of apps may help individuals in understanding their experiences (Radovic et al., 2016).

Participants also placed high value in achieving acceptance. Acceptance was described as the most effective mechanism to cope with the challenges of pregnancy and motherhood. Through acceptance mothers expressed kindness and understanding to themselves, which seemed to help them cope with their worries, fears, and frustration. The notion of using acceptance to achieve well-being and mental health is not new, but the connection between acceptance and well-being in the perinatal period is a unique finding of this study.

Apps are part of life

In general, participants referred to apps as positive tools that were already part of their life. Many disclosed using more than one pregnancy app and offered comparisons among them. This finding corroborates that apps are accessible, and available at all times, having the potential to offer support, promote the achievement of goals, and help alleviate symptoms when is most needed (Radovic et al., 2016; Turvey & Roberts, 2015). This study also corroborates previous findings that the use of app technology increases significantly during pregnancy (Derbyshire & Dancey, 2013; Osma et al., 2016).

Benefits of the in-app EPDS

Women in this study found the EPDS as part of the app as one of the most helpful and important features. They appreciated it was as faster, private, and yielded immediate results, and agreed on the positive role the EPDS had in tracking and identifying their emotions and in gaining insight. This finding validates previous research identifying the EPDS as a fast, widely used, and affordable screening tool with the most established psychometric properties of any depression-screening tool for perinatal populations (Milgrom & Gemmill, 2014; Underwood et al., 2016). It also corroborates the appropriateness of adapting screening and assessment tools to be used as app instruments and the ability of such instruments to rate mood/anxiety levels (Ameringen et al., 2017; Derbyshire & Dancey, 2013; Goodwin et al., 2016; Schlosser et al., 2017).

Teach me something new, now!

Participants wanted the app to offer immediate responses to their needs. They appreciated mindfulness as a beneficial strategy, but its value might derive more from its novelty than for the participant's ability to practice it. This finding confirms previous research indicating pregnant women's interest in health-related apps and information, and the need to develop and test apps for perinatal depression and wellbeing (Osma et al., 2016).

... and please remind me

Participants perceived reminders as a convenient and indispensable part of the app. Women relied on this feature to remember completing the EPDS, watch videos, change behavioral patterns, or develop a mindfulness practice. Without reminders, most women decreased or stopped the number of visits to the app. Other researchers' findings confirm interventions that offer reminders are perceived as useful and motivating in increasing health related behaviors (Fjeldsoe et al., 2010).

Limitations

Although the present study produced meaningful findings, there were some limitations worth addressing. All participants were patients of a maternal-fetal clinic located in South Texas. The clinic services women whose pregnancies are considered high-risk, even with no actual complicating issues, which might have had an effect on the emotions experienced by the participants. The demographic characteristics of the sample were reflective of the clinic's location. Though diverse for a small sample size, results of this study may not represent experiences of women who identify with different or more specific groups or live in different areas. Women were at various stages of pregnancy and some had delivered their babies by the time the focus group was held, but there was not enough data to demonstrate any implications related to the stages of pregnancy. Although the study design included measures to reduce participants' sense of pressure, it is possible the participants felt pressure to conform to use the app.

Implications

Mental health practitioners can find it beneficial to incorporate the use of apps into their practices and embrace it as part of the therapeutic process. These same professionals are also encouraged to advance the creation of ethical and evidence-based app-delivered interventions that focus on mental health as the first author has done. Findings from this study confirm that one way to offer mother-centered care is by promoting insight and acceptance which was a goal of the VeedaMom app.

Therapy, early intervention, and psycho-educational practices could be more effective if they serve to educate women about a whole range of emotions, including pleasant and unpleasant ones. Based on the unique experiences of pregnancy and motherhood, it is necessary to allow for a new definition of perinatal mental health that includes adjustment to changes, instead of classifying the experiences as PND. As important as it is to treat clinical depression, mothers might highly benefit from preventive interventions aimed at promoting healthy adjustment like this app. Because of mothers' unique understanding of their experiences, self- disclosure might not be sufficient in identifying mental and emotional challenges. This study confirms that using screening instruments such as VeedaMom aimed only at depression may not be sufficient but do successfully serve to open important exploratory conversations about perinatal mental health.

Recommendations for future research

This study promotes the importance of investigating the effectiveness and adequacy of existing app- delivered interventions and other possible

applications of this technology in promoting mental health. This study is a response to the need for more research about maternal wellness and mental health starting during pregnancy, to research effective therapeutic approaches and interventions during the perinatal period. Future research on perinatal mental health and the use of apps across the lifespan for different presenting issues can be beneficial for the advancement of more effective and appropriate therapies.

Conclusions

The findings of this study provide a deeper understanding of pregnant women's experiences in relation to perinatal depression while using the VeedaMom app as treatment companion. The participants' descriptions referred to two important aspects of the phenomenon: the experience of motherhood and the experience of using an app during pregnancy. Participants described pregnancy as a time of profound and significant change that might lead them to redefine their own identity. Life as a mother is surrounded by comparisons, judgment, and challenges that bring about a wide range of emotions. Participants seemed to experience emotions that included doubt, guilt, anger, worry, anxiety, frustration, and fear. Nevertheless, they made an effort to clearly distinguish the moods and emotions described in their experiences from perinatal depression. This could be a consequence of stigmatization of mental disorders, a lack of understanding of the disorder, or an effort to define their experiences in their own terms. In any case, the use of disorder terminology seems to be inadequate in describing the experiences of pregnancy.

When asked about emotions, most participants described unpleasant or uncomfortable feelings. Only a few included happiness, joy, or comfort in their revelatory descriptions, although they described how identifying pleasant emotions might have a positive effect in mothers' experiences. An encompassing wellness approach in an app addressing emotions that surround pregnancy and childbirth is a needed companion.

Participants perceived the app as helpful and valuable, especially related to outcomes linked to mother-centered care and the promotion of insight and acceptance. The use of the in-app EPDS was an essential tool to help them accomplish these outcomes. Some of the findings were unique to this study. At the time of this writing, the high value of acceptance during the perinatal period had not been discussed in previous findings. Neither had other researchers explicitly discussed the importance of presenting mothers with new and unique information, nor the essential role reminders play when using an app.

There is still much to be accomplished in advancing supportive interventions and quality of care for perinatal mothers. Through this study we aimed to gain a deeper understanding of pregnant mothers' experiences using the VeedaMom app as a treatment companion. Some findings were consistent with current literature in relation to the use of app technology for mental health care, including specifically its use during the pregnancy period. Unique findings on the experience of motherhood and app technology also emerged from this study. We hope this study inspires further research that will contribute to the understanding of maternal experiences of pregnancy and motherhood, the needs of mothers in the perinatal period, and the best way mental health professionals can address those needs including the use of app technology.

References

American Psychiatric Association. (2013). *Diagnostic and statistical manual of mental disorders* (5th ed.). Author.

Ameringen, M., Turna, J., Khalesi, Z., Pullia, K., Patterson, B., & Van Ameringen, M. (2017). There is an app for that! The current state of mobile applications (apps) for DSM-5 obsessive-compulsive disorder, posttraumatic stress disorder, anxiety and mood disorders. *Depression & Anxiety (1091-4269)*, *34*(6), 526–539. https://doi.org/10.1002/da.22657

Barrera, A. Z., & Nichols, A. D. (2015). Depression help-seeking attitudes and behaviors among an Internet-based sample of Spanish-speaking perinatal women. *Pan American Journal of Public Health*, *37*(3), 148–153.

Broomé, R. E. (2011). *Descriptive phenomenological psychological method: An example of a methodology section from doctoral dissertation*. Saybrook University.

Bunevicius, A., Kusminskas, L., Pop, V. J., Pedersen, C. A., & Bunevicius, R. (2009). Screening for antenatal depression with the Edinburgh Depression Scale. *Journal of Psychosomatic Obstetrics and Gynecology*, *30*(4), 238–243. https://doi.org/10.3109/01674820903230708

Choate, L. H., & Gintner, G. G. (2011). Prenatal depression: Best practice guidelines for diagnosis and treatment. *Journal of Counseling & Development*, *89*(3), 373–381. https://doi.org/10.1002/j.1556-6678.2011.tb00102.x

Derbyshire, E., & Dancey, D. (2013). Smartphone medical applications for women's health: What is the evidence-base and feedback? *International Journal of Telemedicine and Applications*, *2013*, 9. https://doi.org/10.1155/2013/782074

Fisher, J., Cabral de Mello, M., Patel, V., Rahman, A., Tran, T., Holton, S., & Holmes, W. (2012). Prevalence and determinants of common perinatal mental disorders in women in low- and lower-middle-income countries: A systematic review. *Bulletin of the World Health Organization*, *90*, 139–149H.

Fjeldsoe, B. S., Miller, Y. D., & Marshall, A. L. (2010). MobileMums: A randomized controlled trial of an SMS-based physical activity intervention. *Annals of Behavioral Medicine*, *39*(2), 101–111. https://doi.org/10.1007/s12160-010-9170-z

Giorgi, A. (2009). *The descriptive phenomenological method in psychology: A modified Husserlian approach*. Duquesne University Press.

Goodwin, J., Cummins, J., Behan, L., & O'Brien, S. M. (2016). Development of a mental health smartphone app: Perspectives of mental health service users. *Journal of Mental Health*, *25*(5), 434–440. https://doi.org/10.3109/09638237.2015.1124392

Howard, L. M., Piot, P., & Stein, A. (2014). No health without perinatal mental health. *The Lancet, 384*(9956), 1723. https://doi.org/10.1016/S0140-6736(14)62040-7

Knudson-Martin, C., & Silverstein, R. (2009). Suffering in silence: A qualitative meta-data-analysis of postpartum depression. *Journal of Marital and Family Therapy, 35*(2), 145–158. https://doi.org/10.1111/j.1752-0606.2009.00112.x

Leigh, B., & Milgrom, J. (2008). Risk factors for antenatal depression, postnatal depression and parenting stress. *BMC Psychiatry, 8*(1), 24. https://doi.org/10.1186/1471-244X-8-24

March of Dimes (2016, March). *Postpartum depression.* http://www.marchofdimes.org/pregnancy/postpartum-depression.aspx

Marcus, S. M. (2009). Depression during pregnancy: Rates, risks and consequences. *Canadian Journal of Clinical Pharmacology, 16*, 15–22.

Megnin-Viggars, O., Symington, I., Howard, L. M., & Pilling, S. (2015). Experience of care for mental health problems in the antenatal or postnatal period for women in the UK: A systematic review and meta-synthesis of qualitative research. *Archives of Women's Mental Health, 18*(6), 745. https://doi.org/10.1007/s00737-015-0548-6

Milgrom, J., & Gemmill, A. W. (2014). Screening for perinatal depression. *Best Practice & Research Clinical Obstetrics & Gynaecology, 28*(1), 13–23. https://doi.org/10.1016/j.bpobgyn.2013.08.014

New York State Department of Health. (2012). *Understanding maternal depression, a fact sheet for care providers.* https://www.health.ny.gov/community/pregnancy/health_care/perinatal/maternal_factshe

Osma, J., Barrera, A. Z., & Ramphos, E. (2016). Are pregnant and postpartum women interested in health-related apps? Implications for the prevention of perinatal depression. *Cyberpsychology, Behavior, and Social Networking, 19*(6), 412–415. https://doi.org/10.1089/cyber.2015.0549

Puryear, L. J. (2007). *Understanding your moods when you're expecting: Emotions, mental health, and happiness- before, during, and after pregnancy.* Houghton Mifflin.

Puryear, L. J. (2014). Postpartum adjustment: What is normal and what is not. In D. L. Barnes, (Ed..), *Women's reproductive mental health across the lifespan [E-reader version]* (pp. 109–122). https://doi.org/10.1007/978-3-319-05116-1_6

Radovic, A., Vona, P. L., Santostefano, A. M., Ciaravino, S., Miller, E., & Stein, B. D. (2016). Smartphone applications for mental health. *Cyberpsychology, Behavior, and Social Networking, 19*(7), 465–470. https://doi.org/10.1089/cyber.2015.0619

Robertson, E., Grace, S., Wallington, T., & Stewart, D. E. (2004). Antenatal risk factors for postpartum depression: A synthesis of recent literature. *General Hospital Psychiatry, 26*(4), 289–295. https://doi.org/10.1016/j.genhosppsych.2004.02.006

Schlosser, D. A., Campellone, T. R., Truong, B., Anguera, J. A., Vergani, S., Vinogradov, S., & Arean, P. (2017). The feasibility, acceptability, and outcomes of PRIME-D: A novel mobile intervention treatment for depression. *Depression & Anxiety (1091-4269), 34*(6), 546–554. https://doi.org/10.1002/da.22624

Shidhaye, P., & Giri, P. (2014). Maternal depression: A hidden burden in developing countries. *Annals of Medical and Health Sciences Research, 4*, 463–465.

Shivakumar, G., Brandon, A. R., Johnson, N. L., & Freeman, M. P. (2014). Screening to treatment: Obstacles and predictors in perinatal depression (STOP-PPD) in the Dallas Healthy Start program. *Archives of Women's Mental Health, 17*(6), 575–578. https://doi.org/10.1007/s00737-014-0438-3

Siu, A., Bibbins-Domingo, K., Grossman, D. C., Baumann, L. C., Davidson, K. W., Ebell, M., García, F. A. R., Gillman, M., Herzstein, J., Kemper, A. R., Krist, A. H., Kurth, A. E., Owens, D. K., Phillips, W. R., Phipps, M. G., & Pignone, M. P., & the US Preventive

Services Task Force (USPSTF). (2016). Screening for depression in adults: U.S. preventive services task force recommendation statement. *Journal of the American Medical Association, 315*(4), 380–387.

Smith, M. V., Shao, L., Howell, H., Wang, H., Poschman, K., & Yonkers, K. A. (2009). Success of mental health referral among pregnant and postpartum women with psychiatric distress. *General Hospital Psychiatry, 31*(2), 155–162. https://doi.org/10.1016/j.genhosppsych.2008.10.002

Stowe, Z., Hostetter, A., & Newport, D. (2005). The onset of postpartum depression: Implications for clinical screening in obstetrical and primary care. *American Journal of Obstetrics & Gynecology, 192*(2), 522–526. https://doi.org/10.1016/j.ajog.2004.07.054

Thurgood, S., Avery, D., & Williamson, L. (2009). Postpartum depression (PPD). *American Journal of Clinical Medicine, 6*, 17–22.

Turvey, C. L., & Roberts, L. J. (2015). Recent developments in the use of online resources and mobile technologies to support mental health care. *International Review of Psychiatry, 27*(6), 547–557. https://doi.org/10.3109/09540261.2015.1087975

Underwood, L., Waldie, K., D'Souza, S., Peterson, E. R., & Morton, S. (2016). A review of longitudinal studies on antenatal and postnatal depression. *Archives of Women's Mental Health, 19*(5), 711–720. https://doi.org/10.1007/s00737-016-0629-1

Wertz, F. (1983). From everyday to psychological description: Analyzing the moments of a qualitative data analysis. *Journal of Phenomenological Psychology, 14*(1–2), 197. https://doi.org/10.1163/156916283X00108

Wertz, F. (1984). Procedures in phenomenological research and the question of validity. *Exploring the Lived World: Phenomenological Psychology, 23*, 29–48.

Wertz, F., Desai, M., Maynard, E., Misurell, J., Morrissey, M. B., Rotter, B., & Skoufalos, N. (2016, May). *Research methods for person-centered health science: Fordham studies of suffering and transcendence* [Paper presentation]. Paper presented at the Society for Qualitative Inquiry in Psychology Conference, Mahwah, NJ.

Woody, C. A., Ferrari, A. J., Siskind, D. J., Whiteford, H. A., & Harris, M. G. (2017). A systematic review and meta-regression of the prevalence and incidence of perinatal depression. *Journal of Affective Disorders*. Advanced online publication. https://doi.org/10.1016/j.jad.2017.05.003

World Health Organization. (2012). *Depression: A global public health concern* http://www.who.int/mental_health/management/depression/who_paper_depression_wfmh_2012.pdf

World Health Organization. (2016). *Maternal mental health*. Retrieved from http://www.who.int/mental_health/maternal-child/maternal_mental_health/en/

"A Silent Battle": Using a Feminist Approach to Support Couples after Miscarriage

Angela R. Hiefner

ABSTRACT

The lack of recognition and understanding of miscarriage as a significant loss often leaves bereaved parents with less social support to help them navigate their grief. In a phenomenological study of parents' experiences of miscarriage, a theme emerged regarding disenfranchisement and the norm of silence surrounding early pregnancy loss. This theme contributes to overwhelming evidence that miscarriage is a unique loss with additional challenges. This paper will discuss this theme of disenfranchisement and describe how a feminist approach to couples therapy can provide greater support to parents experiencing this loss.

Miscarriage, a pregnancy loss prior to 20 weeks gestation, is estimated to occur in 10–25% of all clinically confirmed pregnancies (American Pregnancy Association, 2015). Despite the frequency of this type of loss, it has been described by Lang et al. (2011) as a disenfranchised grief, an experience defined as a loss that is "not openly acknowledged, publicly mourned, or socially supported" (Doka, 1989, p. 4). Research has identified multiple sources of disenfranchisement after miscarriage, including society (Callister, 2006; Chollete, 2012), family members and friends (McCreight, 2004; Trepal et al., 2005), and healthcare providers (Bellhouse et al., 2019; Lang et al., 2011; Rowlands & Lee, 2010). Though not all parents respond to miscarriage in the same way, for many the impact of this loss is profound and initiates a period of intense grief (Brier, 2008). The lack of recognition and understanding of miscarriage as a significant loss leaves bereaved parents with less social support to help them through the process of grieving the loss of their child (Renner et al., 2000). This paper will review research exploring disenfranchisement and social norms related to pregnancy and early pregnancy loss, present-related findings that emerged in a broader qualitative study of parents' experiences of miscarriage, and describe how a feminist approach may be particularly meaningful in supporting parents who are navigating this type of loss. Together, a growing evidence base for the disenfranchisement experienced by many parents after miscarriage and guidance for clinicians working with this population can increase the availability of support for bereaved parents.

Disenfranchisement after miscarriage

Lack of societal recognition

Though the loss of a baby due to miscarriage is profound, there is minimal societal recognition of the loss as significant and painful (Callister, 2006; Chollete, 2012; Leon, 2008; Renner et al., 2000). Many bereaved parents feel that society generally views this type of loss as 'just a miscarriage' (DeFrain et al., 1996). While a mother's loss is seldom fully recognized and validated, a father's is even less so, because miscarriage is typically not considered an event that is of concern to men, apart from the support they are expected to provide their partners (Rinehart & Kiselica, 2010).

The sense of disenfranchisement is further complicated by the absence of a publicly acknowledged person to bury and no established rituals to structure mourning and gain support, as with other losses (Bellhouse et al., 2018; Brier, 2008; Callister, 2006; McCreight, 2004). Parents may find it difficult to reconcile this lack of acknowledgment of the loss with their sense of connection to their baby (Lang et al., 2011). Many parents have already begun developing a relationship with their baby, such as picking out names, buying furniture and clothes, imagining what their child will be like, and making plans for the future of their growing family (Lang et al., 2011). In addition to the broader societal lack of acknowledgment of this loss, parents' support networks and medical providers also often fail to recognize the significance of the experience of miscarriage (Bellhouse et al., 2018).

Support network

Support systems are a primary factor affecting parents' emotional recovery after miscarriage (Renner et al., 2000; Trepal et al., 2005). While supportive relationships aid parents' abilities to cope with their loss, family members and friends often make statements that minimize the importance of miscarriage (Bellhouse et al., 2018; Trepal et al., 2005) or avoid the topic entirely (Bellhouse et al., 2018). These responses from family members and friends contribute to parents' sense of disenfranchisement and can result in parents feeling they do not have the right or space to grieve for their baby (Trepal et al., 2005).

Many parents may feel disappointed by the lack of support and empathy after their loss (Bellhouse et al., 2018). Bereaved parents may feel that their family and friends do not recognize the loss as being as significant and painful as other deaths (Lang et al., 2011; Wagner et al., 1997). In a paper describing her loss experience, Meyer (2016) poignantly states that phrases often used by others after miscarriage (e.g., "You can always have another"; "It just wasn't your time"; "It's probably better off this way."), would not be acceptable after other losses, and yet are uttered anyway. Though family members and friends often have good intentions of offering support, these responses invalidate parents' experiences of miscarriage (Meyer, 2016).

Medical providers

Healthcare providers encounter individuals and couples experiencing miscarriage in a variety of different medical settings, including outpatient clinics, emergency departments, and obstetrical units (DiMarco et al., 2002). The care these providers offer is particularly important because many bereaved parents do not receive adequate support from family and friends, and may also have little to no prior experience with a major loss (DiMarco et al., 2002; Rowlands & Lee, 2010). Bereaved parents will vary in their need for social and professional support after miscarriage (Bellhouse et al., 2019), but healthcare providers are often parents' first point of contact after miscarriage and can inform them about what is available to them and help them find ways to cope with their loss (DiMarco et al., 2002; Hutti, 2005).

Though empathic care can play a significant role in how parents are able to navigate their loss and grief (Evans, 2012), many parents experience their healthcare providers as dismissing the meaning of the loss (Bellhouse et al., 2019) and viewing miscarriage as routine and trivial (Lang et al., 2011). Research has indicated that only a minority of mothers and even fewer fathers are asked by healthcare providers about how they are coping with the miscarriage, resulting in a general perception of support from these providers as less than optimal (Bellhouse et al., 2019; Conway & Russell, 2000; Lang et al., 2011).

Recommendations in the literature for more effective care after miscarriage include better provision of information to women and their partners (Robinson, 2014; Smith et al., 2006), improving the treatment decision-making process to allow women a more active role (Olesen et al., 2015), educational programs to provide healthcare providers with greater expertise in supporting parents after miscarriage (DiMarco et al., 2002), and developing a strong referral system and resource list (Kong et al., 2010). Though research has highlighted a number of ways that medical providers can improve care post-miscarriage, research has also identified time constraints, lack of resources, and compassion fatigue as barriers to medical providers' greater responsiveness to parents' loss experiences (Jensen et al., 2019). Family therapists are uniquely qualified to provide support after miscarriage due to their systemic training and can partner with medical providers in a way that addresses these barriers and creates greater access to supportive care for parents navigating loss and grief (Hodgson et al., 2018).

Norm of silence

Pregnancy and pregnancy loss are subject to deeply ingrained societal norms and rules regarding what can be discussed and when. Bute et al. (2019) identified three major societal-level privacy rules that govern how individuals and couples share about miscarriage: (1) miscarriage should not be discussed openly, (2) men should not discuss miscarriage and women have more permission to mourn the loss publicly, and (3) news of pregnancy should not be shared too soon in case a miscarriage occurs. These rules contribute to the silence and stigma that impact parents' abilities to mourn and obtain support in their loss.

For parents' support systems, the silence resulting from these societal norms contributes to perpetuating a lack of understanding of the significance of the loss, discomfort with discussing the loss, and difficulty knowing how to provide support, which may result in avoidance of the topic or unintentional minimization of the loss (Bellhouse et al., 2018; Bute et al., 2019). Despite the pervasiveness of disenfranchisement after miscarriage, research indicates that society may have concrete understanding of miscarriage as a loss, but lack the important emotional meaning attached to the loss (Renner et al., 2000). Without emotional understanding of miscarriage, individuals within parents' support systems may have difficulty grasping the impact of the loss unless they have experienced it themselves (Bellhouse et al., 2018). The norm of silence surrounding early pregnancy and miscarriage coupled with few physical markers that indicate a loss has occurred may explain society's lack of understanding of the significance of miscarriage (Bute et al., 2019; McCreight, 2004).

With strict guidelines about when pregnancies should be announced, miscarriage often occurs before important potential sources of support are aware of the pregnancy (Bellhouse et al., 2018). Together, norms related to announcing pregnancy and discussing miscarriage further reduce the availability of support and can result in parents feeling alone and isolated as they attempt to navigate their grief (Bellhouse et al., 2018; Markin & Zilcha-Mano, 2018). The norm of silence also contributes to an underestimation of how commonly miscarriage occurs (Bute et al., 2019), further exacerbating parents' experiences of isolation, as well as stigma (Bellhouse et al., 2018; Frost et al., 2007). Stigma is fueled by the silence and resulting misconceptions about miscarriage, including assumptions that a mother's actions or something she consumed caused the miscarriage and a perceived link between miscarriage and abortion (Frost et al., 2007). Normalization of miscarriage can reduce stigma and isolation, but paired with validation of the meaning of the loss, can help to prevent the loss from feeling minimized as trivial and commonplace.

Until early pregnancy and miscarriage can be more openly discussed, bereaved parents will continue to face a lack of acknowledgment of their loss, stigma surrounding the experience, insufficient support, and the sense of isolation that follows. Many researchers and the participants in their studies have called for greater efforts to break the silence and change societal norms (Bellhouse et al., 2018; Frost et al., 2007; Markin & Zilcha-Mano, 2018). With greater conversation, miscarriage may eventually be viewed as a normal part of reproduction (Frost et al., 2007), and gain recognition and validation as a significant and painful loss. To add to this important conversation, this qualitative study explored parents' experiences of disenfranchisement after miscarriage with the goal of contributing to a growing evidence base for an important aspect of miscarriage that creates significant challenges for parents attempting to navigate grief and loss.

Method

In a broader study of parents' experiences of miscarriage, a descriptive phenomenological approach was utilized to explore partners' dyadic experiences of the loss, particularly in regard to experiences of greater closeness and strength (author). The purpose of the study was to develop a greater understanding of what enables some couples to experience greater strength and closeness after miscarriage. Though experiences of disenfranchisement were not explicitly explored, disenfranchisement emerged as an important theme in this phenomenological study, contributing to a large base of evidence indicating that miscarriage is a unique loss with additional challenges. This article focuses on this finding.

The descriptive phenomenological method was developed by Edmund Husserl and aims to capture rich descriptions of an experience in order to identify essential meanings within a phenomenon (Converse, 2012; Dowling & Cooney, 2012; Giorgi, 2005). In this methodological approach, a phenomenon is studied as it appears in the consciousness of the individuals experiencing it, leading researchers to form general, thematized descriptions of what it means to experience that particular phenomenon for the sample studied (Dowling & Cooney, 2012; Giorgi, 1997). Applied to the study of couples' experiences of miscarriage, a descriptive phenomenological approach contributes to a richer understanding of what it means to navigate this loss as a couple. Findings provide guidance to researchers studying this phenomenon, as well as the clinicians working on the front lines to support individuals, couples, and families impacted by miscarriage.

Sample

This study received IRB approval. Recruitment occurred via purposive sampling through two family medicine clinics at a large metropolitan medical center and through the Collaborative Family Healthcare Association (CFHA) listserv, as well as snowball sampling. A recruitment flyer was utilized for each recruitment method, and interested participants contacted the researcher, who then assessed for eligibility and answered questions about the study.

Potential participants were assessed for four inclusion criteria: (1) opposite sex relationship described as committed by both partners, (2) an awareness of the pregnancy prior to the miscarriage, (3) a desire by both partners for the pregnancy, and (4) the couples' most recent miscarriage occurred within the last four years. Couples were not included in the study if their loss occurred after 20 weeks of gestation, or if partners were separated at the time of the interview.

The study resulted in 18 interviews, collected across 12 participants who made up 6 couples. One couple reported two miscarriages, about a year apart, and the other five couples reported one miscarriage. Participant ages ranged from 20 to 45, and relationship length ranged from three to ten years. Though marital status was not an inclusion criterion, all participating couples were married. Five of the couples had living children at the time of the interview, and one couple had no living children. Three partners identified as Hispanic/Latino, and nine identified as Caucasian. Education level ranged from high school diploma to graduate degree, and annual household income ranged from 20,000 USD – 34,999 USD to 100,000 USD – 149,999. USD

Procedure

Semi-structured interviews were conducted using open-ended questions and follow up probing questions to elicit rich descriptions of the partners' experiences of navigating miscarriage within the context of their relationship (e.g., How is your relationship the same or different after the miscarriage? What do you think contributed to those changes?). In order to capture a broad range of data within each couple dyad, three interviews were conducted with each couple, a conjoint interview followed by an individual interview with each partner. Each interview consisted of the same questions in an effort to develop greater depth in the participants' descriptions, with one additional question added for the individual interview (Were there ways that you coped with the miscarriage that did not include your partner or upset your partner?). The participants were given the option of conducting the interview in person at a location of their choice or via video call, with care taken to ensure that the chosen location maintained participant confidentiality. Each interview was audio-recorded, and brief field notes were taken to capture important non-verbal information (e.g., facial expressions, tone, gestures).

Utilizing both conjoint and individual interviews served multiple functions. First, conjoint interviews support the richness sought by qualitative research through opportunities for participants to elicit responses from each other as they tell their story together (Morgan et al., 2013; Polak & Green, 2016). Second, multiple interviews with a period of time between each enabled participants to reflect on their experience and the stories shared by their partner. Many of the partners shared that the conjoint interview reminded them of forgotten parts of their miscarriage experience, and also that hearing their partner's story gave new shape to their own experience, which they were able to describe in the individual interview. Third, a follow up individual interview creates space for participants to share parts of their story they withheld during the conjoint interview (Morgan et al., 2013). Lastly, conducting both conjoint and individual interviews utilizes the strengths of each, while also increasing the rigor and trustworthiness of the qualitative data by collecting from multiple perspectives and sources (Eisikovits & Koren, 2010).

Data analysis

Data analysis began with the completion of the first set of interviews in order to assess for saturation of themes throughout the course of data collection (Saunders et al., 2018). Recruitment and data collection occurred over a period of eight months and concluded when new themes were no longer emerging. Throughout the process of data collection and analysis, the researcher engaged in a continuous, reflective process of bracketing to ensure the trustworthiness of the data. This process of identifying biases and presuppositions that can influence data collection and analysis is a critical component of Husserl's descriptive phenomenological method and serves to ensure the trustworthiness of qualitative data (Hein & Austin, 2001). Relevant areas of bracketing for this study included the researcher's experience as a woman who has not directly experienced pregnancy loss, but experienced this loss indirectly as a daughter of parents who had multiple miscarriages.

Each interview audio recording was transcribed in preparation for data analysis. With the couple dyad identified as the unit of analysis, each couple's set of three interview transcripts was read together in order to begin obtaining a global sense of each couple's experience. Data analysis then proceeded with a second reading of the data, at which point thematic analysis was utilized to code important categories and themes. These themes were integrated to create a broader sense of the essential meanings within the couples' experiences of miscarriage (Vaismoradi et al., 2013). NVivo 12 (QSR International Pty Ltd, 2018) was then used in a third reading of all interview transcripts for further refinement of the themes. All data were additionally independently reviewed by a Masters-level researcher with a background in psychology to further enhance trustworthiness (Morse et al., 2002).

During this analysis process, experiences of disenfranchisement emerged as an important theme within the couples' descriptions. To further explore this theme, a second analysis was then conducted in a similar manner. This analysis resulted in two major themes: Loss Minimized and Norm of Silence.

Findings

Though disenfranchisement was not specifically explored in the initial study, descriptions of minimization of the loss and the norm of silence emerged repeatedly throughout the couples' narratives. Each of the couples felt they were able to cope successfully with their loss(es), but navigating their grief was made more challenging by the disenfranchised nature of miscarriage.

Loss minimized

Four of the six couples described experiences of their loss being minimized by others. For one couple, this was felt in responses from family members, and for three others this was experienced in interactions with healthcare providers. In addition to these experiences, minimization and invalidation were also described more broadly as a perception of other people's problems as more significant.

Though family members had good intentions for supporting Kim and Juan in their grief, Kim shared that some of their comments unintentionally minimized the loss and framed it as easily replaceable. She stated: "I think they did their best. They said, 'Oh, you can have another one.' But of course that's not what I wanted to hear at that moment, you know." For other couples, the minimization was experienced from healthcare providers. Andrea and Federico did not feel that their physician or the other providers they came in contact with acknowledged their loss as significant. Andrea compared miscarriage to a car accident to illustrate her confusion about several healthcare providers' lack of acknowledgment of the loss:

> There is a process when you go through a car accident. And they say, "Do you need any support?" Like, for the trauma. But why nobody when you are in a miscarriage, why does nobody tell you, "Okay so this miscarriage can last for weeks and you are going to see every single time how your baby is leaving . . . " Why is there no support in that traumatic moment? I mean, to me that's more traumatic than when you have a fender bender. I mean, it's something that is huge. Nobody's even mentioning. Like, "Yeah it's a miscarriage, you will get pregnant again." Excuse me. It was alive. It was a loss for a family. And nobody is even thinking that.

Federico shared a similar sentiment that the miscarriage was treated as "this is no big deal. Yes, it's really sad for you, but it's just part of life." Jenny and Will also experienced minimization from their physician. Jenny shared about the interaction she had with her physician after receiving final confirmation of the miscarriage:

> She told me, "At least we know you can get pregnant." And I was like, "Yeah, but that doesn't fix now. I mean, I'm not gonna go back six weeks later to try to have another baby. Holy crap, no." It's just like, "At least you can move on later on down the road," kind of . . . .There was a moment there where she kinda belittled the situation I feel like. I was upset and she was like, "It's a loss, but it's not a loss."

The experience of feeling the miscarriage was minimized and invalidated as a significant and painful loss seemed to lead to the couples questioning their experience and feeling that other people, more generally, perceive miscarriage as relatively insignificant in comparison with other experiences. Jenny stated:

> I felt like I didn't have a right to be upset because I didn't, you know, my doctor at first was like, "Well you know, it's a loss without being a loss." . . . And a lot of women, they go through stillbirths and they go through so many things, that ours seemed so trivial. Or that's what she kinda made it seem like, that it was just so trivial.

Despite feeling a deep and painful sense of loss, Jenny began to feel she was overreacting after receiving messages from others that her miscarriage was not a significant loss. Nicole expressed a similar sense of not having the right to be upset or the right to ask for support from her physician: "I feel like they're saving quadruplets out there, so someone having a miscarriage is kinda like, 'Okay, well . . . .'" Juan described this experience of questioning his loss as he and Kim began to look at funeral homes and cemeteries:

> I felt almost like I was lying to them, cause we would say it was for a baby, but it almost felt like a lie, because I think most people think of it as a kid that was born and not a kid who's more of an unborn child.

Though the couples experienced their losses as significant and painful, they were frequently confronted with messages that invalidated their loss and contributed to the idea that other people's problems are more significant than miscarriage. Nicole gave voice to the longing she felt for someone to acknowledge her loss:

> I just wanted somebody to tell me, "The stuff you've been through is really hard, and it's okay you're this upset, and it's okay you're having a hard time." Cause I feel like there's a tendency just to, I don't know, "Okay, figure out a way to deal with it, you can be sad, and then you just gotta keep going . . . Everybody has problems." But I needed to hear from somebody else that, "Yes, losing a baby is really hard."

Norm of silence

The norm of silence surrounding pregnancy loss was discussed by four of the couples. Juan observed this in his loss experience and stated: "It's not uncommon in our society, yet it's so hush-hush. It feels so taboo almost." Federico also noticed this norm of silence:

> People don't like to talk about that experience. Even though it happens to so many. So many people told me, "Yes, we went through the same thing one time." Some people would say, "The same thing happened to us four times." And they don't really, people just don't talk about it. And I don't blame them for not talking about it, but it doesn't mean it doesn't happen.

After experiencing a miscarriage, several of the partners were surprised by the number of people in their lives who opened up about their own losses. Andrea said: "When you cross for a miscarriage, you never know the life of anybody around you until basically you say something and people just start sharing." Kim had a similar experience with family members sharing about their losses for the first time:

> And miscarriage and stillbirth are just not really talked about either, at all. And even like Juan was saying, his dad had lost a baby. My stepdad did as well. So he was talking about that, and I never knew he had had [a miscarriage].

Though many family members and friends had experienced miscarriage, it was not openly discussed and would not have been shared had the participants not first shared about their own losses. Learning about family members' and friends' miscarriages made the participants more aware of the norm of silence surrounding miscarriage.

Hearing others' stories of similar losses was described as helpful and comforting because it reduced the sense of isolation. Stephanie described the importance of having friends and family know about the loss and provide support:

> I think it opened doors to hear other women's stories about miscarriage, cause it can be such a silent battle. People don't talk about it. And that was helpful just to hear how common it really is and to know that this wasn't necessarily the end for us. Like, we could potentially have healthy pregnancies.

Talking with others about their experiences gave Stephanie comfort and hope. Juan described an additional aspect of comfort in hearing others' stories, coupled with confusion over the norms that reduce support after miscarriage:

> Just with the frequency of these things happening, it's weird that we as a community, as a society, still seem unwilling or unable to openly talk about these things. And just the lack of awareness kinda surprised me. And just being able to be more, it would be good to be more informed. I don't know, it's just I feel like we're part of a cohort after this experience versus before we were normal people. And really it happens so often and so many people just never mention it. To me, it would be good if it would be more socially addressed.

Miscarriage can feel isolating due to experiences of minimization and lack of understanding from others, but the opportunity to hear others' experiences created a sense that the loss was understood.

Though the couples had individuals in their lives who were able to provide support because they had also experienced miscarriage, there were others who avoided conversation about the loss. Nicole shared that, "People kind of don't want to bring it up ... [because] ... nobody knew what to do with that." Juan gave voice to the lack of understanding others had about miscarriage and their resulting discomfort discussing the loss:

> People don't know how to, people don't really know how to address you. They don't know whether to say, "I'm sorry for your loss," or whether to bring it up. It's awkward to deal with death in a regular sense. With this one it's even more, like, you buried a kid. There's just so much unknown that makes it a bit more weird.

The social support partners received after their loss and knowing they were not alone in their experience was a meaningful part of their ability to cope with miscarriage, but the norm of silence and others' discomfort with talking about miscarriage created a barrier to obtaining the same degree of support that is traditionally available after other types of loss.

Discussion

The disenfranchisement of miscarriage has gained more attention in recent years, creating opportunity for researchers and clinicians to play a part in breaking the norm of silence that makes miscarriage a uniquely challenging loss to navigate (Bellhouse et al., 2018; Frost et al., 2007; Markin & Zilcha-Mano, 2018). The couples' descriptions of disenfranchisement in this study echo the findings of other studies (Bellhouse et al., 2018, 2019; Bute et al., 2019; Lang et al., 2011; Rowlands & Lee, 2010), highlighting the lack of acknowledgment, minimization, and isolation that many parents face after miscarriage. The data from this study and many others repeatedly point to societal norms as the problematic starting point contributing to limited support during a time in which support is critical (Bellhouse et al., 2018; Bute et al., 2019; Frost et al., 2007; Lang et al., 2011; Markin & Zilcha-Mano, 2018).

The minimization and lack of acknowledgment described by the couples in this study spanned multiple sources of potential support, from medical providers to family members and friends. This widespread disenfranchisement contributed to many of the partners' conclusions that others must perceive their loss as less significant and less painful than other types of loss. As Bute et al. (2019) discuss, societal-level rules that discourage parents from talking openly about early pregnancy and miscarriage likely limit opportunities for greater awareness of the frequency of miscarriage and understanding of the meaning and significance of the loss that can grow out of open sharing and conversation.

The couples' reports of the "hush-hush" and "taboo" nature of miscarriage may seem contradictory to their statements of surprise at the number of people in their lives who revealed their own losses. However, this aligns with other research suggesting that sharing about miscarriage can be a risky venture for parents due to the likelihood of receiving responses that minimize and invalidate feelings of loss (Bute et al., 2019). Therefore, individuals may be more likely to share about their loss once they have identified another person as sharing in that same experience, because those individuals are more likely to understand the impact of the loss and respond in a supportive manner (Bellhouse et al., 2018). Hearing about others' similar losses made the *battle* feel less *silent*, and played an important role in reducing feelings of isolation and stigma. Thus, addressing the societal norms that contribute to a deficit of needed support is a necessary next step. As researchers continue to study these societal norms, clinicians can provide support in a number of meaningful ways, particularly through the use of a feminist approach.

Feminist approach to couples therapy after miscarriage

Within a feminist approach to therapy, clinicians are called to collaborate with clients and deconstruct dominant discourses that may overtly or covertly silence clients' perspectives and experiences (Miller & Wieling, 2002). Assumptions are questioned and issues of power and privilege are explored in efforts to give voice to marginalized stories and enable clients to create meaning in their lives apart from societal influences (Gosling & Zangari, 1996; Harvey et al., 2016). For clinicians working with couples experiencing miscarriage, a feminist approach to couples therapy can provide support through validating the meaning of the loss, exploring influences of power within the loss, deconstructing the norm of silence, empowering silenced voices, and depathologizing grief.

Collaborate

A feminist approach to therapy with couples and families is highly collaborative (Gosling & Zangari, 1996; Miller & Wieling, 2002). Within a collaborative therapeutic relationship, the clinician is able to create space for the partners to define their loss. After miscarriage, parents receive many messages from their support system and medical providers regarding the meaning and significance of the loss (Bellhouse et al., 2018; Lang et al., 2011). These messages may or may not be congruent with their loss experience. Through an invitation to describe what the loss has meant to them, couples have an opportunity to define their loss for themselves. As the couple describes their loss, the clinician facilitates a meaning-making process that guides the couple in developing a shared understanding of the loss, which can strengthen resilience during experiences of loss and grief (Walsh, 2019). Understanding the couple's loss experience creates the foundation for clinicians to validate the couple's loss as they define it and empower their own voices and perspectives.

In addition to creating a collaborative relationship with each couple, clinicians can also establish collaborative relationships with medical providers. Because medical providers are often the first individuals with whom couples have contact during their miscarriage experience, partnerships between mental health professionals and medical providers can create clearer pathways for connecting couples to additional support. Medical providers are often experienced by parents as minimizing the loss (Bellhouse et al., 2019; Lang et al., 2011), and though this may in part be due to desensitization as a result of seeing miscarriage so frequently, it may also be a result of time and resource constraints (Jensen et al., 2019). Medical providers may feel more comfortable acknowledging the impact of the loss if they know they have resources to provide when needed, and thus, do not have to be the sole professional source of support. By collaborating with medical providers, mental health professionals can create referral pathways that empower medical providers to acknowledge the psychosocial impact of miscarriage and increase the availability of support for parents. Increased acknowledgment of the loss and availability of professional support may also more broadly help reduce the sense of disenfranchisement within this loss.

Validate

Markin and Zilcha-Mano (2018) propose that the therapeutic relationship provides couples with a place to mourn in the company of someone who is able to acknowledge and validate the meaning of the loss, counteracting the isolation created by disenfranchisement. As described by some of the partners in this study, couples may feel they do not have permission to grieve the loss of their unborn baby or identify as parents who have lost a child. Within the therapeutic relationship, clinicians can acknowledge the partners' grief as legitimate and validate their experiences as grieving parents, freeing partners to explore their feelings of loss and express their grief. Sharing about loss and grief facilitates healing (Walsh, 2019), but couples may not feel able to share with members of their support system, so the therapeutic relationship becomes an important starting point for many couples in their efforts to navigate their grief.

Explore power

Power is present in multiple ways as couples navigate miscarriage. Women are typically given more permission to express feelings of loss and grief (Bute et al., 2019). While both men's and women's grief experiences are marginalized after miscarriage, miscarriage is largely considered a woman's issue, leaving men with even more pressure to remain silent in their grief (Bute et al., 2019). Gender roles also influence the expression of grief and coping strategies after miscarriage, such that it is more acceptable for women to discuss their loss (within the limitations of the norm of silence) and men are expected to be stoic, strong, and provide support to their partner (Rinehart & Kiselica, 2010). These gender norms not only further impede men's ability to grieve the loss, but can also result in women feeling even more isolated in their grief because their partner appears unaffected by the loss (Puddifoot & Johnson, 1997). By addressing these gender norms, clinicians enable couples to explore their loss beyond the constraints of gendered expectations of grieving and come together in their shared loss.

Power can also be seen in interactions between couples and others in their support system, where individuals in positions of authority (e.g., parents, aunts/uncles, boss, medical providers) minimize the significance of the loss. These interactions result in couples feeling they are overreacting about the loss, do not have the right to grieve or cannot identify as parents who have lost a child (Trepal et al., 2005). These experiences exacerbate couples' sense of disenfranchisement and leave them feeling more isolated and alone in their grief (Bellhouse et al., 2018). Through exploring issues of power, clinicians can lead couples in broader discussions that examine and deconstruct dominant societal discourses regarding miscarriage.

Deconstruct

The norm of silence surrounding miscarriage, and the resulting sense of stigma, creates significant barriers to couples' abilities to grieve openly and seek support after miscarriage (Bellhouse et al., 2018; Frost et al., 2007; Markin & Zilcha-Mano, 2018). Bute et al. (2019) suggest that discussing this norm of silence can support couples in navigating disenfranchisement. By deconstructing the norm of silence related to miscarriage, clinicians support couples in identifying the dominant discourse and questioning assumed truths regarding pregnancy and pregnancy loss, which can then create space for marginalized stories of deeply painful loss and grief (Miller & Wieling, 2002). As these conversations are facilitated by the clinician, couples can continue discussing their stories outside the therapy room. By naming their experiences and the influence of the norm of silence, couples give stronger voice to the disenfranchised aspects of their stories.

Empower

Amplifying the voices of marginalized individuals or groups is a major aim of feminist ideology (Harvey et al., 2016). The social norms surrounding early pregnancy and pregnancy loss pressure couples to remain silent in their loss

(Bute et al., 2019). A societal-level rule that miscarriage should not be discussed conveys the message that this loss is not important and is not a loss that should involve grief or mourning. Through a feminist approach, couples are empowered to give voice to silenced and marginalized parts of their loss through space to share their experiences with a clinician who validates their unique stories and facilitates discussion of the ways in which social norms influence grief and mourning. Clinicians also have opportunity to expand the therapy beyond the couple, inviting family members and friends to join one or more sessions. Within a safe space, clinicians can support couples in sharing the silenced parts of their experiences with their support system, as well as assist the couple's support system in providing support in more affirming ways.

Depathologize grief

Part of a feminist family therapist's role is to depathologize experiences that are unnecessarily labeled as problematic (Gosling & Zangari, 1996). Due to the disenfranchised nature of miscarriage, couples' grief can easily be labeled as pathological by those who do not understand the significance of the loss or by those who recognize indicators of complicated grief in couples without acknowledging the broader context of disenfranchisement (Markin & Zilcha-Mano, 2018). Disenfranchisement results in reduced social support for navigating grief and few (if any) culturally sanctioned rituals or traditions that facilitate mourning, leaving many couples feeling lost and stuck in their grief, which can be easily mislabeled as complicated or pathological. Partners also often experience differences between themselves in experiences of grief and coping strategies, and though these differences are normal, they can be misinterpreted by one or both partners as problematic (Lang et al., 2011). By depathologizing grief and grieving differences, clinicians can further validate couples' experiences, free them from barriers to understanding and navigating their grief, and support partners in creating shared meaning in their loss.

Limitations and directions for future research

This study is limited by the small sample size and homogeneous nature of the sample. Each of the couples identified their relationship as committed and strong, therefore, these findings may be specific to couples in more satisfied relationships. The dyadic interviews and the inclusion criterion of a committed relationship may have influenced recruitment toward couples who were more supportive of each other and experienced the miscarriage as a shared loss. The experience of miscarriage and accompanying feelings of disenfranchisement may impact couples in less committed or satisfied relationships differently. The couples in this study were also predominantly Caucasian, well-educated, and middle to upper-middle class.

Greater diversity is needed in research studying miscarriage and disenfranchisement. Few studies have explored this loss in minority populations (Abboud & Liamputtong, 2005). Research exploring disenfranchisement and the norm of silence has largely only involved well-educated, Caucasian participants (Bellhouse et al., 2018, 2019; Bute et al., 2019; Frost et al., 2007; Rowlands & Lee, 2010), leaving important questions regarding the ways in which power, privilege, and intersectionality influence experiences of grief within a disenfranchised loss. Additionally, intervention research has primarily targeted mothers (Bennett et al., 2012; Kersting et al., 2011; Swanson et al., 2009). Next steps include studying diverse samples, evaluating couple and family-level interventions, and exploring collaboration between medical providers and mental health professionals as a pathway for increasing support for parents' silent battle in the experience of miscarriage.

References

Abboud, L., & Liamputtong, P. (2005). When pregnancy fails: Coping strategies, support networks and experiences with health care of ethnic women and their partners. *Journal of Reproductive and Infant Psychology*, *23*(1), 3–18. https://doi.org/10.1080/02646830512331330974

American Pregnancy Association, (2015). *Miscarriage: Signs, symptoms, treatment, and prevention*. https://americanpregnancy.org/pregnancy-complications/miscarriage/

Bellhouse, C., Temple-Smith, M., & Bilardi, J. E. (2018). "It's just one of those things people don't seem to talk about ..." Women's experiences of social support following miscarriage: A qualitative study. *BMC Women's Health*, *18*(1), 176–185. https://doi.org/10.1186/s12905-018-0672-3

Bellhouse, C., Temple-Smith, M., Watson, S., & Bilardi, J. (2019). "The loss was traumatic ... some healthcare roviders added to that": Women's experiences of miscarriage. *Women and Birth*, *32*(2), 137–146. https://doi.org/10.1016/j.wombi.2018.06.006

Bennett, S. M., Ehrenreich-May, J., Litz, B. T., Boisseau, C. L., & Barlow, D. H. (2012). Development and preliminary evaluation of a cognitive-behavioral intervention for perinatal grief. *Cognitive and Behavioral Practice*, *19*(1), 161–173. https://doi.org/10.1016/j.cbpra.2011.01.002

Brier, N. (2008). Grief following miscarriage: A comprehensive review of the literature. *Journal of Women's Health*, *17*(3), 451–464. https://doi.org/10.1089/jwh.2007.0505

Bute, J. J., Brann, M., & Hernandez, R. (2019). Exploring societal-level privacy rules for talking about miscarriage. *Journal of Social and Personal Relationships*, *36*(2), 379–399. https://doi.org/10.1177/0265407517731828

Callister, L. (2006). Perinatal loss: A family perspective. *The Journal of Perinatal & Neonatal Nursing*, *20*(3), 227–234. https://doi.org/10.1097/00005237-200607000-00009

Chollete, M. E. (2012). Through the eyes of a father: A perinatal loss. *International Journal of Childbirth Education*, *27*(2), 33–38. http://eds.a.ebscohost.com.foyer.swmed.edu/eds/pdfviewer/pdfviewer?vid=2&sid=87bbfebf-9f71-4991-845d-139fa916f529%40sessionmgr4007

Converse, M. (2012). Philosophy of phenomenology: How understanding aids research. *Nurse Researcher*, *20*(1), 28–32. https://doi.org/10.7748/nr2012.09.20.1.28.c9305

Conway, K., & Russell, G. (2000). Couple's grief and experience of support in the aftermath of miscarriage. *British Journal of Medical Psychology*, *73*(4), 531–545. https://doi.org/10.1348/000711200160714

DeFrain, J., Millspaugh, E., & Xie, X. (1996). The psychosocial effects of miscarriage: Implications for health professionals. *Family, Systems and Health*, *14*(3), 331–347. https://doi.org/10.1037/h0089794

DiMarco, M., Renker, P., & Medas, J. (2002). Effects of an educational bereavement program on health care professionals' perceptions of perinatal loss. *Journal of Continuing Education in Nursing*, *33*(4), 180–186. https://doi.org/10.3928/0022-0124-20020701-10

Doka, K. J. (1989). *Disenfranchised grief: Recognizing hidden sorrow*. Lexington Books D.C. Health & Co.

Dowling, M., & Cooney, A. (2012). Research approaches related to phenomenology: Negotiating a complex landscape. *Nurse Researcher*, *20*(2), 21–27. https://doi.org/10.7748/nr2012.11.20.2.21.c9440

Eisikovits, Z., & Koren, C. (2010). Approaches to and outcomes of dyadic interview analysis. *Qualitative Health Research*, *20*(12), 1642–1655. https://doi.org/10.1177/1049732310376520

Evans, R. (2012). Emotional care for women who experience miscarriage. *Nursing Standard*, *26*(42), 35–41. https://doi.org/10.7748/ns2012.06.26.42.35.c9160

Frost, J., Bradley, J., Levitas, R., Smith, L., & Garcia, J. (2007). The loss of possibility: Scientisation of death and the special case of early miscarriage. *Sociology of Health & Illness*, *29*(7), 1003–1022. https://doi.org/10.1111/j.1467-9566.2007.01019.x

Giorgi, A. (1997). The theory, practice, and evaluation of the phenomenological method as a qualitative research. *Journal of Phenomenological Psychology*, *28*(2), 235. https://doi.org/10.1163/156916297X00103

Giorgi, A. (2005). The phenomenological movement and research in the human sciences. *Nursing Science Quarterly*, *18*(1), 75–82. https://doi.org/10.1177/0894318404272112

Gosling, A. L., & Zangari, M. (1996). Feminist family therapy and the narrative approach. *Journal of Feminist Family Therapy*, *8*(1), 47–63. https://doi.org/10.1300/J086v08n01_05

Harvey, R., Brown, K. S., Miller, B., Williams-Reade, J., Tyndall, L., & Murphy, M. (2016). Theory into research practice: Reflections and recommendations on collaborative feminist research. *Journal of Feminist Family Therapy*, *28*(4), 136–158. https://doi.org/10.1080/08952833.2016.1235410

Hein, S. F., & Austin, W. J. (2001). Empirical and hermeneutic approaches to phenomenological research in psychology: A comparison. *Psychological Methods*, *6*(1), 3–17. https://doi.org/10.1037/1082-989X.6.1.3

Hodgson, J., Trump, L., Wilson, G., & Garcia-Huidobro, D. (2018). Medical family therapy in family medicine. In T. Mendenhall, A. Lamson, J. Hodgson, & M. Baird (Eds.), *Clinical methods in medical family therapy* (pp. 17–59). Springer International.

Hutti, M. H. (2005). Social and professional support needs of families after perinatal loss. *Journal of Obstetric, Gynecologic, and Neonatal Nursing: JOGNN*, *34*(5), 630–638. https://doi.org/10.1177/0884217505279998

Jensen, K. L. B., Temple-Smith, M. J., & Bilardi, J. E. (2019). Health professionals' roles and practices in supporting women experiencing miscarriage: A qualitative study. *The Australian & New Zealand Journal of Obstetrics & Gynaecology*, *59*(4), 508-513. https://doi.org/10.1111/ajo.12910

Kersting, A., Kroker, K., Schlicht, S., Baust, K., & Wagner, B. (2011). Efficacy of cognitive behavioral internet-based therapy in parents after the loss of a child during pregnancy: Pilot data from a randomized controlled trial. *Archives of Women's Mental Health, 14*(6), 465–477. https://doi.org/10.1007/s00737-011-0240-4

Kong, G. S., Lok, I. H., Lam, P. M., Yip, A. K., & Chung, T. H. (2010). Conflicting perceptions between health care professionals and patients on the psychological morbidity following miscarriage. *Australian & New Zealand Journal of Obstetrics & Gynaecology, 50*(6), 562–567. https://doi.org/10.1111/j.1479-828X.2010.01229.x

Lang, A., Fleiszer, A. R., Duhamel, F., Sword, W., Gilbert, K. R., & Corsini-Munt, S. (2011). Perinatal loss and parental grief: The challenge of ambiguity and disenfranchised grief. *Omega. Journal of Death and Dying, 63*(2), 183–196. https://doi.org/10.2190/OM.63.2.e

Leon, I. (2008). *Helping families cope with perinatal loss. The Global Library of Women's Medicine*. Retrieved April 1, 2010, from. http://www.glowm.com/index.html?p= glowm.cml/section_view&articleid=417

Markin, R. D., & Zilcha-Mano, S. (2018). Cultural processes in psychotherapy for perinatal loss: Breaking the cultural taboo against perinatal grief. *Psychotherapy, 55*(1), 26. https://doi.org/10.1037/pst0000122

McCreight, B. S. (2004). A grief ignored: Narratives of pregnancy loss from a male perspective. *Sociology of Health & Illness, 26*(3), 326–350. https://doi.org/10.1111/j.1467-9566.2004.00393.x

Meyer, M. D. E. (2016). The paradox of time post-pregnancy loss: Three things not to say when communicating social support. *Health Communication, 31*(11), 1426–1429. https://doi.org/10.1080/10410236.2015.1077414

Miller, M. M., & Wieling, E. (2002). Points of connection and disconnection: A look at feminism and postmodernism in family therapy. *Journal of Feminist Family Therapy, 14* (2), 1–19. https://doi.org/10.1300/J086v14n02_01

Morgan, D. L., Ataie, J., Carder, P., & Hoffman, K. (2013). Introducing dyadic interviews as a method for collecting qualitative data. *Qualitative Health Research, 23*(9), 1276–1284. https://doi.org/10.1177/1049732313501889

Morse, J. M., Barrett, M., Mayan, M., Olson, K., & Spiers, J. (2002). Verification strategies for establishing reliability and validity in qualitative research. *International Journal of Qualitative Methods, 1*(2), 13–22. https://doi.org/10.1177/160940690200100202

Olesen, M. L., Graungaard, A. H., & Husted, G. R. (2015). Deciding treatment for miscarriage - experiences of women and healthcare professionals. *Scandinavian Journal of Caring Sciences, 29*(2), 386–394. https://doi.org/10.1111/scs.12175

Polak, L., & Green, J. (2016). Using joint interviews to add analytic value. *Qualitative Health Research, 26*(12), 1638–1648. https://doi.org/10.1177/1049732315580103

Puddifoot, J. E., & Johnson, M. P. (1997). The legitimacy of grieving: The partner's experience at miscarriage. *Social Science & Medicine, 45*(6), 837–845. https://doi.org/10.1016/S0277-9536(96)00424-8

QSR International Pty Ltd. (2018) . *NVivo qualitative data analysis software*. Version 12.

Renner, C. H., Verdekal, S., Brier, S., & Fallucca, G. (2000). The meaning of miscarriage to others: Is it an unrecognized loss? *Journal of Personal and Interpersonal Loss, 5*(1), 65–76. https://doi.org/10.1080/10811440008407847

Rinehart, M. S., & Kiselica, M. S. (2010). Helping men with the trauma of miscarriage. *Psychotherapy Theory, Research, Practice, Training, 47*(3), 288–295. https://doi.org/10.1037/a0021160

Robinson, J. (2014). Provision of information and support to women who have suffered an early miscarriage. *British Journal of Midwifery, 22*(3), 175–180. https://doi.org/10.12968/bjom.2014.22.3.175

Rowlands, I. J., & Lee, C. (2010). 'The silence was deafening': Social and health service support after miscarriage. *Journal of Reproductive and Infant Psychology*, *28*(3), 274–286. https://doi.org/10.1080/02646831003587346

Saunders, B., Sim, J., Kingstone, T., Baker, S., Waterfield, J., Bartlam, B., Burroughs, H., & Jinks, C. (2018). Saturation in qualitative research: Exploring its conceptualization and operationalization. *Quality & Quantity*, *52*(4), 1893–1907. https://doi.org/10.1007/s11135-017-0574-8

Smith, L. F., Frost, J., Levitas, R., Bradley, H., & Garcia, J. (2006). Women's experiences of three early miscarriage management options: A qualitative study. *British Journal of General Practice*, *56*(524), 198–205.

Swanson, K. M., Chen, H., Graham, J. C., Wojnar, D. M., & Petras, A. (2009). Resolution of depression and grief during the first year after miscarriage: A randomized controlled clinical trial of couples-focused interventions. *Journal of Women's Health*, *18*(8), 1245–1257. https://doi.org/10.1089/jwh.2008.1202

Trepal, H. C., Semivan, S. G., & Caley-Bruce, M. (2005). Miscarriage: A Dream Interrupted. *Journal of Creativity in Mental Health*, *1*(3/4), 155–171. https://doi.org/10.1300/J456v01n03_09

Vaismoradi, M., Turunen, H., & Bondas, T. (2013). Content analysis and thematic analysis: Implications for conducting a qualitative descriptive study. *Nursing & Health Sciences*, *15*(3), 398–405. https://doi.org/10.1111/nhs.12048

Wagner, T., Higgins, P., & Wallerstedt, C. (1997). Perinatal death: How fathers grieve. *Journal of Perinatal Education*, *6*(4), 9–16.

Walsh, F. (2019). Loss and bereavement in families: A systemic framework for recovery and resilience. In B. H. Fiese, M. Celano, K. Deater-Deckard, E. N. Jouriles, & M. A. Whisman (Eds.), *APA handbook of contemporary family psychology* (pp. 649-663). American Psychological Association.

Latina Sexual Health Care (IN) the US: Community-based Participatory Research and Her Lived Experience

Angela L. Lamson, Rebekah J. Clark, Roberta W. Bellamy, Jennifer Hodgson, Sharon M. Knight, Eboni J. Baugh and Jasmine Flores

ABSTRACT

There is a continuous upward trend in the number of Latinas living in the US; thus, their need for safe and accessible sexual health care ever-growing. This article addresses the sexual health of Latinas through the framework of critical theory, answering the research question: "What are Latina immigrants' experiences with receiving sexual health care from providers in the United States?" The study was conducted through a community-based participatory research design in collaboration with Latina community members. Seven themes emerged that can enhance Latina's sexual health care cultural humility and the role of family in treatment. Implications for family therapists include advocating for screeners and interventions that are indicated for Latinas.

Introduction

Over the past 30 years, immigration patterns of Latinos/as have shifted dramatically in the United States (US). Currently, 36.1% of all immigrants in the US are from Mexico, El Salvador, Cuba, Guatemala, and the Dominican Republic, a notable difference in contrast to 1990 when these countries made up 30.7% of all immigrants, but even more compelling compared to 1960 when only 7% of immigrants came from these countries (Migration Policy Institute (MPI) tabulation of data from U.S. Census Bureau, 2018). Previously, California and Texas were home to many of the immigrants who were primarily from Mexico;, but in the twenty-first century, a shift began whereby immigration patterns for Latinos/as from North and South America demonstrated an increased presence in many states across the Southeast US (e.g., Georgia, Florida, North Carolina) (Migration Policy Institute (MPI) tabulation of data from U.S. Census Bureau, 2018). In fact, Latinos/as are the fastest growing population in rural areas in the US and now comprise the largest minority group found residing in rural areas at 9% of the total rural population (United States Department of Agriculture [USDA], 2018).

Growth in the number of Latinos/as in rural areas has resulted in a healthcare infrastructure that has struggled to meet their health-care needs (Schminkey et al., 2019). While the rise in and inclusion of immigrant populations has brought many strengths to the US, it has also generated subsequent challenges to ensuring that health and wellbeing needs are met. One example is the inability to meet Latinas' (Latina women's) sexual health-care needs. Latinas' experiences with sexual health care involve many factors, some of which include cultural expectations and language barriers that widen rather than minimize the health disparities between Latinas and their white counterparts.

Receiving quality health care (pertaining to sensitive needs such as those related to sexual health), particularly in smaller, isolated, or rural communities is further complicated through misfires in patient–provider interactions and lack of culturally competent health-care systems (Schminkey et al., 2019). These factors together result in multiple concerns for Latinas' well-being and increase their vulnerability to or progression of unidentified sexual health diagnoses and infections as they navigate support through a complex system of care.

Through the many shifts in US patient demographics and healthcare infrastructure, as referenced above, the adoption of multidisciplinary care teams has emerged. Through these systems, a variety of health-care professionals may extend treatment to patients (i.e., clients) as part of their health-care visit. As such, the term provider in the context of this article includes medical (e.g., MD, nurse, nurse practitioner, physician assistant) and behavioral health (e.g., family therapist, psychologist, social worker) professionals. In many instances, participants in this study referenced their visit with a medical provider; however, the message about their experiences is also intended for behavioral health providers (such as family therapists), who are increasingly seeking employment in health-care settings (American Association for Marriage and Family Therapy, 2018). Therefore, the reader will notice the terms provider or professional throughout the article instead of clinician, and patient rather than client.

The purpose of this article is to investigate Latinas' experiences of receiving sexual health care from providers in the US and offer recommendations that promote their rights to safe and accessible sexual health care. Throughout this article, the authors (a) describe the prevalence and prognosis of sexually transmitted infections (STIs; i.e. the bacteria, viruses, and parasites that can be passed on via sexual contact) for Latina immigrants in context of Latino/a culture and immigration experiences, including factors that are not often understood by health-care providers who seek to evaluate and treat Latinas' sexual health concerns, (b) discuss the framework of critical theory (in relation to critical feminist theories (Sharma, 2019)) and how it grounds the research question: "What are Latina immigrants' experiences with receiving sexual health care from providers in the United States?" (c) highlight a community-based participatory research study that involves

Latina community members as part of the research team, and (d) offer previously unexplored ways that health-care providers (i.e., both medical and behavioral health professionals) can develop cultural sensitivity and humility in order to better meet the needs of Latina immigrants. Finally, this article offers implications for family therapists by recognizing the ways in which critical theory and feminist theories can help to reduce sexism, racism, and classism in the care received by Latinas, so that they may be able to better navigate and access safe treatment for sexual health. Implications include opportunities to support advocacy toward screeners and interventions that are indicated for Latinas – giving voice to their specific needs.

Prevalence and Prognosis of STIs for Latina Immigrants

Researchers have provided evidence that Latinos/as who come to the US to live and work are at a higher risk for contracting the human immunodeficiency virus (HIV), as well as other STIs, than those who live and work in their homeland (Althoff et al., 2017; Hong et al., 2015; Magis-Rodriguez et al., 2009; National Center for Farmworker Health, Inc, 2017). Along the US and Mexico border regions, Latinas' primary risk factor for contracting HIV is having a sexual partner who has migrated to the US (Persichino & Ibarra, 2012). Researchers have recognized Latinas' vulnerability to STIs (including those beyond HIV) for a number of years (Ertl et al., 2018; Mann et al., 2016), including reports of health outcomes aligned with heterosexual contact as primary transmission mode for women (Centers for Disease Control and Prevention, 2016). In fact, Latina heterosexual women comprise one of the fastest growing sub-population for STIs in the US (Centers for Disease Control and Prevention, 2019), and the south alone holds over half of the nation's HIV cases (Centers for Disease Control and Prevention, 2017). The prevalence and prognosis for STIs become even more complicated given that a growing percentage of Latinos/as live in small towns and rural areas (Lichter et al., 2016; Schminkey et al., 2019), hence the geographical focus of this article.

The shift in STI prevalence for women has been on a global radar now for nearly 15 years (UNAIDS, 2004). The fourth global report from the Joint United Nations Program on HIV/AIDS stated that 50% of new infections occur between spouses, calling this a movement toward the "feminization of HIV/AIDS" (UNAIDS, 2004, p. 8), making the prevalence and prognosis of STIs with Latinas an important focus for clinicians, researchers, and policymakers. The most recent patterns of immigration and subsequent increase of Latino/a residents in small rural communities have found providers unprepared to meet the health-care needs of the immigrant communities (Schminkey et al., 2019). Generally speaking, rural communities have fewer resources with which to address health-care issues, including provider shortages and lack of adequate services that can be provided to patients in their indigenous languages

(Schminkey et al., 2019). In particular, a lack of resources as well as an absence in cultural competency exists in relation to Latinas' sexual health care for STIs (Mann et al., 2016). These unmet needs and health disparities surrounding Latinas' sexual health require health-care providers, researchers, and policy-makers to learn more from the voice of Latinas about cultural roles and expectations that influence the patient–provider relationship and provider's sense of cultural awareness and humility.

Influence of Culture and Oppression of the Latina Voice

Many Latina immigrants face patient-provider language barriers, high costs for their health care, and lack of family support. Latinas may be separated from their social support temporarily or permanently due to immigration status or regulations associated with work visas. These barriers all increase Latinas' likelihood for heath disparities (López-Cevallos & Harvey, 2016; Mann et al., 2016; Schminkey et al., 2019). These disparities include Latinas' (a) tendency to enter treatment later than their white counterparts (Chen et al., 2012; Lopez-Quintero et al., 2016), (b) reduced likelihood to engage in STI testing or having health-care tests confirmed (Ganguli et al., 2013; Liddicoat et al., 2006; Parra et al., 2001), (c) lack of remaining in treatment after diagnosis (Lopez-Quintero et al., 2016; Torrone et al., 2010), and (d) ability to access medications or adhere to medication management (Fortuna et al., 2019; Zhang et al., 2013) across their lifespan (Chen et al., 2012).

Health disparities in the Latino community are multifaceted and are often due to provider and/or institutional sexism, racism, or classism (Sharma, 2019) implicit bias, or discrimination as it interfaces with people of color's experiences with historical oppression (Schminkey et al., 2019; Wiltz, 2015). For many, the cultural roles of Latinos/as within the family (i.e., roles that are influenced by ethnic, religion, or geographic rituals, traditions, or systemic oppression), including gender roles, are contributors to the complexity of seeking and sustaining sexual health care. Furthermore, traditional gender and family system roles, such as *machismo*, which is an emphasis on male dominance and masculinity, and *familismo*, which is an emphasis on loyalty to the family in Latino/a culture, play at least some part in whether Latinas feel able to voice concerns about their own sexual health within a relationship (Hargreaves et al., 2010; Lindsey, 2018; Mann et al., 2016; Tung, 2012). Sexual health disparities for this community are especially concerning, given that Latinas are at a heightened risk for being victimized by sexual assault or abuse (Fortun`a et al., 2019).

Researchers found traditional gender roles influence Latinas' view of self and autonomy (or lack thereof) in relation to decision-making about sexual and reproductive health (Hargreaves et al., 2010; Mann et al., 2016; Parrado et al., 2005; Persichino & Ibarra, 2012; Viadro & Earp, 2000). Some suggested that the traditional machismo lens is a facilitator for Latina submissiveness to their partners (Hargreaves et al., 2010; Stephens et al., 2017), which can result in a marginalized voice when navigating sexual health decision-making (Hargreaves et al., 2010; Parrado et al., 2005; Peragallo Montano et al., 2019). Furthermore, Latinas' attention to *familismo* ensures that the needs of her family are placed before her own. Researchers found *familismo* to be a contributor for Latina dropout rates in relation to healthcare treatment (Hargreaves et al., 2010). These factors, when interfaced with highly stigmatized health issues, such as sexual health symptoms or diagnoses, result in a heightened disparity. Latino/as are then left with a reduced likelihood for seeking or sustaining health care or psychosocial treatment.

While only barriers to Latinas' health care have been described to this point, facilitators are also known to exist that help to improve Latinas' sexual health, and as such are important to acknowledge. Researchers have recognized that positive patient–provider relationships and interactions (once treatment has been sought out) may facilitate better health-care experiences and opportunities for Latinas (Beach et al., 2010; Lazcano-Ponce et al., 2004; Mann et al., 2016; Saha et al., 2013; Schuster et al., 2005), as well as improve patients' perceptions of health-care providers (Infante et al., 2006; Schuster et al., 2005).

Providers have been identified as culturally sensitive to Latino/a patients when they embrace *personalismo* (i.e., the Latino/a sense of belonging, attachment to others, developing personal connections), *simpatía*, (i.e. kindness), and *respeto*, (i.e., respect) (Juckett, 2013). *Personalismo* is a cultural value shared among Latinos that emphasizes the importance of establishing a personal relationship with a health-care provider before pursuing treatment (Mogro-Wilson et al., 2016), and is noted in previous research to be an important cultural value that effects treatment adherence (Antshel, 2002). Simpatía and respeto are two examples of cultural competence in the clinical setting associated with equitable treatment and quality of care (Mann et al., 2016; Saha et al., 2013), both of which align strongly with feminist standpoint theory (i.e., understanding power differentials in structural practices; Harding, 1986). While barriers and facilitators to Latino/a health-care experiences appear in past literature, almost no research exists on Latinas' experiences with health-care providers in the US. As such, the following provides a theoretical foundation and community-based participatory research design to answer this research question: What are Latina immigrants' experiences with receiving sexual health care from providers in the United States?

Theoretical Foundation

The historical context that the US shares with the countries of Latin America is extensive (Chambers et al., 1987; Fernandez-Armesto, 2014; Goldfield et al., 2004) and riddled with oppressive outcomes (e.g., colonization, enslaving of indigenous peoples, women receiving fewer rights) that are morally unjustified

(Chambers et al., 1987; Fernandez-Armesto, 2014). The resulting societal structures and social positions continue to support the dominant race, while holding stagnant and less empowered the state of minority cultures and ethnicities (Fernandez-Armesto, 2014; Habermas, 1981, p. 1984). Critical theory (Habermas, 1981, p. 1984) provides us with a lens that highlights unjust power structures and brings attention to the need for emancipatory endeavors (e.g., advocacy toward political movement) (McCarthy, 1989). These tenants also intersect with numerous feminist theories as they interface with health-care systems (Sharma, 2019) and the need for promoting emancipatory knowledge.

According to critical theory (Habermas, 1981, p. 1984), *emancipatory knowledge* is self-reflection that produces a liberation from such social forces as institutions or environmental powers that stand to limit the control one has over their own lives. Critical theory was used to ground this study and give voice to Latina sexual health-care experiences in the US; which was further enhanced through a community-based participatory research (CBPR) design (Israel et al., 2013).

Given the sensitivity of this health topic (i.e., Latinas' sexual health), CBPR was adopted in partnership with non-researchers who identified as Latina immigrants, constructed the research questions, developed the research protocol, and analyzed the study's findings. CBPR focuses on an equitable collaboration between community organizations or elders and university researchers to improve a community's public health and health outcomes (Israel et al., 2013; Springer & Skolarus, 2019). There is a growing appreciation for the use of CBPR as a vehicle to explore and better understand health outcomes, specifically within minority populations (De Las Nueces et al., 2012; Viswanathan et al., 2004; Wallerstein et al., 2017). While attending to power differentials and validating voices within the targeted research sample, CBPR researchers are ultimately charged with the production of quality data via an ethical and rigorous research method.

The CBPR team assembled for this study, included multiple university-based bilingual researchers, as well as an executive director and members of a local grassroots Latino/a organization (that did not identify as researchers). The CBPR team's community members included advocates who promote community participation and prosperity of Mexican and Latino/a immigrants. Together, this team unified around critical theory Habermas (1981, p. 1984) as the foundation for this study and proceeded to co-construct the research questions and process of analyzing the data.

Method

This team utilized the transcendental phenomenology of Husserl (1960) to develop a CBPR project (grounded in Habermas' critical theory (Habermas, 1981, p. 1984) that was approved by both the social science and biomedical university IRBs (IRB00000705, IRB00003781). The interview questions and research topic were developed in close collaboration with all members of the

CBPR team in keeping with CBPR principles (Israel et al., 2013). Regular and confidential meetings between the university researchers and community advocates were key to fostering a well-developed study, quality data collection, and productive outcomes (Israel et al., 2013; Viswanathan et al., 2004). While CBPR can be qualitative, quantitative, or mixed method in design, the team chose to implement a qualitative study to address the research question: "What are Latina immigrants' experiences with receiving sexual health care from providers in the United States?"

Phenomenology was deemed an appropriate strategy of inquiry for this study, as it aligned with the core components and principles of CBPR (Israel et al., 2013), and promoted self-knowledge and reflection that is advocated for by critical theory (Habermas, 1962, p. 1989). It was determined that of all the qualitative designs, phenomenology would allow the team to explore and interpret a phenomenon through the eyes of the participant population studied (Husserl, 1960) consistent with critical theory (Habermas, 1981, p. 1984) and critical feminist theories (Sharma, 2019). This strategy of inquiry has been described as more of a method of questioning than a method of answering (Van Manen, 2014), thus selected as the design of best fit by the CBPR team.

Participants

The CBPR team worked collaboratively to create English and Spanish recruitment flyers that would be placed at mainly rural-based health departments and clinics in one US southeastern state. Inclusion criteria for participant selection included: (a) identified as a first-generation Latina immigrant, (b) provided a sexual history in the context of a medical appointment with a health-care provider, and (c) was at least 18 years old. Exclusion criteria ensured that potential candidates were not selected if: (a) they had not received health care in their life, (b) had not been asked about their sexual history in a health-care setting, or (c) were currently pregnant.

Interview Guide

An in-depth interview guide was co-created for this study (see Figure 1) by the CBPR team. The team developed 17 semi-structured and open-ended questions and determined that all interviews would be competed face-to-face. The interview guide was constructed such that participants could describe their experiences with receiving health care for sexual health concerns or being asked about their sexual histories during a medical visit in the US. The interview then moved into more specific questions about their health-care experiences and concluded with a final question encouraging the participant to add any additional information that they felt would be relevant to the study's purpose.

Grand Tour Question

- Describe any experiences that you have had with your doctors, or other health care providers, in your home country and the United States who have asked to complete a sexual history, screening, and/or assessment regarding sexually transmitted infections or diseases.

Mini-Tour Questions

- Without disclosing any names, can you tell me about your thoughts or feelings about the last provider that you went to for care?
  - How did the provider assess for sexual health concerns? STIs?
  - Did this appointment take place in the US or in your home country?
- Without disclosing any names, tell me why you chose to go to this provider?
  - In what ways was the experience a good one for you?
  - What did you not like about the visit?
- What concerns you most about going to a health care provider like a doctor for some problems you have been experiencing/have experienced?
- What health problems would be most difficult to talk about with a doctor?
  - What makes these discussions most difficult to discuss?
- If there comes a time when you are concerned about a sexually transmitted infection, who would you be most likely to talk to about it?
  - How confident are you that this information would be accurate?
- If you ever had to talk to a doctor about a sexually transmitted infection, what do you think would make that discussion go the best way possible?
  - What do you think would make the discussion go as badly as possible?
- What concerns would you have, if any, about talking with your doctor about sexually transmitted infections?
- If you had concerns or questions about HIV who would you talk to about those concerns?
- What messages do people receive from the community about being tested for sexually transmitted infections?
- What messages do people receive from the community about being tested for HIV?
- What do you think would improve the chances that Latina immigrants would get screened for sexually transmitted infections or diseases, or HIV?
- What do you think would improve the chances that Latina immigrants would talk with a doctor or other health care provider about sexually transmitted infections or diseases, or HIV?
- What do you wish US providers learned from providers in your home country about assessing for sexual health concerns, STIs, and HIV?
- What do you wish the providers in your home country learned from US providers about assessing for sexual health concerns, STIs, and HIV?
- Describe your preferred provider for sexual health issues: age, gender, ethnicity, etc.

Interview Closing

- What have we not yet talked about that you think is important for me to know in relation to the purpose of this study?

Figure 1. Interview Guide.

A 21-question demographic survey (e.g., nationality, time lived in US, age, marital status, education level, gender, and questions about healthcare appointment attendance both in the US and home country) was also constructed. The survey was intended to give more context to the qualitative interview responses without having to extend the length of the qualitative portion of the interview. Participants filled out the demographic survey after completing the informed consent.

Procedure

The interviews were conducted by a university-based bilingual researcher and a bilingual, bicultural research assistant. Each participant was informed about the study's purpose, its risks and benefits, and their confidentiality rights before being enrolled. Upon completion, participants received a gift card in the amount of 25 USD. To protect participant identity, during the data analysis process, researchers used a coding and numbering system in place of actual names.

Interviews lasted approximately one and a half hours and participants were informed that they could stop at any time. Participants were offered a choice of interview setting. Of the 11 face to face interviews conducted, seven interviews took place in participants' homes and four took place at a local grassroots organization's office. The latter was a location commonly used for regular meetings specific to Latino/a issues and was considered by the CBPR team to be a safe environment.

Analysis

Interviews were professionally transcribed from Spanish into English and non-identifying numbers replaced actual participant names. Following the transcription of the English recordings, Giorgi's method (Giorgi, 2009) was applied to the data coding process. Giorgi's four-step method was selected because it closely followed Husserl's writings on phenomenology, which promoted theoretical consistency throughout the study. Giorgi's method involves multiple reviews of the data and the development of "units of meaning" that help to establish significant themes from the data. These themes were then crossed-checked by consulting the literature, as well as discussing the results with members of the local organization who served as research collaborators.

The intended sample size for a phenomenological study is determined when the major thematic content reaches a point of saturation, namely, when the themes arising from new participants begin to replicate those found in previous participant's answers. In this study, the research reached a point of saturation after 11 interviews. The point of saturation was confirmed through the multiple review process conducted by the CBPR team. This multi-review process further strengthened the indicators of rigor applied to the research study.

Indicators of Rigor

To ensure credibility and transferability, field notes and research logs were utilized by the team in order to highlight and attend to personal biases during the research process. Each team member wrote and periodically revisited his or her own bias statement, acknowledging systemic influences in keeping with a CBPR approach. The researchers also regularly engaged with the Latino/a

community as a way to better understand participants' responses in the context of culture. The time spent by the CBPR team in co-constructing each component of the study and analyzing the data from the interviews solidified the rigor that afforded Latina voices (involved in this study) to be shared with communities of interest and professional audiences (Cypress, 2017).

Results

Sample

Eleven Latina immigrants between the ages of 31 and 64 participated in the study, with 46 as the mean age. All but one of the interviewees immigrated from Mexico; the remaining participant immigrated from Honduras. With one exception, interviews were conducted in Spanish. Six of the participants were married at the time of the interview, while four were single or "other," and one was divorced. Seven of the participants earned a high school diploma or GED, two reported less than 2 years of higher education, and two reported a primary school level of education. Five of the women had no medical insurance at the time of the interview. The average number of years since immigration was 15 and ranged between 1 and 21 years.

Identified Themes

A total of 7 themes and 15 subthemes emerged from the interviews, constructed from 266 separate units of meaning. The themes are organized in Table 1 from the most commonly mentioned to the least commonly mentioned. Specifically, Table 1 shares the percentage of the 266 units of meaning that related to each particular theme. The identified themes punctuate elements that both facilitated and negatively influenced Latina immigrants' experiences with sexual health care in the US, often in contrast to experiences encountered in their home country.

The most commonly identified theme related to cultural differences in health care is *communication style* among Latina women and their health-care providers. Communication style was particularly connected to the subthemes of personalismo and directive vs. nondirective communication styles. *Personalismo* was captured as a connection with the provider that included but extended beyond a caring atmosphere. This concept seemed to more deeply reveal a sense of belonging that participants felt when *personalismo* was present in treatment. One participant explained that when Latinas feel as though *personalismo* is absent in the health-care setting "that the doctor just doesn't really care … [they are] much less likely to want to share anything." A second subtheme associated with communication direct vs. nondirective styles. Participants described how challenging it was when health-care professionals

Table 1. Themes and Subthemes Related to Latinas' Perceptions of Sexual Health Care in the US.

Themes	Units of Meaning	Subthemes	Thematic Examples	Quote
1. Communication Style	21%	A. Personalismo B. Directive vs. Non-Directive	A. Provider establishes a warm, caring atmosphere. B. Clear, direct communication from the health care provider.	A. "If many think that the doctor [in the US] just doesn't really care … [they are] much less likely to want to share anything." B. "[Doctors in Mexico] give you the advice straightforward … whereas here it's more ambiguous, in the United States."
2. Capacity of the Health Care System	21%	A. Inclusion of sexual health assessments B. Ability of the healthcare system to meet health care needs	A. Sexual health is more often assessed in US than in the country of origin. B. Medical concerns are unaddressed or left unresolved.	A. "In [the US] … it's much more normal that they ask you questions about it." B. "Here [in the United States] there is a lot of running around and making appointments and just so much information that nothing is being done."
3. Access to Care	18%	A. Long wait times B. Lack of doctors C. Travel distance D. High costs/Lack of insurance E. Language barriers	A, B. Provider carries heavy caseload and full schedule. C. Healthcare facility requires extensive travel capability. D. Insurance is not available or does not cover important tests, procedures, and/or treatments. E. Interpreters and patients often know each other outside the medical setting.	A, B. "[T]hey took way too long – two hours – for me to be seen [in the US] … there were no doctors." C. "Over there [in Mexico], the reason I went to that doctor is because he was the most reachable." D. "Money do a lot with how you take care of yourself, because … you might find something that is going on with you and you don't have either the insurance or the money to pay for it [in the US]." E. "A counsel with a doctor [in the US] … it's like going to confession." "[I]t's much harder for me to be able to tell the [US] doctor everything … because the interpreter belongs to the community."
4. Time Orientation	15%	A. Present time vs. Future Time	A. Healthcare culture in the US tends to ask preventative, or future-oriented, questions.	A. "When I got pregnant, I was asked [by the US provider] if I wanted the AIDS test and I was thinking that maybe he thought that I was sleeping around."
5. Stigma	13%	A. Community perception of HIV/STIs B. Provider perception of HIV/STIs	A. Latinas face discrimination concerning their sexual behaviors in their countries of origin. B. Latinas fear provider judgment regarding their sexual health.	A. "If I was in Mexico, I would stay quiet [if I had an STI]." B. "The people think that the [US] doctors will tell them that these are just degenerates, sexual beings."
6. Familismo	7%	A. Cultural practice of placing the needs of the family before those of the individual B. Increased comfort levels with community members than with professionals	A. Family needs can become a barrier to attending to healthcare needs. B. Discussing healthcare-related topics is more comfortable with family or peers present.	A. "Everything comes before health … the children, to make food, her job. She can't miss work." B. "[I prefer] that [the doctor] didn't tell me alone, that maybe he would tell me with three other friends."
7. Perceptions of Risk	5%	A. Community members do not always understand when they are at risk for contracting STIs.	A. Married women feel that they are safe from the risk of sexual disease.	A. "A lot of people think because they are married and they have their spouse that they are safe, that it can't happen to them."

in the US used ambiguous or confusing words when asking questions or discussing treatment. "[Doctors in Mexico] give you the advice straightforward … whereas here it's more ambiguous, in the United States" was given as one example. Participants described their comfort in receiving more direct communication as they had often received in their home country.

Almost as prevalent was a theme related to the *capacity of the healthcare system* to address the Latina participant's ability to feel adequately heard and treated by their health-care providers. Many expressed a belief that their health needs had not been met by the system, discouraging them from seeking further care. One participant expressed her frustration that "there is a lot of running around and making appointments and just so much information that nothing is being done." A third and similar theme was that of *access to care*. Participants described their struggle to access appropriate health care due to long wait times, not enough providers on staff, inability to travel to their providers, inability to afford services, lack of health insurance, and finally, language barriers when communicating with providers. Often rural health-care systems utilize interpreters from their patients' communities to navigate the patient's health-care visit; one participant lamented that "a counsel with a doctor … is like going to confession."

Occurring as a theme in 15% of the total number of meaning units, *time orientation* was coded when participants expressed what the researchers identified as a conflict between the time orientation of a participant's culture of origin and that of the US. health-care provider. Specifically, present time orientation (e.g., accessing health care only when there is a problem or symptoms) of their native culture sometimes clashed with the future time orientation (e.g., accessing health care for preventive care) of their new home country (Galanti, 2008). Some participants expressed concern that when providers ask proactive future-oriented questions about their sexual health, these providers are asking because they assume risky sexual behavior has occurred. This feeling ties into Latina concerns about how society perceives them, as evidenced through this quote: "When I got pregnant, I was asked [by the US provider] if I wanted the AIDS test and I was thinking that maybe he thought that I was sleeping around."

Specifically, *stigma* was another theme that emerged, with participants expressing the taboo surrounding a discussion of HIV or other STIs in their native cultures. They suggested that in the US questions pertaining to sexual health were always the hardest questions to answer. If asked questions about STIs in their home country, they would stay quiet. Providers in the US ask proactive and open questions about sexual health as part of their practice; however, one participant feared that her provider considered Latinas to be "degenerates, sexual beings."

There was a theme in the data related to *familismo*, the cultural practice in Latino/a families of placing family needs before individual concerns. Specifically, the Latinas in the study felt it was self-serving to attend to their own health-care needs at length, taking resources and time away from their family responsibilities. One participant explained that "everything comes before health … the children, to make food, her job. [Latinas] can't miss work." *Familismo* highlights the importance of the family system in Latino culture and is essential to understanding this culture. Some mentioned that they would be more inclined to discuss sexual health concerns with a family member than speaking about such issues with a health-care professional. Furthermore, participants mentioned a comfort in having a family member or friend join them in their health-care visit.

The final theme that emerged from the participants was their *perceptions of the risk* of contracting an STI or HIV. Many did not feel that their heterosexual relationships could lead to infection. As one participant stated, "A lot of people think because they are married and they have their spouse that they are safe, that it can't happen to them." In fact, some believed that if a Latina woman was married then she was not at risk for a STI. Others felt that their religion would protect them from contracting a disease.

The Phenomenological Exhaustive Description: The Latina Voice

The Latina immigrants in our study encountered health care in a way that is unique to a bicultural immigrant experience (Ali & Johnson, 2016). Access to sexual health care for Latina immigrants was limited due to explicit barriers (e.g., long wait times, insufficient number of doctors, travel distance, language barriers, cost, and lack of health insurance), as well as concerns regarding communication. Interpreters were often needed to help Latinas navigate their health-care visits and sexual health-care encounters. These encounters with interpreters created a strong cause for concern about confidentiality and often resulted in highly stigmatized communication. Stigmatized interactions meant that they did not feel safe and held back questions intended for the health-care professional. In some instances, participants mentioned they would not seek out sexual health information or access health care for sexual issues at all. The lack of access was further complicated by time orientation. They noted that health-care professionals in participants' home countries do not typically extend preventative care; thus, sexual health assessments in the US felt stigmatizing and confirmatory of poor sexual health decisions. In their native cultures, health-care professionals only assessed for what they thought was potentially a problem. Participants shared that when health-care professionals in the US did not take time to build rapport with the patient, participants often became uncomfortable. This lack of *personalismo* left them wondering if the provider is making a moral judgment about their character or suspecting that she may actually have a STI.

Overall, Latinas in this study experienced health care as confusing and sometimes left visits not understanding what their diagnoses were. Whether due to language barriers or a deliberate avoidance of care due to stigma, they did not have a clear understanding of STIs/HIV, nor the ability to ask the questions that were necessary for clarification. Participants stated they would feel more comfortable if sexual health screenings were normalized (described as questions they ask all patients/clients) and that information be given to them routinely, in order to further normalize the otherwise taboo topic and experience. Furthermore, they mentioned that the presence of a family or friend as part of their health-care visit would likely enhance their experiences. They shared that particularly they would want a family member present if they were receiving news relate to sexual health. *Familismo* was shared as an important component of Latinas' health care, in the following ways: (a) safety and trust were more easily established when a family member was part of the visit, (b) more *personalismo* was experienced when health-care professionals asked about or involved her family members in the discussion, and (c) understanding how their own sexual health may influence the lives of their unborn or living children.

Discussion

Using critical theory (Habermas, 1981, p. 1984) as our guide, we employed a CBPR research study (Israel et al., 2013) as a culturally sensitive way to explore the sexual health-care experiences of Latina immigrants. Through critical theory, we sought to promote *emancipatory knowledge* by asking questions that invoked self (and other) reflection, institutional forces in health care, and the potential for outcomes from this study to influence Latina and family health care positively.

Critical theory (Habermas, 1981, p. 1984) (in alignment with critical feminist theories (Sharma, 2019)) was present throughout the CBPR design (Israel et al., 2013), giving attention to the importance of communities and universities mutually working together on issues that influence Latina and family health. Through this study, the CBPR team aimed for equity between all partners throughout the research process (Israel et al., 2013) and promoted the voice of Latinas through their US-based health-care experiences. While the research aim was the primary focus, unquestionably the university research team and the community advocacy members gained new skill sets that would have otherwise not occurred without a CBPR design (e.g., the university team would have missed the theme of time orientation in the analysis and the community team would not have understood the intricacies of research ethics).

Recommendations

While recommendations could be put forth for each theme, recommendations will instead be aimed at bridging research findings with women's health through *peronsalismo, familismo*, and feminist family therapy healthcare practices. A focus on these three topics may be most influential in carrying the voices of the Latina who participated in this study into direct clinical care.

Throughout the interviews, participants stated that it was important to them that they develop a relationship with health-care professionals before beginning any screenings, assessments, or treatment interventions. The cultural concept known as *personalismo* extends beyond the very quick joining process that commonly occurs at the start of any session or health-care visit. Latinas' reported safety was based on a sense of connection or belonging with health-care professionals, often absent in biomedicine's patriarchal dominance stance (Sharma, 2019).

Regardless of the work context, but perhaps especially in systems that are fast-paced, it is important for family therapists and other health-care professionals to nurture *personalismo*. Moving too quickly to assessment or treatment could fracture relationships or deepen experiences of oppression. Health-care professionals may benefit from recognizing that *personalismo* is a biological, psychological, social, and often spiritual (i.e., attributing meaning-making to a person or experience) connection to people and experiences. As such, it is recommended that health-care professionals take time with Latina patients to establish the relationship. Investing time in learning more about their cultural connections to health will likely promote a safer environment for care that can improve their health outcomes.

The Latinas and CBPR team put forth the following specific recommendations to family therapists in relation to *personalismo*: (a) construct a first visit that emphasizes getting to know the client, her culture, and experiences that are meaningful to her, (b) address sexual health matters with Latina patients in a normalizing way. Explain that these questions are asked as part of good sexual health care for all clients in the practice regardless of gender, sexual orientation, ethnicity, etc., and (c) include sexual health-care questions or assessments indicated for their practice and the population served in that practice. Two or three assessment questions could be integrated into an intake or part of sessions with the provider to normalize the conversation. These questions may help to ensure that a safe environment exists in the health-care setting and that the client is biologically, psychologically, and socially safe in the health-care encounter. This is recommended not only for females, but also for Latino males, in order to further normalize the conversation.

Participants also highlighted the concept of *familismo* as important to the health-care visit. This aligns with previous research (Hargreaves et al., 2010). Unfortunately, some researchers have documented *familismo* as a barrier to care or contributor to dropout rates in health care (e.g., Hargreaves et al., 2010). While it is important to attend to previous research, it is also important for family therapists and others on the health-care team to explore with patients' ways in which *familismo* can be more central to their healthcare experience (i.e., encourage Latinas to bring a support person to their health-care visits and/or ask questions that attend to her relational safety, satisfaction, and well-being).

Latinas did share that they often put the needs of their children before their own needs. However, participants in this study also suggested that emphasizing the importance of STI screenings for Latinas for the sake of their children's health could be an effective approach to increasing the chances that they will get tested for HIV and STIs. The CBPR team added to this recommendation by clarifying that this should not be through a pathologizing conversation or one that is coercive or punishing but rather, a conversation that offers psychoeducation about how STIs can influence an unborn child. This conversation would be consistent with the goal of normalizing assessment and discussions pertaining to sexual health.

Familismo is a concept that is expected to be known and applied by family therapists who are well trained in and attuned to diverse family systems, even when treating an individual client. Consistent with family therapists systemic training, it is essential to ensure that the family (however that is defined by the client) is present through descriptions, stories, or rituals even when they are unable to be physically present. The underscore cannot be pronounced enough around the role of safety when it comes to *familismo*. Clients will often know ahead of time (per communication within the community) which practices and providers are safer than others to go to for care. Another level of safety scanning will take place once a patient/client arrives to ensure that family-based conversations can occur about any physical, psychological, relational, and/or spiritual concerns. While *familismo* may not have been the most frequently cited theme in this study, its role in a Latina's life guides most of her health-care decisions.

As part of the US healthcare system, family therapists can provide such a positive influence on the care of Latinas and other immigrants that seek health care and a best life in the US. Their competency in relational health makes them an important collaborator for any health-care provider who extends sexual health-care education, screenings, assessments, and interventions. The Latina voices from this study along with inclusion of a diverse CBPR team offer a call to action for family therapists to engage in practice and research that can be more culturally sensitive and open up a self-reflection for both clients and health-care professionals to enhance our cultural humility toward a better healthcare system and improved health-care outcomes for all.

Conclusion

Community-based participatory research can be part of the feminist solutions that challenge the power dynamics which have historically subjugated vulnerable populations. If, through the avenues of CBPR, researchers are able to partner with Latino community organizations and community members in research, to be co-producers of knowledge, then knowledge can be exchanged for the sake of improving community health outcomes. Together, clinical researchers (such as family therapists) in tandem with community partners can influence present social structures and social issues that may inadvertently impede access to health care for Latinos/as. This research is an important contribution to science as it involves the Latina community both as co-researchers and participants in order to better understand sexual health-care practices in the US in contrast to the home countries of Latina immigrants. In addition, this research provides significant outcomes that health-care professionals, such as family therapists can implement in order to reduce stigma, build trust, and bridge the divide between treatments and psychoeducation received in Latinas' home countries and the US. Through this research (grounded in critical theory and aligned with critical feminist theories), Latinas were able to voice many barriers and facilitators to accessing sexual health care and participating in conversations around sexual health. By recognizing and honoring the many cultural differences that Latinas experience in the US, health-care providers can begin to offer a more culturally sensitive, feminist-informed, and humble approach to important screenings, diagnoses, and treatments for sexual health with their Latina immigrant patients/clients.

ORCID

Jennifer L. Hodgson http://orcid.org/0000-0001-5363-0215

References

Ali, P. A., & Johnson, S. (2016). Speaking my patient's language: Bilingual nurses' perspective about provision of language concordant care to patients with limited English proficiency. *Journal of Advanced Nursing, 73*(2), 421–432. https://doi.org/10.1111/jan.13143

Althoff, M. D., Theall, K., Schmidt, N., Hembling, J., Gebrekristos, H. T., Thompson, M. M., Muth, S. Q., Friedman, S. R., & Kissinger, P. (2017). Social support networks and HIV/STI risk behaviors among Latino immigrants in a new receiving environment. *AIDS and Behavior, 21*(12), 3607–3617. http://dx.doi.org/10.1007/s10461-017-1849-8

American Association for Marriage and Family Therapy. (2018). *Competencies for family therapists working in healthcare settings*. AAMFT. www.aamft.org/healthcare

Antshel, K. M. (2002). Integrating culture as a means of improving treatment adherence in the Latino population. *Psychology, Health & Medicine, 7*(4), 435–449. https://doi.org/10.1080/1354850021000015258

Beach, M. C., Saha, S., Korthuis, P. T., Sharp, V., Cohn, J., Wilson, I. B., Eggly, S., Moore, R., Cooper, L. A., Roter, D., & Sankar, A. (2010). Differences in Patient–Provider Communication for Hispanic Compared to Non-Hispanic White Patients in HIV Care. *Journal of General Internal Medicine, 25*(7), 682–687. https://doi.org/10.1007/s11606-010-1310-4

Centers for Disease Control and Prevention. (2016). *CDC fact sheet: New HIV infections in the United States*. National Center for HIV/AIDS, Viral Hepatitis, STD, and TB Prevention; Division of HIV/AIDS Prevention. https://www.cdc.gov/nchhstp/newsroom/docs/factsheets/new-hiv-infections-508.pdf

Centers for Disease Control and Prevention. (2017). *HIV Surveillance Report*. National Center for HIV/AIDS, Viral Hepatitis, STD, and TB Prevention; Division of HIV/AIDS

Prevention. https://www.cdc.gov/hiv/pdf/library/reports/surveillance/cdc-hiv-surveillance-infographic-2017.pdf

Centers for Disease Control and Prevention. (2019). *HIV in the United States and Dependent Areas*. National Center for HIV/AIDS, Viral Hepatitis, STD, and TB Prevention; Division of HIV/AIDS Prevention. https://www.cdc.gov/hiv/pdf/statistics/overview/cdc-hiv-us-ataglance.pdf

Chambers, M., Grew, R., Herlihy, D., Rabb, T. K., & Woloch, I. (Eds.). (1987). *The western experience to 1715* (Vol. 1). Knopf, Inc.

Chen, N. E., Gallant, J. E., & Page, K. R. (2012). A systematic review of HIV/AIDS survival and delayed diagnosis among Hispanics in the United States. *Journal of Immigrant and Minority Health, 14*(1), 65–81. https://doi.org/10.1007/s10903-011-9497-y

Cypress, B. S. (2017). Rigor or reliability and validity in qualitative research: Perspectives, strategies, reconceptualization, and recommendations. *Dimensions of Critical Care Nursing, 36*(4), 253–263. https://doi.org/10.1097/DCC.0000000000000253

De Las Nueces, D., Hacker, K., DiGirolamo, A., & Hicks, L. S. (2012). A systematic review of community-based participatory research to enhance clinical trials in racial and ethnic minority groups. *Health Research and Educational Trust, 47*(3), 1363–1386. https://doi.org/10.1111/j.1475-6773.2012.01386.x

Ertl, M. M., Dillon, F. R., Cabrera Tineo, Y. A., Verile, M., Jurkowski, J. M., & De La Rosa, M. (2018). Sexual risk during initial months in US among Latina young adults. *AIDS Care, 30* (3), 353–360. https://doi.org/10.1080/09540121.2017.1368442

Fernandez-Armesto, F. (2014). *Our America: A Hispanic history of the United States*. W.W. Norton & Company, Inc. https://doi.org/10.1002/polq.12259

Fortuna, L. R., Noroña, C. R., Porche, M. V., Tillman, C., Pratima, A. P., Wang, Y., Algeria, M., & Markle, S. L. (2019). Trauma, immigration, and sexual health among Latina women: Implications for maternal-child well-being and reproductive justice. *Infant Mental Health Journal, 40*(5), 640–658. https://doi.org/10.1002/imhj.21805

Galanti, G. A. (2008). *Caring for patients from different cultures* (4th ed.). University of Pennsylvania Press. https://doi.org/10.1111/maq.12079

Ganguli, I., Collins, J. E., Reichmann, W. M., Losina, E., Katz, J. N., Arbelaez, C., Walensky, R. P., & Donnell-Fink, L. A. (2013). Missed opportunities: Refusal to confirm reactive rapid HIV tests in the emergency department. *PLOS One, 8*(1), 1–7. http://dx.doi.org/10.1371/journal.pone.0053408

Giorgi, A. (2009). *The descriptive phenomenological method in psychology: A modified Husserlian approach*. Pennsylvania: Duquesne University Press. https://doi.org/10.1163/156916210x526079

Goldfield, A., Anderson, A., Argersinger, B., & Weir, (Eds.). (2004). *The American journey: A history of the United States* (1 ed.). Pearson. https://trove.nla.gov.au/work/7052878

Habermas, J. (1962, translated 1989). *The structural transformation of the public sphere: An inquiry into a category of bourgeois society*. MIT Press. https://doi.org/10.1177/144078339102700310

Habermas, J. (1981, translated 1984). *Lifeworld and system: A critique of functionalist reason*. (T. McCarthy, Trans.)… Beacon Press. https://doi.org/10.2307/1955926

Harding, S. (1986). *The science question in feminism*. Cornell University Press.

Hargreaves, M., Hidalgo, J., Burd, V., Bagchi, A., & Kim, J. (2010, August). *Strategies for Engaging and Retaining Latinas in HIV Care. [PDF file]. Mathematica Policy Research.* https://www.mathematica.org/download-media?MediaItemId={59A41350-846F-43BB-B9D0-76DFE7A08142}

Hong, Y. A., Murga, A. L., Plankey-Videla, N., & Chavez, M. J. (2015). HIV/STI risks in Latino day laborers in central Texas: A mixed-method study. *Health Psychology and Behavioral Medicine, 3*(1), 315–322. https://doi.org/10.1080/21642850.2015.1100541

Husserl, E. (1960). *Cartesian meditations: An introduction to phenomenology*. D. Cairns, Trans.) Springer Science & Business Media. (Original work published in 1960)... https://books.google.com/books?id=PdHrCAAAQBAJ&printsec=frontcover&source=gbs_ge_summary_r&cad=0#v=onepage&q&f=false

Infante, C., Zarco, A., Cuadra, S. M., Morrison, K., Caballero, M., Bronfman, M., & Magis, C. (2006). HIV/AIDS-related stigma and discrimination: The case of health care providers in Mexico. *Salud Publica Mexico, 48*(12), 141–150. http://search.ebscohost.com/login.aspx?direct=true&AuthType=ip,shib&db=mdc&AN=16619870&site=ehost-live&scope=site

Israel, B. A., Eng, E., Schulz, A. J., & Parker, E. A. (2013). *Methods for community-based participatory research for health* (2nd ed.). Wiley & Sons, Inc.

Juckett, G. (2013). Caring for Latino patients. *American Family Physician, 87*(1), 48–54. https://www.clinicalkey.com/#!/content/playContent/1-s2.0-S0002838X12604560

Lazcano-Ponce, E., Angeles-Llerenas, A., Alvarez-del Rio, A., Salazar-Martinez, E., Allen, B., Hernandez-Avila, M., & Kraus, A. (2004). Ethics and communication between physicians and their patients with cancer, HIV/ AIDS,and rheumatoid arthritis in Mexico. *Archives of Medical Research, 35*(1), 66–75. https://doi.org/10.1016/j.arcmed.2003.06.007

Lichter, D. T., Parisi, D., & Taquino, M. C. (2016). Emerging patterns of Hispanic residential segregation: Lessons from rural and small-town America. *Rural Sociology, 81*(4), 483–518. https://doi.org/10.1111/ruso.12108

Liddicoat, R. V., Losina, E., Kang, M., Freedberg, K. A., & Walensky, R. P. (2006). Refusing HIV testing in an urgent care setting. *Results from the "Think HIV" Program. AIDS Patient Care and STDs, 20*(2), 84–92. https://doi.org/10.1089/apc.2006.20.84

Lindsey, E. W. (2018). Cultural values and co-parenting quality in families of Mexican origin. *Journal of Cross-Cultural Psychology, 49*(10), 1523–1538. https://doi.org/10.1177/0022022118803182

López-Cevallos, D. F. & Harvey, S. *M.* (2016). Foreign-born Latinos living in rural areas are more likely to experience health care discrimination: Results from Proyecto de Salud para Latinos.Journal of Immigrant and Minority Health, 18, 928–934. doi.10.1007/s10903-015-0281-2

Lopez-Quintero, C., Rojas, P., Dillon, F. R., Varga, L. M., & De La Rosa, M. (2016). HIV testing practices among Latina women at risk of getting infected: A five-year follow-up of a community sample in South Florida. *AIDS Care, 28*(2), 137–146. https://doi.org/10.1080/09540121.2015.1071769

Magis-Rodriguez, C., Lemp, G., Hernandez, M. T., Sanchez, M. A., Estrada, F., & Bravo-García, E. (2009). Going North: Mexican migrants and their vulnerability to HIV. *Journal of Acquired Immune Deficiency Syndrome, 51*, S21–S25. https://doi.org/10.1097/QAI.0b013e3181a26433

Mann, L., Tanner, A. E., Sun, C. J., Erausquin, J. T., Siman, F. M., Downs, M., & Rhodes, S. D. (2016). Listening to the voices of Latina women: Sexual and reproductive health intervention needs and priorities in a new settlement state in the United States. *Health Care for Women International, 37*(9), 979–994. https://doi.org/10.1080/07399332.2016.1174244

McCarthy, T. (1989). *The critical theory of Jurgen Habermas*. The MIT Press. (Original work published 1979).

Migration Policy Institute (MPI) tabulation of data from U.S. Census Bureau. (2018). American Community Surveys (ACS), and 2000 Decennial Census; data for 1960 to 1990 are from Campbell J. Gibson and Emily Lennon, "Historical Census Statistics on the Foreign-Born Population of the United States: 1850 to 1990" (Working Paper No. 29,

U.S. Census Bureau, Washington, DC, 1999). https://www.migrationpolicy.org/programs/data-hub/charts/immigrants-countries-birth-over-time

Mogro-Wilson, C., Rojas, R., & Haynes, J. (2016). A cultural understanding of the parenting practices of Puerto Rican fathers. *Social Work Research*, *40*(4), 237–248. https://doi.org/10.1093/swr/svw019

National Center for Farmworker Health, Inc. (2017). *HIV/AIDS Agricultural Worker Factsheet*. National Center for Farmworker Health, Inc. http://www.ncfh.org/uploads/3/8/6/8/38685499/fs-hiv_aids.pdf

North Carolina Department of Health and Human Services. (2016). *North Carolina's integrated HIV prevention and care plan including the statewide coordinated statement of need, CY 2017-2021*. https://epi.dph.ncdhhs.gov/cd/hiv/docs/NC2017-2021_IntegratedPreventionandCarePlan_9-30-16.pdf

Parra, E. O., Doran, T. I., Ivy, L. M., Ramirez Aranda, J. M., & Hernandez, C. (2001). Concerns of pregnant women about being tested for HIV: A study in a predominately Mexican-American population. *AIDS Patient Care and STDs*, *15*(2), 83–93. https://doi.org/10.1089/108729101300003681

Parrado, E. A., Flippen, C. A., & McQuiston, C. (2005). Migration and relationship power among Mexican women. *Demography*, *42*(2), 347–372. https://doi.org/10.1353/dem.2005.0016

Peragallo Montano, N., Cianelli, R., Villegas, N., Gonzalez-Guarda, R., Williams, W. O., & de Tantillo, L. (2019). Evaluating a culturally tailored HIV risk reduction intervention among Hispanic women delivered in a real-world setting by community agency personnel. *American Journal of Health Promotion*, *33*(4), 566–575. https://doi.org/10.1177/0890117118807716

Persichino, J., & Ibarra, L. (2012). HIV and Latino migrant workers in the USA. *Ethnic and Racial Studies*, *35*(1), 120–134. https://doi.org/10.1080/01419870.2011.594167

Saha, S., Korthuis, P. T., Cohn, J. A., Sharp, V. L., Moore, R. D., & Beach, M. C. (2013). Primary care provider cultural competence and racial disparities in HIV care and outcomes. *Journal of General Internal Medicine*, *28*(5), 622–629. https://doi.org/10.1007/s11606-012-2298-8

Schminkey, D. L., Liu, X., Annan, S., & Sawin, E. M. (2019). Contributors to health inequalities in rural Latinas of childbearing age: An integrative review using an ecological framework. *Sage Open*, *9*(1), 1–20. https://doi.org/10.1177/2158244018823077

Schuster, M. A., Collins, R., Cunningham, W. E., Morton, S. C., Zierler, S., Wong, M., & Kanouse, D. E. (2005). Perceived discrimination in clinical care in a nationally representative sample of HIV-infected adults receiving health care. *Journal of General Internal Medicine*, *20*(9), 807–813. https://doi.org/10.1111/j.1525-1497.2005.05049.x

Sharma, M. (2019). Applying feminist theory to medical education. *The Lancet*, *393* (10171 doi:10.1016/S0140-6736(18)32595-9), 570–578. doi: 10171

Springer, M. V., & Skolarus, L. E. (2019). Community-based participatory Research: Partnering with communities. *Stroke*, *50*(3), 48–50. https://doi.org/10.1161/STROKEAHA.118.024241

Stephens, D. P., Eaton, A. A., & Boyd, B. (2017). Hispanic college men's perceptions of appropriate strategies for initiating sexual intercourse with women. *Sex Roles*, *77*(3–4), 239–253. https://doi.org/10.1007/s11199-016-0709-8

Torrone, E. A., Wright, J., Leone, P. A., & Hightow-Weidman, L. B. (2010). Pregnancy and HIV infection in young women in North Carolina. *Public Health Reports*, *125*(1), 96–102. https://doi.org/10.1177/003335491012500113

Tung, W. (2012). HIV among Hispanic/Latino populations in the United States. *Health Care Diversity*, *24*, 153–155. https://doi.org/10.1177/1084822311435544

UNAIDS. (2004). 2004 report on the global AIDS epidemic. http://www.unaids.org/sites/default/files/en/media/unaids/contentassets/documents/unaidspublication/2004/GAR2004_en.pdf

United States Department of Agriculture. (2018). *Rural America at a glance: 2018 edition.* USDA Economic Research Service. https://www.ers.usda.gov/webdocs/publications/90556/eib-200.pdf?v=5899.2

Van Manen, M. (2014). *Phenomenology of practice.* Left Coast Press, Inc. http://www.maxvanmanen.com/files/2014/10/MvM-Phen-of-Practice-113.pdf

Viadro, C. I., & Earp, J. A. L. (2000). The sexual behavior of married Mexican immigrant men in North Carolina. *Social Science & Medicine, 50*(5), 723–735. https://doi.org/10.1016/S0277-9536(99)00305-6

Viswanathan, M., Ammerman, A., Eng, E., Gartlehner, G., Lohr, K. N., Griffith, D., ... Whitener, L. (2004). *Community-based participatory research: Assessing the evidence. [PDF File].* Agency for Healthcare Research and Quality. AHRQ publication 04-E022-2. https://pdfs.semanticscholar.org/943e/172f45ef9a6c1ada24cb48ce5f1541252acb.pdf

Wallerstein, N., Duran, B., Oetzel, J. G., & Minkler, M. (2017). *Community-based participatory research for health: Advancing social and health equity* (3rd ed.). John Wiley & Sons, Inc. https://doi.org/10.1177/1524839918809007

Wiltz, T. (2015, August 14). *Hispanic poverty in rural areas challenges states.* Pew Research Center. The Pew Charitable Trusts. https://www.pewtrusts.org/en/research-and-analysis/blogs/stateline/2015/08/14/hispanic-poverty-in-rural-areas-challenges-states

Zhang, S., Senteio, C., Felizzola, J., & Rust, G. (2013). Racial/Ethnic Disparities in Antiretroviral Treatment Among HIV-Infected Pregnant Medicaid Enrollees, 2005–2007. *American Journal of Public Health, 103*(12), e46–353. https://doi.org/10.2105/AJPH.2013.301328

Sexual Health of Women with Obesity: A Review of the Literature

Özlem Köse, Jennifer Hodgson and Karlene Cunningham

ABSTRACT
While sexual health problems due to obesity is more pronounced in women than men, which biopsychosocial factors compound this effect is not clear. In this systematic review, the authors collected 63 studies that met the inclusion and exclusion criteria on the biopsychosocial factors associated with sexual problems in women with obesity and highlighted the gaps. More research and clinical attention on social context and intersectionality and its connections to other biopsychosocial factors are needed to better serve women with obesity and their romantic partners, as well as combat obesity and sexual health disparities. Recommendations for clinicians and researchers are provided.

Obesity is a global epidemic (Friedrich, 2017). Mounting evidence indicates the negative impacts of obesity on different aspects of life including physical and psychosocial health (Değirmenci et al., 2015; de Zwaan et al., 2009). More recently, researchers have identified evidence of adverse effects of obesity on sexual health (Træen et al., 2016). Within this literature, sexual health is often focused on the presence or absence of sexual dysfunction. For example, abdominal obesity was found to be a risk factor sexual dysfunction (Esposito et al., 2010), and weight loss interventions were helpful for improving sexual functioning and sexual quality (Conason et al., 2017). However, the World Health Organization (WHO) has encouraged clinicians and researchers to define sexual health more broadly to include sexual wellbeing. To do this, one must examine the state of biological, psychological, and interpersonal factors concerning sexuality and sexual experiences (World Health Organization, 2006).

A biopsychosocial model of sexual health in women with obesity

The biopsychosocial model is a theoretical framework developed by Engel (1977, 1980) that conceptualizes health as a biological, psychological, and social experience. Among studies focused on women with obesity and impacts on sexual health, psychosocial factors such as body image, depression, and relationship quality, directly and indirectly, contribute to sexual problems (Sarwer et al., 2013). Similarly, relationship-related factors, including perceived relationship quality and conflict, affect women's sexual satisfaction and frequency among those in heterosexual romantic relationships (Kwon & Schafer, 2017). Biological factors, such as a women's reproductive stage may also contribute to obesity being a risk factor for sexual dysfunction (Esposito et al., 2010). Lastly, there is evidence to suggest that women with obesity report more sexual dysfunction than their male counterparts (Østbye et al., 2011); however, most published studies focus mainly on male sexual health. Taken together, these research findings suggest there are unique psychological, interpersonal, and biological challenges among women with obesity; however, there are limited available reviews of these unique factors related to their sexual health.

Dynamic biopsychosocial model of health

The dynamic biopsychosocial model of health (Lehman et al., 2017), an expansion of Engel's (1977, 1980) biopsychosocial model, is chosen to identify the existing research and ground the analyses for this review as its main principles are relevant to better understand the multidimensional nature of the relationship between obesity and women's sexual health. First, the model posits that each factor of overall health mutually interacts with each other, and the impacts of these dynamic and ongoing interactions on one's health change over time. In the context of obesity and women's sexual health, this means that sexual problems are not to be explained with individual factors (e.g., higher body mass index, low self-esteem, or gender), but rather we must account for how these individual factors interact with one another over time and how these interactions shape the impact of obesity-related sexual problems on women's and their partners' health and wellbeing. In addition to explaining the dynamic nonlinearity between biopsychosocial factors, the model exclusively focuses on the systemic interplay of interpersonal and contextual factors and their direct and indirect effects on health and development. Given the recent efforts to capture the role of social health determinants in the treatment of women's obesity and sexual health (Kwon & Schafer, 2017), the authors utilized the dynamic biopsychosocial model to ground the search methodology for collecting the existing research on biological, psychological, and interpersonal health factors affecting the relationship between women's obesity and sexual health.

Defining sexual health

To appreciate the scope of the literature involved in this review, it is important to understand what sexual health is. Defining sexual health as the nonexistence of sexual problems and dysfunction is an oversimplification. The World

Health Organization (2006) concurs stating, sexual health is more than the absence of sexual problem or dysfunction, rather it includes a subjective evaluation of sexual wellbeing. Sexual health is a state of biological, psychological, interpersonal wellbeing in relation to sexuality and sexual experiences (World Health Organization, 2006). The mere presence of sexual dysfunction may not always lead to clinical distress or dissatisfaction with sexual life (Ferenidou et al., 2008). In fact, women can still report having a satisfying sex life with their partner despite having sexual difficulties or absence of sexual activity with a partner (Thomas & Thurston, 2016). Several factors, including individual, partner, and relationship-related domains, contribute to a satisfying sex life (Velten & Margraf, 2017). Therefore, the authors take a multidimensional approach to sexual health to include all relevant studies.

Sexual health reaches beyond sexual functioning and includes consideration of one's subjective evaluation of their sexual experiences such as sexual quality, sexual satisfaction, and sexual desire (World Health Organization, 2006). The current conceptualization of female sexual functioning involves the biopsychosocial wellbeing of women in relation to the domains of sexual response including desire, arousal, lubrication, orgasm, satisfaction, and pain (McCabe et al., 2016). Female sexual dysfunction, based on the criteria of The Diagnostic and Statistical Manual of Mental Disorders – Fifth Edition (DSM-5; American Psychiatric Association, 2013), is defined as the presence of an impairment in sexual response cycle (i.e., desire, arousal, lubrication, orgasm, satisfaction, and pain) leading to distress. The terms dysfunction and problem are used interchangeably throughout this review.

Sexual quality is defined as the negative and positive evaluations of sexual activity with a partner (Shaw & Rogge, 2016). Sexual satisfaction is used to describe the subjective global evaluation of one's enjoyment of their sexual life (Lawrance et al., 2011). Sexual desire can be defined as an individual's interest in searching, initiating, or participating in sexual activity when a sexual stimulus is presented (Brezsnyak & Whisman, 2004). Research that investigated the associations between obesity and sexual health predominantly focused on sexual functioning, sexual desire, sexual satisfaction, and health- and weight-related sexual quality of life in women (Enzlin et al., 2009; Træen et al., 2016). While growing attention has been paid to reviewing the relationship between obesity and sexual functioning (Kolotkin et al., 2012), no published reviews to date investigated the biological, psychological, and interpersonal factors of sexual health in relation to women's obesity.

Method

This systematic review was conducted to answer the primary research question: What is known about the relationship between obesity and sexual health among women? The authors followed Cooper's (2017) seven-step model and the recommended guidelines for search and evaluation str[...] the Preferred Reporting Items for Systematic Reviews and Meta[...] (PRISMA) statement (Moher et al., 2009). With the assistance of a [...] science librarian, searches were completed using five different databases: [...] PubMed, (b) PsychInfo, (c) CINAHL, (d) SocINDEX, and (e) Cochrane Libraries (i.e., Central Register of Controlled Trials, and Cochrane Database of Systematic Reviews). Medical subject headings, subject terms, and keywords were entered into each database in consultation with a health sciences librarian. Each keyword was also searched as a text word in titles and abstracts to ensure that there was no mismatch between the database and subject terms in databases. Both the first author and the librarian repeated the searches with the same keywords and methodology to ensure consistency of results. The total number of the articles initially identified was 3,003.

The lead author and a coauthor went through the 3,003 titles and abstracts and applied the inclusion and exclusion criteria. Articles were admitted if: (a) the study focused on the relationship between obesity and sexual health, (b) the sample was conducted with human participants and women who were 18 years old or older; and (c) the study was published in English in a peer-review journal. Articles were excluded if: (a) they were unpublished scientific work (e.g. conference papers, thesis/dissertation, and abstracts, etc.), (b) the participants were adolescents, and (c) the participants were pregnant. After applying the inclusion and exclusion criteria, 212 articles remained in the review.

The lead author and a coauthor went through the remaining articles. A third coauthor was brought into the article review process when there was uncertainty about whether or not an article met the criteria for inclusion and assisted with the identification of themes to explain the findings. The remaining coauthors reviewed the tables and discussion of results to ensure that the themes and summarized data were representative of the reported findings. One hundred and fifty additional articles were excluded for not meeting the inclusion and exclusion criteria. Reference lists of the 62 articles were searched, and one additional article was identified that met the review criteria. In total, the final number of articles admitted into the review was 63. The results are provided in the proceeding section.

Results

The 63 articles selected for this review quantitatively studied the relationship between obesity and sexual functioning, as well as constructs of sexual experience (e.g., sexual satisfaction, sexual desire, and sexual quality). The studies included in this review defined sexual dysfunction based on the assessments that are grounded in Masters and Johnson (1966) linear model of human sexual response. Most of the studies with women assessed female sexual function by using the Female Sexual Function Index (FSFI; Brown et al., 2000). All of the items of the FSFI were summed, and the clinical cutoff score (i.e. ≤26.5) was used for defining female sexual dysfunction. Three studies with women only used the McCoy Sexual Questionnaire (McCoy, 2000), which is a measure that considers changes in hormonal levels due to menopause, as well as factors associated with the sex partner. Similarly, the studies with older women used the sexuality domain of Cervantes Scale (Palacios et al., 2004) to measure sexual function after menopause. The following two themes emerged to better analyze the findings: (a) biological factors (which included subthemes of weight indices and sexual functioning) and (b) psychosocial factors (which included subthemes of body image issues, self-esteem, depression, cultural influences, and the romantic partner's health impacts).

Biological factors

To evaluate biological factors associated with obesity and women's sexual health, the majority of the selected articles focus on the association between obesity indices (i.e., body mass index [BMI] and waist circumference [WC]) and sexual dysfunction in women. A large portion of these studies was cross-sectional. In this section, the authors discuss the findings regarding the relationship between obesity indices and women's sexual health as well as the definition and assessment of sexual dysfunction in the included studies.

The majority of the cross-sectional studies selected for this review concluded that women with higher BMI report lower overall sexual functioning scores as compared to women with normal BMI (e.g., Assimakopoulos et al., 2006). This problem also has a global reach. For example, a cross-sectional study with Iranian women found 85.9% with obesity or overweight status reported experiencing sexual dysfunction (Rabiepoor et al., 2017). Unlike cross-sectional studies, longitudinal and population studies examining this association found no association between BMI and sexual dysfunction, sexual desire, and frequency of partnered intercourse. Overall, most studies finding a negative association between BMI and overall female sexual functionin were cross-sectional, and their sample size was low. Only four of the articl selected for this review collected longitudinal data. Even though the cro sectional design has potential time and cost benefits for researchers, t provide limited information in terms of capturing interactions of biopsy social factors of health over time (Trump & Mendenhall, 2017). More l itudinal research with a consideration of multiple factors underlyi relationship between obesity and sexual functioning as well as their i tions with one another is needed.

Some of the published studies investigated the relationship between BMI and subdomains of sexual functioning (i.e., desire, lubrication, arousal, orgasm, satisfaction, and pain) assessed by FSFI (Brown et al., 2000), but yielded mixed results. For example, some studies showed that higher BMI predicted greater impairment in arousal, lubrication, satisfaction, and orgasm, but not desire and sexual pain. Contrarily, two other studies found that both bodyweight predicted diminished sexual desire in women. Eftekhar et al. (2014) found that higher BMI predicted greater difficulties with female arousal. The researchers argued that low sexual desire may be explained with the association between obesity and changes in androgen levels (Kirchengast et al., 1996). They also posit that decreasing sexual desire may be due to a negative association between obesity and women's perception of sexual attractiveness (Eftekhar et al., 2014). Overall, there is a lack of clarity regarding the predictive role of BMI on overall sexual functioning as well as its subdomains particularly in desire. Given that low desire is highly prevalent, affecting up to 40% of women (Brotto, 2017), more research determining individual, systemic, and contextual factors that explain decreased desire for sex in the context of obesity is critically important.

Given the inconsistency regarding the predictive role of BMI on sexual health problems in women, researchers argued that BMI may not be a valid measure for diagnosing obesity as it cannot differentiate fat and lean body mass, particularly in women (Banack et al., 2018). Researchers found that BMI does not accurately predict obesity in Black and Asian populations, and different cutoff points based on race/ethnicity are needed for defining the isk for obesity-related health problems (e.g., Carroll et al., 2008). Some argued t indicators of visceral obesity such as waist circumference and waist-to- ht ratio are reportedly better than BMI at detecting obesity and comorbid s (i.e., metabolic syndrome, cardiometabolic diseases, and polycystic ndrome (PCOS)). In fact, larger waist circumference was associated levels of sexual functioning in women with obesity. Moreover, larger waist circumference reported decreased sexual activity, as xual desire. It should be noted that most of these findings are al samples of women who presented with obesity-related ., diabetes, PCOS, and metabolic syndrome), which might the negative relationship between waist and sexual pro- not enough evidence to conclude that abdominal obesity BMI at predicting sexual dysfunction in women with ould clarify if there is a direct relationship between o-height ratio, waist-to-hip ratio, and body com- l health.

Psychosocial factors

In addition to biological factors of health, sexual health in women with obesity can be influenced by several psychological factors, including body image (Sarwer et al., 2012). Researchers noted a positive relationship between obesity and body image dissatisfaction. They highlighted the fact that body image dissatisfaction is more common in women than men with obesity, as well as among women with normal weight. Interestingly, several research teams found that body image dissatisfaction among women with extreme obesity impacts their sexual functioning more than men's.

Besides sexual functioning issues among women with obesity, a few studies examined the mediating role of body image on women's reported sexual quality. For example, Træen et al. (2016) found that body image mediates the negative relationship between obesity and sexual satisfaction. Lower BMI was associated with increased body satisfaction, which led to higher sexual satisfaction. Among young women (18–25 years old), affective body image (i.e., having positive feelings about one's body) mediated the relationship between body fat percentage and sexual satisfaction (Milhausen et al., 2015). On the other hand, Pujols et al. (2010) found a relationship between BMI and various aspects of body image (i.e., cognitive distraction during sexual activity and body esteem), but not between BMI and sexual satisfaction among women between the ages of 18 and 49 years. Taken together, studies indicating the link between body weight and body image problems in regards to sexual satisfaction is limited to young and middle-aged women (18–49 years old). Given the compounding effect of age on women's body image and how they view their body weight, more research with older cohorts is needed.

Besides body image concerns, researchers studying women's obesity considered self-esteem as a key factor for the understanding weight-related quality of life. In the studies comparing men and women, women reported more impairments in their self-esteem compared to their male counterparts. White et al. (2004), for example, studied racial differences and found that White women reported lower self-esteem than Black women. Further, cross-sectional research found no differences in self-esteem when comparing North American and Spanish women with morbid obesity, and BMI was not correlated with self-esteem. Similarly, there were no differences in sexual esteem, a construct measuring one's self-evaluation of being a good sexual partner, between normal-weight women and overweight women. However, they argued that their results might be due to small sample size. While both self-esteem and sexual quality are instrumental to understanding women's health in regard to their obesity, none of the studies reviewed investigated to what extent self-esteem is associated with declines in sexual quality in women with obesity. Clearly, more studies enhancing and expanding our understanding of how self-esteem influences the relationship between obesity and sexual quality in women are needed.

Given that the relationship between depression and sexual functioning is robust, several studies included in this review investigated it in relation to women's obesity. Both higher scores of depression and antidepressant use were found to be associated with more impairments in sexual functioning as well as sexual quality in women with obesity. Further, Assimakopoulos et al. (2006) found that depression was linked with subdomains of female sexual functioning including desire, arousal, and satisfaction although depression severity did not affect the link between overall sexual functioning and obesity. Overall, these studies underscore the critical importance of addressing depressive mood symptoms in order to better capture the link between obesity and sexual health.

Along with psychological factors, research consistently supports the critical importance of evaluating the interdependence of both partners' sexual functioning and sexual quality in the context of romantic relationships (Heiman et al., 2007). When a partner has a medical condition causing sexual difficulties, not only does it impact their own sexual quality of but also their partner's (Rottmann et al., 2017). In the context of heterosexual relationships, the male partner's health condition affects their female partner's sexual health more than their own sexual health (Eisemann et al., 2014). Only one study examined the adverse effects of the male partner's obesity illness on their female partner's sexual health (Kwon & Schafer, 2017). In a sample of older adult couples (57–85 years old), Kwon and Schafer (2017) found that among older heterosexual couples, male obesity was not associated with the frequency of partnered sex while obesity in women was. Their study indicated that couples with female partners with extreme obesity (BMI > 40) and male partners with normal weight (BMI 18.5–24.9) reported less partnered sex as opposed to the couples with both partners within normal weight. Lastly, the couples were less likely to have vaginal sex when the male partner was within normal weight but the female partner was obese. Researchers found women's weight is more important than men's for the frequency of sexual activity and vaginal intercourse. Although enlightening, the generalizability of these findings is limited due to the age range of their sample. More research with a larger age-range of women and their partners are needed. Furthermore, there is a gaping hole in regard to how obesity impacts couples' sexual relationship of same-sex couples. Overall, more research with women of other age groups, relationship status, and sexual orientation is needed to clarify the understanding of the influence of body weight on women's and their partners' sexual quality within a romantic relationship context.

Besides weight status, the male partner's sexual functioning is a key factor for sexual health among heterosexual couples where the heterosexual woman has obesity. In a sample of Canadian women, women whose partners had difficulty with erection or premature ejaculation reported lesser frequency of orgasm and lower desire as compared with women who did not report their partner's having sexual dysfunction (Gruszecki et al., 2005). Similarly, Kwon and Schafer (2017) found that the couples reported decreased sexual activity when the male partner had erection problems. Although these findings support the interdependence of partner's sexual functioning and women's sexual health, to what extent these partner-related factors impact the sexual quality of women with obesity and their male partners' is not clear. Other partner-related related factors such as partners' body image problems might provide further insight into the relationship between obesity and women's sexual health.

Finally, cultural influences might be important for understanding women's sexual behavior and overall sexual health in relation to their obesity. However, only a few articles selected for this review discussed the role of culture in understanding sexual health and behavior. For example, a cross-sectional study with young uncircumcised Egyptian women (18–25 years old) found no difference between a group of women with obesity and their normal weight counterparts regarding their overall sexual functioning score (Elnashar et al., 2015). The authors explained that cultural values, beliefs and education status might explain why excessive weight is not a concern for these women's sexual functioning. Unfortunately, they did not discuss the specific values and norms that are different than Western cultures and how they might influence Egyptian women's perceptions of their weight and sexual functioning.

As culture is often defined based on racial and ethnic differences in the United States (Amaro et al., 2002), studies with American women compared White and African Americans in terms of their weight-related sexual quality. What they found is that White people with obesity reported greater risk for lower sexual functioning as compared with African Americans. In fact, one study with African American women only found a positive association between BMI and sexual satisfaction. Only one cross-cultural study compared Spanish and North American women with morbid obesity in regard to their weight-related sexual quality and found that Spanish participants reported higher impairments in their sexual life due to their weight. While these studies are helpful for moving closer to understanding women's sexual health and obesity from a dynamic biopsychosocial perspective, insufficient evidence prevents us from determining the influence of culture on obesity-related sexual problems. That said, more cross-cultural studies are needed to shed light on how culture and macrosystem level factors (e.g., healthcare policies, laws, norms, and economic conditions) shape and maintain obesity-related sexual health problems among women.

Discussion

While research on the biological, psychological, and interpersonal factors affecting the sexual health of women is increasing, the association between obesity and women's sexual health has not been fully explored. The systematic review aimed to update the literature on biological, psychosocial factors impacting women's obesity and sexual health by answering the following research question: What is known about the relationship between obesity and sexual health among women? Several gaps were identified. Recommendation for future research and clinical work is provided below that will hopefully guide work in this area.

Recommendations for future research

A large portion of the studies included in this review examined the relationship between obesity and overall female functioning and defined dysfunction based on the clinical cutoff total score (i.e. ≤26.5) of FSFI (Wiegel et al., 2005). However, given ongoing debates and gender politics involved regarding how to define female sexual dysfunction, a more careful use of measures assessing it is advised. Measures such as FSFI are grounded in traditional theories of human sexual response that views the phases of sexual response (i.e., excitement, plateau, orgasm, and resolution) as a linear process and in a particular order. Sex researchers critique the linear model of human sexual response (Masters & Johnson, 1966) for its inability to capture the complexity and variability of women's partnered sexual experiences. There is a call to redefine women's sexual response considering the relationship- and partner-related factors, sexual and non-sexual outcomes of sexual encounters, and sexual motivation (Basson, 2012, 2015; Tiefer, 2001) and to move beyond the emphasis on "functioning" and focusing on women's sexual experiences such as sexual quality and sexual satisfaction (Brotto, 2017; Kolotkin et al., 2012). Therefore, the dyadic conceptualization of obesity through dyadic analysis techniques (e.g., Actor-Partner Interdependence Models) would help researchers explore the interdependence between women's sexual health and their partners' sexual health.

While several sex researchers recognized the impact of social context on sexual health (e.g., Marvan & Trujillo, 2009; Rosenthal & Lobel, 2018), existing research on obesity-related sexual problems does not account for social locations and the role intersectionality (e.g., relationship between our many social locations and our positions in society; Crenshaw, 1989) plays. More recent reviews on this topic explicitly emphasized the role of studying sex and gender differences in regards to adverse effects of obesity on sexual health (e.g., Kolotkin et al., 2012), but only a few published work focused on social locations including race, sexual orientation, ethnicity, and gender, and how they influence sexual health. Thus, more research accounting for the role of sexual orientation and gender on the associations between obesity-related biopsychosocial factors and sexual health is needed. There is also a need to investigate similarities and differences in obesity-related impairments in sexual health among heterosexual, gay, and lesbian couples.

Another gap is the lack of research on the direct and indirect effects of interpersonal factors on the relationship between obesity and sexual health. Although interpersonal factors are key to understanding women's sexual health, very little research considers their role in the context of women's obesity (Kwon & Schafer, 2017; Williams & Merten, 2013). No studies were identified addressing the impact of obesity on same-sex couples. Given that gender is a social construct accounting for the influence of cultural norms, values, and perceived gendered roles on women's sexual experiences (Paine et al., 2019; Springer et al., 2012), same-sex couples differ from heterosexual couples in terms of how they deal with health issues as a dyadic unit, as well as their sexual experiences.

Finally, very little was found in terms of how women's obesity contributes to their sexual experience, such as sexual quality. Sexual quality in the context of obesity was researched as a subdomain of weight-related impairments in quality of life using assessments such as the Laval Questionnaire (Donini et al., 2017) and the Impact of Weight on Quality of Life Measures (IWQOL & IWQOL-Lite; Kolotkin et al., 2001, 1995). Given that sexual quality is more complex than the absence of impairments and involving both negative and positive sexual experiences (Shaw & Rogge, 2016), more research using instruments that measure the multidimensional nature of sexual quality is needed, inclusive of participants' social locations and intersectionality. All of the emerging and needed research will hopefully translate into more resources for clinicians working directly with women who struggles with obesity and sexual health complications related to it.

Recommendations for clinical work

The dynamic biopsychosocial model of health posits that human's health is impacted by the actual or perceived effects of interpersonal factors (Lehman et al., 2017). Clinicians who work with couples could help them to understand the shared burden of obesity on each partner's sexual health and treat it relationally and not just with the symptom bearer. Based on systemic perspective that sees sexual health problems as a symptom of the couple's dynamics rather than the responsibility of the partner with the symptom (Atwood et al., 2006; Conaglen & Conaglen, 2017; Wagner et al., 2000), including the partner in the assessment and treatment phase of the care may enhance the treatment outcomes and help destigmatize and remove blame from the patient.

This review confirms that an interdisciplinary approach is critical for assessing and treating women's obesity and sexual health problems (Træen et al., 2016). Creating a network of care and coordinating referrals for presenting issues helps to advance the practice of biopsychosocial care and pave the way for more comprehensive treatment for women. Utilizing a multidisciplinary treatment approach such as integrated sex therapy (Perelman, 2007, 2008) will help optimize treatment outcomes as it views human sexual response as a dynamic interaction of biomedical, psychosocial, and cultural factors. Using valid and obesity-specific biopsychosocial screening tools (e.g., IWQOL-Lite; Kolotkin et al., 2001) to regularly assess patients and their partners may help clinicians improve the early detection and treatment of sexual difficulties and integrate and/or refer to a behavioral health or sexual health specialist. However, clinicians should also note that single women with obesity are also at risk for sexual functioning concerns (Assimakopoulos et al., 2011; Steffen et al., 2017). Therefore, it is recommended that clinicians practice using a biopsychosocial approach and provide therapeutic options for women who are not partnered.

Interventions should also be applied that are considerate to clients' social locations (e.g., age, sexual orientation, race/ethnicity, SES; Hankivsky, 2012), and their intersectionality (e.g., relationship between one's many social locations and position in society; Crenshaw, 1989). Addressing sexual health problems often becomes a challenge for clinicians due to differences between them and their clients' social locations, as well as lack of time and training (Gott et al., 2004; Hughes et al., 2014). Isomorphic to providers' experience, women are usually reluctant to seek help from their providers about their sexual health due to the lack of awareness of the problem and its symptoms, denial, and lack of availability and affordability of sexual health services (Azar et al., 2013). Clinicians should empower women to share their sexual health problems through a safe, non-judgmental, and culturally humble approach. For example, clinicians may want to use Galanti's (2015) four Cs of culture: call (i.e., What do you call what you are experiencing?), cause (i.e., What do you think caused it to happen?), cope (i.e., How do you cope with it?), and concerns (i.e., What concerns do you have about it?). This helps to structure the client interview so that they feel empowered and providers are less driven by their own biases to assess and diagnose the type and severity of sexual health problems.

Given that both biological sex and gender are shaped by culture, their impact on sexual health should be conceptualized considering the interactions of biological factors, multiple social locations (e.g., race/ethnicity, class, income, education, ability, age, sexual orientation, immigration status, and geography), and healthcare factors. In addition to the intersections of these multiple biopsychosocial factors, Smith (2019) advises clinicians to address sizeism, a result of intersectional fat stigma, to fully support and empower women with obesity. She defines sizeism as "oppression based on body size" (p.61). She also cautions clinicians to be aware of how weight stigma intersects with the other social locations in women's lives as well as recognizing their beliefs and personal experiences about their own sizeism. Taken altogether, both researchers and clinicians should integrate social context and intersectionality perspectives into their work when working with women with obesity and their sexual health problems. Hence, recommendations for research and clinical work considering this gap are also provided.

Limitations

This review is not without limitations. First of all, the authors only included peer-reviewed studies that were published in English language. The studies published in a foreign language and gray literature (i.e., dissertations, conference papers, and abstracts) were excluded. It might be that these studies provide additional information regarding the association between obesity and sexual health in women. Second, it is possible that the authors might have overlooked or failed to find articles due to search terms or human error. Lastly, the search results found articles that were associated with co-morbidities related to obesity such as diabetes, polycystic ovary syndrome (PCOS), and metabolic syndrome. Although these studies were included in this review, to what extent these comorbid conditions compound the relationship between obesity and sexual health were not analyzed separately as it was beyond the scope of this current review and search strategy.

Conclusion

This systematic review helps reinforce that sexual health is comprised of biological, psychological, and interpersonal factors that have a direct and/or indirect impact on women with obesity, particularly relative to sexual functioning and quality of sex. However, most researchers have focused on sexual dysfunction while neglecting the other dimensions such as sexual desire, sexual satisfaction, sexual quality, and the partner- and relationship-related factors. Equally as important is the need for more research and clinical attention to social context, social location, and intersectionality. This expanded focus is needed to better serve women with obesity and their romantic partners, as well as combat obesity and sexual health-related health disparities.

ORCID

Jennifer Hodgson http://orcid.org/0000-0001-5363-0215
Karlene Cunningham http://orcid.org/0000-0001-5325-933X

References

* Articles included in the systematic review.

Amaro, H., Navarro, A. M., Conron, K. J., & Raj, A. (2002). Cultural influences on women's sexual health. In G. M. Wingood & R. J. DiClemente (Eds.), *Handbook of women's sexual and reproductive health* (pp. 71–92). Kluwer Academic/Plenum Publishers.

American Psychiatric Association. (2013). *Diagnostic and statistical manual of mental disorders* (5th ed. ed.). Author.

Assimakopoulos, K., Karaivazoglou, K., Panayiotopoulos, S., Hyphantis, T., Iconomou, G., & Kalfarentzos, F. (2011). Bariatric surgery is associated with reduced depressive symptoms and better sexual function in obese female patients: A one-year follow-up study. *Obesity Surgery*, *21*(3), 362–366. https://doi.org/10.1007/s11695-010-0303-z

*Assimakopoulos, K., Panayiotopoulos, S., Iconomou, G., Karaivazoglou, K., Matzaroglou, C., Vagenas, K., & Kalfarentzos, F. 2006. Assessing sexual function in obese women preparing for bariatric surgery. *Obesity Surgery*, *16*(8), 1087–1091. https://doi.org/10.1381/09608920 6778026442

Atwood, J. D., Klucinec, E., & Neaver, E. (2006). A combined-constructionist therapeutic approach to couples experiencing erectile dysfunction: Part II. *Contemporary Family Therapy*, *28*(4), 403–418. https://doi.org/10.1007/s10591-006-9022-y

Azar, M., Bradbury-Jones, C., & Kroll, T. (2013). Patterns of help-seeking in women when problems arise in their sexual life: A discussion paper. *Journal of Clinical Nursing*, *22*(23–24), 3587–3596. https://doi.org/10.1111/jocn.12374

Banack, H. R., Wactawski-Wende, J., Hovey, K. M., & Stokes, A. (2018). Is BMI a valid measure of obesity in postmenopausal women? *Menopause*, *25*(3), 307–313. https://doi.org/10.1097/ GME.0000000000000989

Basson, R. (2012). Women's sexuality and sexual dysfunction. In R. S. Gibbs & D. N. Danforth (Eds.), *Danforths obstetrics and gynecology* (pp. 742–758). Lippincott Williams & Wilkins.

Basson, R. (2015). Human sexual response. In M. P. Islam & S. E. Roach (Eds.), *Handbook of clinical neurology* (pp. 415–434). Elsevier.

Brezsnyak, M., & Whisman, M. A. (2004). Sexual desire and relationship functioning: The effects of marital satisfaction and power. *Journal of Sex & Marital Therapy*, *30*(3), 199–217. https://doi.org/10.1080/00926230490262393

Brotto, L. A. (2017). Evidence-based treatments for low sexual desire in women. *Frontiers in Neuroendocrinology*, *45*, 11–17. https://doi.org/10.1016/j.yfrne.2017.02.001

Brown, R. C., Heiman, J., Leiblum, S., Meston, C., Shabsigh, R., Ferguson, D., & D'Agostino, R. (2000). The female sexual function index (FSFI): A multidimensional self-report instrument for the assessment of female sexual function. *Journal of Sex & Marital Therapy*, *26*(2), 191–208. https://doi.org/10.1080/009262300278597

Carroll, J. F., Chiapa, A. L., Rodriquez, M., Phelps, D. R., Cardarelli, K. M., Vishwanatha, J. K., ... Cardarelli, R. (2008). Visceral fat, waist circumference, and BMI: Impact of race/ethnicity. *Obesity*, *16*(3), 600–607. https://doi.org/10.1038/oby.2007.92

Conaglen, H. M., & Conaglen, J. V. (2017). Integrating sexual partners into pharmacological sex therapy. In Z. D. Peterson (Ed.), *The wiley handbook of sex therapy* (pp. 453–467). John Wiley & Sons, Ltd. https://doi.org/10.1002/9781118510384.ch28

Conason, A., McClure Brenchley, K., Pratt, A., & Geliebter, A. (2017). Sexual life after weight loss surgery. *Surgery for Obesity and Related Diseases*, *13*(5), 855–861. https://doi.org/10. 1016/j.soard.2017.01.014

Cooper, H. M. (2017). *Research synthesis and meta-analysis: A step-by-step approach*. SAGE Publications.

Crenshaw, K. (1989). Demarginalizing the intersection of race and sex: A black feminist critique of antidiscrimination doctrine, feminist theory and antiracist politics. *University of Chicago Legal Forum, 140*(1), 136–167.

*de Zwaan, M., Petersen, I., Kaerber, M., Burgmer, R., Nolting, B., Legenbauer, T., ... Herpertz, S. 2009. Obesity and quality of life: A controlled study of normal-weight and obese individuals. *Psychosomatics, 50*(5), 474–482. https://doi.org/10.1016/S0033-3182(09)70840-0.

Değirmenci, T., Kalkan-Oğuzhanoğlu, N., Sözeri-Varma, G., Özdel, O., & Fenkçi, S. (2015). Psychological symptoms in obesity and related factors. *Noro Psikiyatri Arsivi, 52*(1), 42–46.

Donini, L. M., Rosano, A., Di Lazzaro, L., Poggiogalle, E., Lubrano, C., Migliaccio, S., ... Lenzi, A. (2017). Validation of the italian version of the laval questionnaire: Health-related quality of life in subjects with obesity. *Health and Quality of Life Outcomes, 15*(1), 101–107. https://doi.org/10.1186/s12955-017-0671-3

*Eftekhar, T., Sohrabvand, F. Zabandan, N., Shariat, M., Haghollahi, F., & Ghahghaei-Nezamabadi, A. 2014. Sexual dysfunction in patients with polycystic ovary syndrome and its affected domains. *Iranian Journal of Reproductive Medicine, 12*(8), 539–546.

Eisemann, N., Waldmann, A., Rohde, V., & Katalinic, A. (2014). Quality of life in partners of patients with localised prostate cancer. *Quality of Life Research, 23*(5), 1557–1568. https://doi.org/10.1007/s11136-013-0588-1

*Elnashar, A. R. M., Ibrahim, N. H., Ahmed, H., Hassanin, A. M., & Elgawady, M. A. 2015. Assessment of female sexual function in a group of uncircumcised obese egyptian women. *International Journal of Impotence Research, 27*(5), 178–181. https://doi.org/10.1038/ijir.2015.12.

Engel, G. L. (1977). The need for a new medical model: A challenge for biomedicine. *Science, 196*(4286), 129–136. https://doi.org/10.1126/science.847460

Engel, G. L. (1980). The clinical application of the biopsychosocial model. *American Journal of Psychiatry, 137*(5), 535–544. https://doi.org/10.1176/ajp.137.5.535

*Enzlin, P., Rosen, R., Wiegel, M., Brown, J., Wessells, H., & Gatcomb, P. 2009.,The DCCT/EDIC research group. Sexual dysfunction in women with type 1 diabetes: Long-term findings from the DCCT/EDIC study cohort. *Diabetes Care, 32*(5), 780–785. https://doi.org/10.2337/dc08-1164.

*Esposito, K., Maiorino, M., Bellastella, G., Giugliano, F., Romano, M., & Giugliano, D. 2010. Determinants of female sexual dysfunction in type 2 diabetes. *International Journal of Impotence Research, 22*(3), 179–184. https://doi.org/10.1038/ijir.2010.6.

Ferenidou, F., Kapoteli, V., Moisidis, K., Koutsogiannis, I., Giakoumelos, A., & Hatzichristou, D. (2008). Presence of a sexual problem may not affect women's satisfaction from their sexual function. *The Journal of Sexual Medicine, 5*(3), 631. https://doi.org/10.1111/j.1743-6109.2007.00644.x

Friedrich, M. J. (2017). Global obesity epidemic worsening. *Jama, 318*(7), 603. https://doi.org/10.1001/jama.2017.10693

Galanti, G. A. (2015). *Caring for patients from different cultures* (5th ed. ed.). University of Pennsylvania Press.

Gott, M., Galena, E., Hinchliff, S., & Elford, H. (2004). "Opening a can of worms": GP and practice nurse barriers to talking about sexual health in primary care. *Family Practice, 21*(5), 528–536. https://doi.org/10.1093/fampra/cmh509

Gruszecki, L., Fisher, W. A., & Forchuk, C. (2005). Factors associated with common sexual concerns in women: New findings from the canadian contraception study. *The Canadian Journal of Human Sexuality, 14*(1–2), 1–13.

Hankivsky, O. (2012). Women's health, men's health, and gender and health: Implications of intersectionality. *Social Science & Medicine, 74*(11), 1712–1720. https://doi.org/10.1016/j.socscimed.2011.11.029

Heiman, T., Bailen, O., Rosenberg, P., & Bavendam. (2007). Sexual function and satisfaction in heterosexual couples when men are administered sildenafil citrate (viagra) for erectile dysfunction: A multicentre, randomised, double-blind, placebo-controlled trial. *BJOG: An International Journal of Obstetrics & Gynaecology, 114*(4), 437–447. https://doi.org/10.1111/j.1471-0528.2006.01228.x

Hughes, A. K., Rostant, O. S., & Curran, P. G. (2014). Improving sexual health communication between older women and their providers: How the integrative model of behavioral prediction can help. *Research on Aging, 36*(4), 450–466. https://doi.org/10.1177/0164027513500055

*Kirchengast, S., Hartmann, B., Gruber, D., & Huber, J. 1996. Decreased sexual interest and its relationship to body build in postmenopausal women. *Maturitas, 23*(1), 63–71. https://doi.org/10.1016/0378-5122(95)00954-X.

Kolotkin, R. L., Crosby, R. D., Kosloski, K. D., & Williams, G. R. (2001). Development of a brief measure to assess quality of life in obesity. *Obesity, 9*(2), 102–111. https://doi.org/10.1038/oby.2001.13

Kolotkin, R. L., Head, S., Hamilton, M., & Tse, C. K. J. (1995). Assessing impact of weight on quality of life. *Obesity Research, 3*(1), 49–56. https://doi.org/10.1002/j.1550-8528.1995.tb00120.x

Kolotkin, R. L., Zunker, C., & Østbye, T. (2012). Sexual functioning and obesity: A review. *Obesity, 20*(12), 2325–2333. https://doi.org/10.1038/oby.2012.104

*Kwon, S., & Schafer, M. H. 2017. Obesity and sexuality among older couples: Evidence from the national social life, health, and aging project. *Journal of Aging and Health, 29*(5), 735–768. https://doi.org/10.1177/0898264316645541.

Lawrance, K., Byers, E. S., & Cohen, J. N. (2011). Interpersonal exchange model of sexual satisfaction questionnaire. In T. D. Fisher, C. M. Davis, W. L. Yarber, & S. L. Davis (Eds.), *Handbook of sexuality-related measures* (pp. 525–530). Routledge.

Lehman, B. J., David, D. M., & Gruber, J. A. (2017). Rethinking the biopsychosocial model of health: Understanding health as a dynamic system. *Social and Personality Psychology Compass, 11*(8), e12328-n/a. https://doi.org/10.1111/spc3.12328

Marvan, M. L., & Trujillo, P. (2009). Menstrual socialization, beliefs, and attitudes concerning menstruation in rural and urban Mexican Women. *Health Care for Women International, 31* (1), 53–67. https://doi.org/10.1080/07399330902833362

Masters, W. H., & Johnson, V. E. (1966). *Human sexual response* (1st ed.). Little, Brown, & Co.

McCabe, M. P., Sharlip, I. D., Atalla, E., Balon, R., Fisher, A. D., Laumann, E., Lee, S. W., Lewis, R., & Segraves, R. T. (2016). Definitions of sexual dysfunctions in women and men: A consensus statement from the fourth international consultation on sexual medicine 2015. *The Journal of Sexual Medicine, 13*(2), 135–143. https://doi.org/10.1016/j.jsxm.2015.12.019

McCoy, N. L. (2000). The McCoy female sexuality questionnaire. *Quality of Life Research, 9*(6), 739–745. https://doi.org/10.1023/A:1008925906947

Milhausen, R. R., Buchholz, A. C., Opperman, E. A., & Benson, L. E. (2015). Relationships between body image, body composition, sexual functioning, and sexual satisfaction among heterosexual young adults. *Archives of Sexual Behavior, 44*(6), 1621–1633. https://doi.org/10.1007/s10508-014-0328-9

Moher, D., Liberati, A., Tetzlaff, J., Altman, D. G., & Group, P. R. I. S. M. A. (2009). Preferred reporting items for systematic reviews and meta-analyses: The PRISMA statement. *PLoS Medicine, 6*(7), e1000097. https://doi.org/10.1371/journal.pmed.1000097

*Østbye, T., Kolotkin, R. L., He, H., Overcash, F., Brouwer, R., Binks, M., . . . Gadde, K. M. 2011. Sexual functioning in obese adults enrolling in a weight loss study. *Journal of Sex & Marital Therapy*, *37*(3), 224–235. https://doi.org/10.1080/0092623X.2011.564530.

Paine, E. A., Umberson, D., & Reczek, C. (2019). Sex in midlife: Women's sexual experiences in lesbian and straight marriages. *Journal of Marriage and Family*, *81*(1), 7–23. https://doi.org/10.1111/jomf.12508

Palacios, S., Ferrer-Barriendos, J., Parrilla, J. J., Castelo-Branco, C., Manubens, M., Alberich, X., & Cervantes, G. (2004). Health-related quality of life in the Spanish women through and beyond menopause. Development and validation of the cervantes scale. *Medicina Clínica*, *122*(6), 205. https://doi.org/10.1016/S0025-7753(04)74198-6

Perelman, M. A. (2007). Clinical application of CNS-acting agents in FSD. *The Journal of Sexual Medicine*, *4*(Suppl 4), 280–290. https://doi.org/10.1111/j.1743-6109.2007.00611.x

Perelman, M. A. (2008). Integrated sex therapy: A psychosocial-cultural perspective integrating behavioral, cognitive, and medical approaches. In C. C. Carson, R. S. Kirby, I. Goldstein, & M. E. G. Wyllie (Eds.), *Textbook of erectile dysfunction* (pp. 298–305). Informa Healthcare.

Pujols, Y., Seal, B. N., & Meston, C. M. (2010). The association between sexual satisfaction and body image in women. *The Journal of Sexual Medicine*, *7*(2 Pt 2), 905–916. https://doi.org/10.1111/j.1743-6109.2009.01604.x

*Rabiepoor, S., Khalkhali, H., & Sadeghi, E. 2017. What kind of sexual dysfunction is most common among overweight and obese women in reproductive age? *International Journal of Impotence Research*, *29*(2), 61–64. https://doi.org/10.1038/ijir.2016.46.

Rosenthal, L., & Lobel, M. (2018). Gendered racism and the sexual and reproductive health of black and latina women. *Ethnicity & Health*, *25*(3), 367-392. https://doi.org/10.1080/13557858.2018.1439896

Rottmann, N., Hansen, D. G., Christensen, R., Hagedoorn, D., Frisch, M., M., Nicolaisen, A., & Johansen, C. (2017). Satisfaction with sex life in sexually active heterosexual couples dealing with breast cancer: A nationwide longitudinal study. *Acta oncologica*, *56*(2), 212–219. https://doi.org/10.1080/0284186X.2016.1266086

*Sarwer, D., Spitzer, J. C., Wadden, T. A., Rosen, R. C., Mitchell, J. E., Lancaster, K. B. A., . . . Christian, N. J. 2013. Sexual functioning and sex hormones in persons with extreme obesity and seeking surgical and nonsurgical weight loss. *Surgery for Obesity and Related Diseases*, *9*(6), 997–1007. https://doi.org/10.1016/j.soard.2013.07.003.

Sarwer, D. B., Lavery, M., & Spitzer, J. C. (2012). A review of the relationships between extreme obesity, quality of life, and sexual function. *Obesity Surgery*, *22*(4), 668–676. https://doi.org/10.1007/s11695-012-0588-1

Shaw, A. M., & Rogge, R. D. (2016). Evaluating and refining the construct of sexual quality with item response theory: Development of the quality of sex inventory. *Archives of Sexual Behavior*, *45*(2), 249–270. https://doi.org/10.1007/s10508-015-0650-x

Smith, C. A. (2019). Intersectionality and sizeism: Implications for mental health practitioners. *Women & Therapy*, *42*(1–2), 59–78. https://doi.org/10.1080/02703149.2018.1524076

Springer, K. W., Hankivsky, O., & Bates, L. M. (2012). Gender and health: Relational, intersectional, and biosocial approaches. *Social Science & Medicine*, *74*(11), 1661–1666. https://doi.org/10.1016/j.socscimed.2012.03.001

*Steffen, K. J., King, W. C., White, G. E., Subak, L. L., Mitchell, J. E., Courcoulas, A. P., Flum, D. R., Strain, G., Sarwer, D. B., Kolotkin, R. L., Pories, W., & Huang, A. J. 2017. Sexual functioning of men and women with severe obesity before bariatric surgery. *Surgery for Obesity and Related Diseases*, *13*(2), 334–343. https://doi.org/10.1016/j.soard.2016.09.022.

Thomas, H. N., & Thurston, R. C. (2016). A biopsychosocial approach to women's sexual function and dysfunction at midlife: A narrative review. *Maturitas*, *87*, 49–60. https://doi.org/10.1016/j.maturitas.2016.02.009

Tiefer, L. (2001). A new view of women's sexual problems: Why new? Why now? *Journal of Sex Research, 38(2)*, 89–96. https://doi.org/10.1080/00224490109552075

*Træen, B., Markovic, A., & Kvalem, I. 2016. Sexual satisfaction and body image: A cross-sectional study among Norwegian young adults. *Sexual & Relationship Therapy, 31* (2), 123–137. https://doi.org/10.1080/14681994.2015.1131815.

Trump, L. J., & Mendenhall, T. J. (2017). Couples coping with cardiovascular disease: A systematic review. *Families, Systems & Health, 35*(1), 58. https://doi.org/10.1037/fsh0000232

Velten, J., & Margraf, J. (2017). Satisfaction guaranteed? How individual, partner, and relationship factors impact sexual satisfaction within partnerships. *PloS One, 12*(2), e0172855. https://doi.org/10.1371/journal.pone.0172855

Wagner, G., Fugl-Meyer, K. S., & Fugl-Meyer, A. R. (2000). Impact of erectile dysfunction on quality of life: Patient and partner perspectives. *International Journal of Impotence Research, 12*(4), 144–146. https://doi.org/10.1038/sj.ijir.3900594

* White, M., O'Neil, P., Kolotkin, R., & Byrne, T. 2004. Gender, race, and obesity-related quality of life at extreme levels of obesity. *Obesity Research, 12*(6), 949–955. https://doi.org/10.1038/oby.2004.116.

Wiegel, M., Meston, C., & Rosen, R. (2005). The female sexual function index (FSFI): Cross-validation and development of clinical cutoff scores. *Journal of Sex & Marital Therapy, 31*(1), 1–20. https://doi.org/10.1080/00926230590475206

Williams, A. L., & Merten, M. J. (2013). Romantic relationships among women experiencing obesity: Self-Perception and weight as barriers to intimacy. *Family and Consumer Sciences Research Journal, 41*(3), 284–298. https://doi.org/10.1111/fcsr.12020

World Health Organization. (2006). *Defining sexual health: Report of a technical consultation on sexual health.* 28–31 January 2002 Sexual Health Document Series. Geneva, Switzerland: Special Programme of Research, Development, and Research Training in Human Reproduction. http://www.who.int/reproductivehealth/topics/sexual_health/sh_definitions/en/

Impact of Sexual and Interpersonal Violence and Trauma on Women: Trauma-Informed Practice and Feminist Theory

Jennifer V. Pemberton and Tamra B. Loeb

ABSTRACT
Women experience disproportionate rates of both sexual assault and intimate partner violence (CDC, 2019). This article describes the physical, sexual, and mental health impact of these traumas for women and the parallels between feminist theory and SAMSHA's six principles for trauma-informed care that include 1. Safety; 2. Trustworthiness and Transparency; 3. Peer Support; 4. Collaboration and Mutuality; 5. Empowerment, Voice and Choice; and 6. Cultural, Historical, and Gender Issues. By utilizing a trauma-informed framework and feminist perspective, clinicians and practitioners can better conceptualize the impact of trauma and the healing journey for survivors. Future research is needed to better understand the impact of interpersonal violence across cultures and how this trauma-informed approach can be effective in recovery.

Sexual violence and intimate partner violence (IPV) are global public health crises with significant psychological and health-related consequences for women (Basile & Smith, 2011; Centers for Disease Control and Prevention [CDC], 2019; Wyatt, Davhana-Maselesele et al., 2017). Women are overwhelmingly, although not the only, targets of these types of assaults (CDC, 2019). Therefore, as clinicians and practitioners working with survivors, utilizing a trauma-informed approach that is tailored to women is essential to both understand and treat trauma. Substance Abuse and Mental Health Services Administration [SAMHSA] (2017) has outlined a trauma-informed framework for providing care for survivors of trauma. By using this framework, along with a feminist perspective, clinicians and practitioners will have a more comprehensive conceptualization regarding the impact of trauma, as well as how to help survivors heal from traumatic experiences.

Sexual assault

Prevalence and definition

Sexual assault affects a substantial portion of women in the United States (U.S.) and globally; the lifetime prevalence of sexual assault among women is approximately 1 in 3; the prevalence of rape is estimated to be 1 in 6 among national samples of females (Kilpatrick et al., 2007; Tjaden & Thoennes, 2006). Sexual assault, or sexual behavior that occurs without consent being obtained or freely given includes rape, attempted rape, forcing the victim to perform sexual acts (oral sex or penetration), and fondling (Loeb, Gaines et al., 2011; Centers for Disease Control and Prevention, 2019; Mental Health America, 2019; Rape, Abuse & Incest National Network [RAINN], 2019). These behaviors include, but are not limited to, those involving physical force; they also include coercion, manipulation, threats, and situations in which the victim is not able to provide consent (RAINN, 2019). The perpetrator of sexual assault is usually someone known to the victim (CDC, 2019). Prevalence rates are thought to be underestimated as many victims do not report their experiences due to feelings of embarrassment and/or shame, beliefs about not being believed, fears associated with telling the police or others, and threats of harm made by the perpetrator (CDC, 2019). Sexual assault frequently co-occurs with other types of trauma, including interpersonal violence (McFarlane et al., 2005).

Sexual assault and mental health

The associations between sexual victimization and adverse psychological outcomes have been well documented. Short-term effects include feelings of shock, disbelief, confusion, shame, guilt, self-blame, withdrawal, flashbacks of the assault, and insomnia (Basile & Smith, 2011; CDC, 2019). Reports of emotional numbness, hypervigilance and avoidance of reminders of the event, as well as disruptions to daily routines, are also common (Koss et al., 1994). Frequently, survivors report intense fear of the perpetrator, fears related to another attack, and suffer anxiety regarding issues related to disclosure (Basile & Smith, 2011). Of great concern are the negative changes in world view reported by survivors and the effect these negative shifts in belief systems have on survivors' subsequent experiences (Basile & Smith, 2011).

National data and meta-analyses suggest that victims of rape or sexual assault are at increased risk for the development of numerous long-term adverse psychological outcomes, including posttraumatic stress disorder (PTSD), depression, generalized anxiety disorder, substance use disorders, eating disorders, sleep disorders, anxiety disorders, and suicide attempts, regardless of the age of the victim at the time of the assault (Chen et al., 2010; Sarkar & Sarkar, 2005; Zinzow et al., 2012). There is evidence that the development of some psychiatric disorders, including depression and PTSD, may vary according to circumstances surrounding the assault; for example, the type of coercion or rape tactic the victim experienced (Basile & Smith, 2011). Rape tactics refer to the methods a perpetrator uses to coerce a victim into engagement in or exposure to a sexual behavior (Basile et al., 2014).

The relationships between the psychological and physical effects of sexual violence tend to be examined in isolation; however, these variables frequently co-occur. For instance, less frequent engagement in physical activity has been found to mediate the relationship between more severe symptoms of PTSD and depression and poorer health status (Rutter et al., 2013). Research identifying the trajectories leading to these differential outcomes is needed.

Sexual assault and physical and sexual health

Several lines of research have detailed the many deleterious physical health consequences associated with sexual violence for women. Victims may sustain injuries from the assault itself, including genital injuries (Sommers, 2007; Weaver, 2009), abrasions, and broken bones (Basile & Smith, 2011). Numerous gynecological issues that present post-rape include pregnancy, sexually transmitted infections (STIs), and HIV transmission (Basile & Smith, 2011; CDC, 2019). The transmission of STIs is of particular concern, as STIs are associated with long-term health complications, including pelvic inflammatory disease, infertility, cervical cancer, tubal or ectopic pregnancy, and perinatal or congenital infections in infants born to infected mothers (Hawks et al., 2019; National Institute of Health [NIH] & National Institute of Allergy and Infectious Diseases, 2015). Further, infection with some STIs actually increases risks of HIV transmission (National Institute of Health [NIH] & National Institute of Allergy and Infectious Diseases, 2015).

Experiences of rape also impact women's reproductive and sexual functioning. Compared to women who have never experienced rape, those that have been raped report more abnormalities with ovulation and menstruation, endometriosis, dyspareunia, and chronic pelvic pain (National Institute of Health [NIH] & National Institute of Allergy and Infectious Diseases, 2015; Weaver, 2009). Other sexual health problems include reduced interest in or avoidance of sex as well as less frequent arousal and orgasms (Becker et al., 1986; CDC, 2019). One of the strongest predictors of sexual and physical revictimization is a previous history of sexual assault (Wyatt, Loeb et al., 2012) and subsequent negative consensual sexual experiences (Loeb, Gaines et al., 2011). These behaviors, in turn, are associated with increased risk of STI transmission and unsafe sexual behaviors (Loeb, Williams et al., 2002). Posttraumatic stress disorder may be an important mediator between sexual violence and sexual health outcomes, as symptoms may inhibit the cognitive processes necessary for accurately gauging sexual risks, negotiating safe sexual behaviors, and adopting health-promoting practices (Weaver, 2009).

Survivors of sexual violence commonly present to primary care doctors with high levels of somatic concerns; physicians who are not trained to ask about experiences of trauma may be unable to determine the etiology of these diverse symptoms (Loeb, Joseph et al., 2018; Creed et al., 2012). This can feel frustrating and may potentially leave victims feeling invalidated, and confused, as well as reduce confidence and trust in healthcare professionals. Common somatic complaints include musculoskeletal pain, headache, pelvic pain and gastrointestinal problems (Loeb, Joseph et al., 2018). Links between sexual abuse and the diagnosis of somatic disorders have also been reported (Paras et al., 2009), as have associations between histories of trauma and adversity, including experiences of sexual assault and interpersonal violence, and the severity of somatic symptoms experienced among a sample of ethnically diverse women (Loeb, Joseph et al., 2018). Symptoms of posttraumatic stress and depression have been found to partially mediate the associations between histories of trauma and adversity and severity of somatic symptoms, suggesting that both exposure to trauma and adversity as well as the development of posttraumatic and depressive symptoms influence the development of somatic concerns (Loeb, Joseph et al., 2018).

Gastrointestinal symptoms and illnesses, including gastrointestinal disorder and irritable bowel syndrome, are also associated with sexual violence (CDC, 2019). Survivors of sexual violence have elevated risks of certain types of cancer (A. L. Coker et al., 2009), cardiovascular disease (CDC, 2019), and chronic neck, head, facial and back pain (Koss et al., 1994). Finally, survivors of sexual violence have been found to engage in negative health behaviors more frequently than women who have not experienced sexual violence. These health compromising behaviors include smoking, substance abuse, alcohol abuse, and engaging in high-risk sexual behaviors (CDC, 2019; Hawks et al., 2019; Lang et al., 2003; Weaver, 2009).

Intimate partner violence

Definition and prevalence

IPV is common, affecting approximately 1 in 4 women in the U.S. annually, causing significant physical and mental health consequences (Smith et al., 2018). Although not limited to females, women are disproportionately affected by severe physical violence by an intimate partner, with lifetime prevalence rates of 22.3% for women and 14% for men (Breiding et al., 2014). Most definitions of IPV include physical and sexual violence, psychological aggression, and stalking perpetrated by current or former spouses, boyfriends or girlfriends, dating partners, or ongoing sexual partners (Basile et al., 2014;

CDC, 2019). Different types of IPV can coexist (Smith et al., 2018). Broader specifications of the characteristics that constitute an intimate partner also exist. Basile et al. (2014) characterize an intimate partner as:

> A person with whom one has a close personal relationship that may be characterized by the partners' emotional connectedness, regular contact, ongoing physical contact and sexual behavior, identity as a couple, and familiarity and knowledge about each other's lives. The relationship need not involve all of these dimensions. (p. 14)

Many victims of IPV experience significant mental and/or physical health consequences.

IPV and mental health

Female victims impacted by IPV have an increased risk of numerous mental health symptoms and disorders, including symptoms of depression, posttraumatic stress, substance abuse and low self-esteem, clinical depression, suicide attempts, PTSD, and other anxiety and substance use disorders (Devries et al., 2013, 2011; Karakurt et al., 2014). A meta-analysis by Beydoun et al. (2012) described moderate to strong associations between experiences of IPV and depression, with a substantial proportion of cases of elevated symptoms of depression, postpartum depression, and major depressive disorder due to exposure to IPV. (Physical IPV has specifically been associated with increased risks for substance use and symptoms of depression (A. Coker et al., 2002)).

Most women who experience physical violence also experience sexual violence, and those who experience both may be at heightened risk for some mental health outcomes, including PTSD, in comparison to women who experience physical violence alone (McFarlane et al., 2005). While the negative effects of IPV have been well documented, less attention has been given to identifying the trajectories of mental health effects due to one or several types of IPV (for instance, physical violence in the absence of other types of IPV) (Delara, 2016). The relationships between IPV and mental health are complex; more studies are needed to clarify relationships between different types of IPV and associated mental health outcomes. Further, specific pathways from exposure to IPV and mental health outcomes have yet to be elucidated, with numerous psychological, environmental and biological risk factors increasing the likelihood of to poor mental health (Chandan et al., 2019).

IPV and physical and sexual health

Research has demonstrated numerous deleterious health consequences associated with experiences of IPV. The most obvious immediate health problems include physical injury sustained during intimate partner violence (Campbell et al., 2002). Physical injury related to IPV is a common occurrence for women in the U.S., affecting approximately 41% of women who are IVP survivors (CDC, 2019). Intimate partner violence can also result in death; approximately 1 in 6 homicides in the U.S. are perpetrated by an intimate partner. Intimate partners are responsible for more than half of female homicides in the U.S. for which circumstances were known (Petrosky et al., 2017). Approximately 1 million women in the U.S. have been shot or shot at by an intimate partner, and 4.5 million report having had an intimate partner threaten them using a gun (Sorenson & Schut, 2018).

Physical violence has been associated with health problems, measures of poor health, and increased risks for chronic diseases (A. Coker et al., 2002; Mathew, Smith, Marsh, & Houry, 2013). Intimate violence victims are at increased risk for chronic pain, cardiovascular, gastrointestinal, musculoskeletal, nervous system, and gynecological problems (Campbell et al., 2002; CDC, 2019). Female survivors of IPV are also at higher risk for engaging in health compromising behaviors, including substance abuse, binge drinking, smoking, and high-risk sexual behaviors (CDC, 2019). Intimate partner violence is common in pregnancy, with lifetime prevalence rates ranging between 3% and 13% percent (Campbell et al., 2002). Numerous pregnancy-related risks have been documented, including inconsistent or delayed prenatal care, engaging in sexual risks, and poor personal health behaviors, including poor diet, smoking, use of alcohol and substance use (Alhusen et al., 2015). Experiencing IPV during pregnancy is also associated with increased symptoms of depression, PTSD, homicide, and suicide (Alhusen et al., 2015). Although studies do not always specify which specific IPV behaviors are responsible for negative health outcomes, there is evidence that women who experience both sexual and physical violence are at increased risk for both immediate and long-term health problems (Campbell et al., 2002).

Trauma-informed practice and feminist theory

Given that sexual assault and interpersonal violence impact women at disproportionate rates compared to men and are coercive, interpersonal attacks that result from power inequities, the healing journey for survivors must take such issues into account. By utilizing SAMSHA's (SAMHSA, 2016, 2017) trauma-informed care framework and feminist theory, clinicians are afforded a comprehensive approach in understanding of the impact of trauma on women's overall health and how best to help them deal with the aftermath. Many of the hallmark concepts of feminist theory are encapsulated within SAMSHA's trauma framework. SAMSHA's six principles of trauma-informed care include: 1. Safety; 2. Trustworthiness and Transparency; 3. Peer Support; 4. Collaboration and Mutuality; 5. Empowerment, Voice and Choice; and 6. Cultural, Historical, and Gender Issues (SAMHSA, 2017).

Safety

Starting with safety, enhancing a sense of physical and emotional safety is priority. The continued aftermath of symptoms following victimization that include hypervigilance, intense fear of the perpetrator, fears related to another attack, and anxiety regarding issues related to disclosure (Basile & Smith, 2011; Koss et al., 1994) create continued feelings of being unsafe. Using psychoeducation regarding the impact of trauma on emotional, mental, neurobiological, and social functioning can help normalize many of the victim/survivor experiences that contribute to such feelings of lack of safety and can increase self-compassion (Brown, 2006). Trauma-informed feminist practitioners can assist clients understand how their symptoms and behaviors are a means of coping with the traumatic experiences. This non-pathological and non-victim-blaming approach enables the client to be less judgmental and more empathic regarding their trauma-responses (Walker, 1990). Interventions that can be effective in enhancing safety are included in the evidence-based treatment program for victims of trauma, Seeking Safety (Navajitz, 2002). By increasing safer and healthier coping skills to manage anxiety, depression, and other mental and physiological symptoms, the survivor can begin to experience more emotional and physiological stability. Feminist practitioners also help their clients to understand the cognitions they hold regarding their trauma experiences (Walker, 1990). Cognitive behavior therapy interventions that include trauma narratives and cognitive restructuring are helpful for practitioners in utilizing effective trauma-informed approaches that incorporate feminist therapy values. Another important component for practitioners to address with their traumatized clients is environmental safety. Is the client currently in a violent relationship? Is the perpetrator a continued threat? Developing a comprehensive safety plan that addresses safety in the current relationship, safety from physical threats, cyber threats, etc. is critical to minimize risk and help the client establish safety. Such safety plans are readily available on-line, in the research literature, and can be tailored to meet the needs of the client.

Trustworthiness and transparency

As victims of trauma are often victimized from known perpetrators, the external world can feel unsafe. Trustworthiness and transparency are important factors as many victims have experienced trauma at the hands of a "trusted" person (CDC, 2019; Conley & Griffith, 2016). This continued stance of being unsafe and the inability to trust others is exacerbated when survivors seek medical attention for somatic complaints that are associated to the trauma but misdiagnosed by physicians (Loeb, Joseph et al., 2018). Therefore, the ability to trust becomes impaired, including trusting clinicians and practitioners as well as mental health providers. A trauma-informed feminist approach can build trust through clear and explicit expectations and policies, thereby effectively being transparent on the part of the clinician. Clinicians can create safety for survivors by approaching them with acceptance, validation, belief in their experiences, and having a non-judgmental stance that can otherwise further a survivors' feelings of guilt and shame. Further, self-awareness on the part of the clinician and practitioner can promote role modeling for survivors and increasing protect against potential unconscious bias (Brown, 2006). Feminist therapists may utilize self-disclosure as a means of enhancing trustworthiness and transparency and achieving a more egalitarian relationship (Bohan, 1992). Further, treatment goals are driven by the client, not imposed by the therapist; feminist therapists work in collaboration to build the therapeutic relationship. In some instances, and not uncommon, the client's goal may be to remain in a violent relationship. Even in these conditions, the trauma-informed feminist practitioner respects the client's decisions and assists the client in achieving their goals of treatment.

Peer support

An atmosphere of peer support is important as it combats tendencies toward isolation and withdrawal and builds a network and community for survivors. As noted, survivors often experience shame, guilt, and self-blame (Basile & Smith, 2011; CDC, 2019). Parsons et al. (1998) emphasize how building connections through small groups can provide validation for the survivor's traumatic experiences and can help in decreasing self-blame and enhance mutual support. Brown (2004) highlights the focus in feminist therapy on the importance of networking for social change and the positive impact of normalizing trauma experiences through social connection. This can be done both in encouragement in individual work, but is also incredibly impactful through group work. Effective group interventions that are both trauma-informed and have feminist underpinnings can focus on sharing personal experiences, cultural values, and current and past traumatic experiences. In doing so, clients will notice similarities in their experiences and support each other in developing and achieving personal goals. Group members can also gain a better and mutual understanding of not only their unique personal, familial and cultural experiences, but the group as a whole can come together and understand the experience of womanhood in the community and social context and how this larger context is related to traumatic experiences. These experiences can combat a tendency to isolate in recovery.

Collaboration and mutuality

Given that sexual and interpersonal traumatization places women in a position of submission and coercion, counteracting these experiences through collaboration and mutuality is important (SAMHSA, 2017). Collaboration and mutuality can be accomplished with an approach of partnering with survivors in shared decision making in their treatment, whether medical or mental health. Fem[illegible] practice embraces equality in the therapeutic relationship, [illegible]llaborating as a means of enhancing empowerment (Worell & Jo[illegible]97) which is consistent with mutuality. The relationship partner[illegible]ist and client can be healing as the trauma-informed feminist [illegible]creates an equal partnership with the victim/survivor that can be [illegible]odel for other relationships with partners, families, and society. [illegible]ioner encourages self-expression, assertiveness, and a space to [illegible]nd challenge discussions, belief systems, and experiences. This [illegible]ased approach is compassionate and empathic, and meets the client [illegible]ey are at in their lives and experiences (Brown, 2004; Courtois & Ford, [illegible]Herman, 1997). Further, Sommers-Flanagan and Sommers-Flanagan [illegible] emphasizes the need for the practitioner to honor the client's trauma experiences, reformulate and redefine mental illness, and participate in a comprehensive understanding of trauma and oppression.

Empowerment, voice and choice

SAMSHA's principles of empowerment, voice and choice overlap with the fundamental core tenets of feminist theory (Enns, 2011). The act of victimization through sexual assault and interpersonal violence takes place as a result of coercion, disempowerment, and control. Not only is the victim unable to protect themselves, they are often silenced through coercion and/or shame, and often re-victimized (Wyatt, Loeb et al., 2012). Heath et al. (2011) describe the importance of helping survivors challenge oppressive beliefs that may have contributed to traumatization. The feminist idea of empowering individuals by helping them identify the pow[illegible] relationship inequities in society and how to create social change can [illegible] beneficial for survivors of trauma (Gutierrez & Lewis, 1999), especiall[illegible] paralleling these inequities to the trauma experience. Walker ([illegible] describes the importance for feminist practitioners to help women[illegible] how to gain and use power in relationships, and how to enha[illegible] utilize their strengths. The relationship between the therapist a[illegible] provides the opportunity for empowerment. Given the inhere[illegible] inequity that exists between therapist and client, by identi[illegible] inequities in relationships and providing a collaborative, su[illegible] strong therapeutic alliance, the client can be empowered an[illegible] these strengths in other relationships (Sommers-Flanigan[illegible] Flanigan, 2018). Bohan (1992) also emphasizes the import[illegible] tioners to be cognizant of the impact of the power differe[illegible] family, and the reality of the roles the client has in te[illegible] decision making, finances, and employment, as w[illegible] understanding of what it means to be a woman within the societal context. As the practitioner listens, questions, and helps the client analyze these issues in the session, power and empowerment ... through the therapeutic relationship as the client becomes ... and better able to understand their familial and social context ... traumatic experiences have impacted their lives. A further under... can be gained for many women who continue to be victims in ... relationships. Lack of employment, caretaking responsibilities and a ... of financial resources are often legitimate reasons that create barriers ... women who may want to leave an IPV relationship but are unable t... (Whiting, 2016). Assisting women in looking at options and creating resources may be helpful in providing some hope and possibilities for change.

Enhancing self-esteem is a key factor in helping traumatized victims gain empowerment, voice and choice. Years of victimization often results in feelings of low self-worth, not valued as a human being, and often times feeling like the abuse and assault may be deserved (Whiting, 2016). Common self-beliefs that include feeling worthless, damaged, and at fault lead to an inability to create change or having a life driven by their choosing and control (Cravens et al., 2015). Therefore, interventions ...ed at improving hope and a strong sense of self are beneficial. ...tioners can help clients focus on strengths, accomplishments, and ...passion. Interventions aimed at developing and enhancing asser- ...kills, including role-playing, can strengthen their voice. ...he importance of self-care and self-nurturance can be effec- ... enhancing self-esteem and creating empowerment and ...en are bombarded by their many roles that require ... For many women, caretaking of the self is not ...n feel selfish or not deserved (Whiting, 2016). ...f self-care and beginning to regard one-self as ...v toward self-worth and value, from victim ...n also be enhanced by utilizing decision ...n routinely discuss and delineate situa- ...ns related to the various options in

...be
by
...990)
learn
...ce and
...d client
...at power
...ying such
...portive and
... able to use
& Sommers-
...nce for practi-
...ntials within the
...ms of caretaking
...ll as gaining

... historical, and gender issues in the ... addresses the importance of incor- ...ects, honors, and embraces diver- ...hes that are relevant to the varied ... It is also helpful in providing a framework to identify the intersectionality, a multicultural feminist theoretical concept (Collins, 2000), of culture, gender and the social climate that place women at risk for sexual and interpersonal victimization. Although sexual and interpersonal violence can potentially affect all women, there are economic, ethnic, and geographical disparities in exposure rates (Hart & Klein, 2013). Native American, Black and Latina females tend to experience higher rates of IPV than white women; however, some research suggests that poverty, rather than ethnicity, is a powerful contributor to these rates. Further, poverty exacerbates the challenges faced by victims of IPV due to lack of accessibility and resources both in the prevention and recovery of trauma (Hart & Klein, 2013). The social climate plays a role in perpetuating violence against women, such a climate includes rape culture. Conley and Griffith (2016) describe rape culture as:

> The societal conditions that allow sexual violence to take place. These societal conditions include, but are not limited to, (a) tolerance of sexual harassment and violent pornography, (b) the belief that women who have consumed alcohol are sexually available, (c) restrictive ideas about masculinity (e.g., men don't cry), (d) the belief that women should be responsible for keeping themselves safe (e.g., victim blaming), (e) jokes about rape, and (f) the belief that certain groups are better than others (e.g., sexism, racism). (p. 279)

Taking an educative stance regarding rape culture and the societal conditions that perpetuate violence against women is imperative in the healing and empowerment of survivors (Conley & Griffith, 2016). Further, the political and social climate that rejects immigrants and undocumented individuals can also place these marginalized women at increased risk for sexual and interpersonal trauma (Kaltman et al., 2011). The feminist idea that focuses on the personal as political enables survivors to identify both internal and external conditions associated with trauma (Nylund & Nylund, 2003).

Future directions

Recommendations for future research on the impact of sexual and interpersonal trauma on women's health include primarily focusing on SAMSHA's last principal of cultural, historical, and gender issues. This review of the research through the feminist lens confirms a lack of diversity found throughout traditional conceptualizations of sexual and interpersonal violence, which disproportionately affect women and have misconceptualized, minimized, and at times blamed victims while dismissing the pervasive impact of the patriarchial societal power structure on violence against women.

Conducting a gender, cultural, and historical analysis in the therapy session with victims and survivors of sexual and interpersonal trauma can be helpful in increasing an understanding of these issues. For example, a gender analysis that looks at how the division of labor, roles and responsibilities in the family, availability of resources, and their position in their families and society can contribute to continued disempowerment can be eye-opening for many women, trauma victims and survivors in particular. Bohan (1992) described the importance for feminist practitioners to understand the impact of sexism inherent in our society and thereby promote roles for trauma victims and survivors that go beyond cultural or gender stereotypes. Bohan (1992) encourages clinicians to help clients participate in their gender role journey. Such a journey would need to include the messages that come from their particular culture, religious beliefs, and historical experiences based on their race and ethnicity that can impact and sustain traumatic experiences.

Conclusion

Given the prevalence of sexual assault and interpersonal violence against women, it is important to identify the health and mental health implications. For women, the intersectionality of gender, race, and social climate play a role in their risks for victimization. Therefore, in working with women survivors, the trauma-informed framework (SAMHSA, 2017) and feminist theory can help clinicians and practitioners gain a comprehensive understanding of the impact of trauma and the necessary components toward healing. By incorporating the principles of Safety; Trustworthiness and Transparency; Peer Support; Collaboration and Mutuality; Empowerment, Voice and Choice; and Cultural, Historical, and Gender Issues (SAMHSA, 2017) in therapy with trauma victims and survivors, feminist tenets and theoretical underpinnings are woven throughout the framework. This approach enables trauma victims and survivors to experience a more respectful, accepting, non-judgmental egalitarian relationship between the therapist and client that enables healing and empowerment, unlike traditional hierarchical therapist-client relationships.

Practice implications include a therapeutic approach of validation, acceptance, respect, and non-judgment that honors and empathizes with the client's experiences. Psychoeducation and evidence-based practices such as Cognitive Behavior Therapy and Seeking Safety can be useful in establishing safety and an understanding of the impact of trauma. A collaborative partnership enables the client to establish and set their own goals. Skill-based interventions such as role-playing can be effective in increasing assertiveness thereby enhancing empowerment, voice and choice. Finally, by addressing the cultural, historical, social/political and gender issues in the context of sexual and interpersonal trauma among women, as a result, the client can gain a holistic understanding of how the intersectionality of these issues impacts their journey from victim to survivor.

Funding

This work was supported by the National Institutes of Health, Lung, and Blood Institute [U01HL142109] for the second author.

References

Alhusen, J. L., Ray, E., Sharps, P., & Bullock, L. (2015). Intimate partner violence during pregnancy: Maternal and neonatal outcomes. *Journal of Women's Health (2002)*, *24*(1), 100–106. https://doi.org/10.1089/jwh.2014.4872

Basile, K. C., & Smith, S. G. (2011). Sexual violence victimization of women: Prevalence, characteristics, and the role of public health and prevention. *American Journal of Lifestyle Medicine*, *5*(5), 407–417. https://doi.org/10.1177/1559827611409512

Basile, K. C., Smith, S. G., Breiding, M. J., Black, M. C., & Mahendra, R. (2014). *Sexual violence surveillance: Uniform definitions and recommended data elements version 2.0*. Centers for Disease Control and Prevention. https://www.cdc.gov/violenceprevention/pdf/sv_surveillance_definitionsl-2009-a.pdf

Becker, J. V., Skinner, L. J., Abel, G. G., & Cinchon, J. (1986). Level of post assault sexual function in rape and incest victims. *Archives of Sexual Behavior*, *15*(1), 37–49. https://doi.org/10.1007/BF01542303

Beydoun, H. A., Beydoun, M. A., Kaufman, J. S., Lo, B., & Zonderman, A. B. (2012). Intimate partner violence against adult women and its association with major depressive disorder, depressive symptoms and postpartum depression: A systematic review and meta-analysis. *Social Science & Medicine (1982)*, *75*(6), 959–975. https://doi.org/10.1016/j.socscimed.2012.04.025

Bohan, J. S. (1992). *Replacing women in psychology: Readings toward a more inclusive history*. Kendall Hunt Publishers.

Breiding, M. J., Smith, S. G., Basile, K. C., Walters, M. L., Chen, J., & Merrick, M. T. (2014). Prevalence and characteristics of sexual violence, stalking, and intimate partner violence victimization–national intimate partner and sexual violence survey, United States, 2011. *Morbidity and Mortality Weekly Report. Surveillance Summaries (Washington, D.C.:2002)*, *63*(8), 1–18.

Brown, L. S. (2006). Still subversive after all these years: The relevance of feminist therapy in the age of evidence-based practice. *Psychology of Women Quarterly*, *30*(1), 15–24. https://doi.org/10.1111/j.1471-6402.2006.00258.x

Campbell, J., Jones, A. S., Dienemann, J., Kub, J., Schollenberger, J., O'Campo, P., Gielen, A. C., & Wynne, C. (2002). Intimate partner violence and physical health consequences. *Archives of Internal Medicine*, *162*(10), 1157–1163. https://doi.org/10.1001/archinte.162.10.1157

Centers for Disease Control and Prevention (CDC). (2019). *Injury prevention & control, violence prevention: Preventing sexual violence*. U.S. Department of Health & Human Services. https://www.cdc.gov/violenceprevention/sexualviolence/fastfact.html?CDC_AA_refVal=https%3A%2F%2Fwww.cdc.gov%2Fviolenceprevention%2Fsexualviolence%2Fconsequences.html

Chandan, J., Thomas, T., Bradbury-Jones, C., Russell, R., Bandyopadhyay, S., Nirantharakumar, K., & Taylor, J. (2019). Female survivors of intimate partner violence and risk of depression, anxiety and serious mental illness. *The British Journal of Psychiatry*, 1–6. https://doi.org/10.1192/bjp.2019.124

Chen, L. P., Murad, M. H., Paras, M. L., Colbenson, K. M., Sattler, A. L., Goranson, E. N., Elamin, M. B., Seime, R. J., Shinozaki, G., Prokop, L. J., & Zirakzadeh, A. (2010). Sexual abuse and lifetime diagnosis of psychiatric disorders: Systematic review and meta-analysis. *Mayo Clinic Proceedings, 85*(7), 618–629. https://doi.org/10.4065/mcp.2009.0583

Coker, A., Davis, K., Arias, I., Desai, S., Sanderson, M., Brandt, H., & Smith, P. (2002). Physical and mental health effects of intimate partner violence for men and women. *American Journal of Preventive Medicine, 23*(4), 260–268. https://doi.org/10.1016/S0749-3797(02)00514-7

Coker, A. L., Hopenhayn, C., DeSimone, C. P., Bush, H. M., & Crofford, L. (2009). Violence against women raises risk of cervical cancer. *Journal of Women's Health, 18*(8), 1179–1185. https://doi.org/10.1089/jwh.2008.1048

Collins, P. H. (2000). *Black feminist thought: Knowledge, consciousness, and the politics of empowerment* (2nd ed.). Routledge.

Conley, A. H., & Griffith, C. (2016). Trauma-informed response in the age of Title IX: Considerations for college counselors working with survivors of power-based personal violence. *Journal of College Counseling, 19*(3), 276–288. https://doi.org/10.1002/jocc.12049

Courtois, C. A., & Ford, J.D. (Eds.). (2009). Treating complex traumatic stress disorders: An evidence-based guide. Guilford Press.

Cravens, J. D., Whiting, J. B., & Aamar, R. O. (2015). Why I stayed/left: An analysis of voices of intimate partner violence on social media. *Contemporary Family Therapy, 37*(4), 372–385. https://doi.org/10.1007/s10591-015-9360-8

Creed, F. H., Davies, I., Jackson, J., Littlewood, A., Chew-Graham, C., Tomenson, B., Macfarlane, G., Barsky, A., Katon, W., & McBeth, J. (2012). The epidemiology of multiple somatic symptoms. *Journal of Psychosomatic Research, 72*(4), 311–317. https://doi.org/10.1016/j.jpsychores.2012.01.009

Delara, M. (2016). Mental health consequences and risk factors of physical intimate partner violence. *Mental Health in Family Medicine, 12*(1), 119–125. https://doi.org/10.25149/1756-8358.1201004

Devries, K. M., Mak, J. Y., Bacchus, L. J., Child, J. C., Falder, G., Petzold, M., Watts, C. H., & Astbury, J. (2013). Intimate partner violence and incident depressive symptoms and suicide attempts: A systematic review of longitudinal studies. *PLoS Medicine, 10*(5), e1001439. https://doi.org/10.1371/journal.pmed.1001439

Devries, K. M., Watts, C., Yoshihama, M., Kiss, L., Schraiber, L. B., Deyessa, N., Heise, L., Durand, J., Mbwambo, J., Jansen, H., Berhane, Y., Ellsberg, M., & Garcia-Moreno, C. (2011). Violence against women is strongly associated with suicide attempts: Evidence from the WHO multi-country study on women's health and domestic violence against women. *Social Science & Medicine, 73*(1), 79–86. https://doi.org/10.1016/j.socscimed.2011.05.006

Enns, C. Z. (2011). Feminist counseling as a pathway to recovery. In T. Bryant-Davis (Ed.), *Surviving sexual violence: A guide to recovery and empowerment* (pp. 160–178). Rowman & Littlefield.

Gutierrez, L. M., & Lewis, E. A. (1999). *Empowering women of color.* Columbia University Press.

Hart, B. J., & Klein, A. R. (2013). *Practical implications of current intimate partner violence research for victim advocates and service providers.* NCJRS Library collection: US Department of Justice. https://ncjrs.gov/App/Publications/abstract.aspx?ID=266429

Hawks, L., Woolhandler, S., Himmelstein, D. U., Bor, D. H., Gaffney, A., & McCormick, D. (2019). Association between forced sexual initiation and health outcomes among US women. *JAMA Internal Medicine, 179*(11), 1551. https://doi.org/10.1001/jamainternmed.2019.3500

Heath, N. M., Lynch, S. M., Fritch, A. M., McArthur, L. N., & Smith, S. L. (2011). Silent survivors: Rape myth acceptance in incarcerated women's narratives of disclosure and reporting of rape. *Psychology of Women Quarterly, 35*(4), 596–610. https://doi.org/10.1177/0361684311407870

Herman, J. L. (1997). Trauma and recovery: the aftermath of violence-from domestic abuse to political terror. New York: Basic Books.

Kaltman, S., Mendoza, A. H., Gonzales, F. A., Serrano, A., & Guarnaccia, P. J. (2011). Contextualizing the trauma experience of women immigrants from Central America, South America, and Mexico. *Journal of Traumatic Stress, 24*(6), 635–642. https://doi.org/10.1002/jts.20698

Karakurt, G., Smith, D., & Whiting, J. (2014). Impact of intimate partner violence on women's mental health. *Journal of Family Violence, 29*(7), 693–702. https://doi.org/10.1007/s10896-014-9633-2

Kilpatrick, D. G., Resnick, H. S., Ruggiero, K. J., Conoscenti, L. M., & McCauley, J. (2007). *Final report submitted to the national institute of justice. Drug-facilitated, incapacitated, and forcible rape: A national study*. U.S. Department of Justice. https://www.ncjrs.gov/pdffiles1/nij/grants/219181 pdf

Koss, M. P., Goodman, L., Browne, A., Fitgerald, L., Keita, G. P., & Russon, N. F. (1994). *No safe haven*. American Psychological Association.

Lang, A. J., Rodgers, C. S., Laffaye, C., Satz, L. E., Dresselhaus, T. R., & Stein, M. B. (2003). Sexual trauma, posttraumatic stress disorder, and health behavior. *Behavioral Medicine, 28* (4), 150–158. https://doi.org/10.1080/08964280309596053

Loeb, T. B., Gaines, T., Wyatt, G. E., Zhang, M., & Liu, H. (2011). Associations between child sexual abuse and negative sexual experiences and revictimization among women: Does measuring severity matter? *Child Abuse & Neglect, 35* (11), 946–955. PMCID: PMC3262588. https://doi.org/10.1016/j.chiabu.2011.06.003

Loeb, T. B., Joseph, N. T., Wyatt, G. E., Zhang, M., Chin, D., Thames, A., & Aswad, Y. (2018). Predictors of somatic symptom severity: The role of cumulative history of trauma and adversity in a diverse community sample. *Psychological Trauma: Theory, Research, Practice, and Policy, 10* (5), 491–498. PMID 29154595. https://doi.org/10.1037/tra0000334

Loeb, T. B., Williams, J. K., Carmona, J. V., Rivkin, I., Wyatt, G. E., Chin, D., & Asuan-O'Brien, A. (2002). Child sexual abuse: Associations with the sexual functioning of adolescents and adults. *Annual Review of Sex Research, 13*, 307–345.

Mathew, A., Smith, L. S., Marsh, B., & Houry, D. (2013). Relationship of intimate partner violence to health status, chronic disease, and screening behaviors. Journal of Interpersonal Violence, 28(12),2581-2592. doi:doi.10.1177/0886260513497312

McFarlane, J., Malecha, A., Watson, K., Gist, J., Batten, E., Hall, I., & Smith, S. (2005). Intimate partner sexual assault against women: Frequency, health consequences, and treatment outcomes. *Obstetrics & Gynecology, 105* (1), 99–108. PMID: 15625149. https://doi.org/10.1097/01.AOG.0000146641.98665.b6

Mhanational.org. (2019). *MHA | Mental Health America*. [online]. Retrieved September 22, 2019 from. Mental Health America. https://www.mhanational.org/

National Institute of Health (NIH), National Institute of Allergy and Infectious Diseases. (2015). Sexually Transmitted Diseases. https://www.niaid.nih.gov/diseases-conditions/sexually-transmitted-diseases

Navajitz, L. (2002). *Seeking safety: A treatment manual for PTSD and substance abuse.* Guilford Press.

Nylund, D., & Nylund, D. A. (2003). Narrative therapy as a counter-hegmonic practice. *Men and Masculinities, 5*(4), 386–394. https://doi.org/10.1177/1097184X03251086

Paras, M. L., Murad, M. H., Chen, L. P., Goranson, E. N., Sattler, A. L., Colbenson, K. M., Elamin, M. B., Seime, R. J., Prokop, L. J., & Zirakzadeh, A. (2009). Sexual abuse and lifetime diagnosis of somatic disorders: A systematic review and meta-analysis. *Jama, 302*(5), 550–561. https://doi.org/10.1001/jama.2009.1091

Parsons, R. J., Gutierrez, L. M., & Cox, E. O. (1998). A model for empowerment practice. In L. M. Gutierrez, R. J. Parsons, & E. O. Cox (Eds.), *Empowerment in social work practice: A sourcebook* (pp. 3–27). Brooks/Cole.

Petrosky, E., Blair, J. M., Betz, C. J., Fowler, K. A., Jack, S. P., & Lyons, B. H. (2017). Racial and ethnic differences in homicides of adult women and the role of intimate partner violence — United States, 2003–2014. *MMWR. Morbidity and Mortality Weekly Report, 66*(28), 741–746. https://doi.org/10.15585/mmwr.mm6628a1

Rape, Abuse, & Incest National Network (RAINN). (2019). https://www.rainn.org

Rutter, L. A., Weatherill, R. P., Krill, S. C., Orazem, R., & Taft, C. T. (2013). Posttraumatic stress disorder symptoms, depressive symptoms, exercise, and health in college students. *Psychological Trauma: Theory, Research, Practice, and Policy, 5*(1), 56–61. https://doi.org/10.1037/a0021996

Sarkar, N. N., & Sarkar, R. (2005). Sexual assault on woman: Its impact on her life and living in society. *Sexual and Relationship Therapy, 20*(4), 407–419. https://doi.org/10.1080/14681990500249502

Smith, S. G., Zhang, X., Basile, K. C., Merrick, M. T., Wang, J., Kresnow, M., & Chen, J. (2018). *The National Intimate Partner and Sexual Violence Survey (NISVS): 2015 data brief—Updated release.* National Center for Injury Prevention and Control, Centers for Disease Control and Prevention.

Sommers, M. S. (2007). Defining patterns of genital injury from sexual assault: A review. *Trauma, Violence & Abuse, 8*(3), 270–280. https://doi.org/10.1177/1524838007303194

Sommers-Flanagan, J., & Sommers-Flanagan, R. (2004). Counseling and psychotherapy theories in context and practice: Skills, strategies, and techniques. Hoboken, NJ: J. Wiley & Sons

Sommers-Flanigan, J., & Sommers-Flanigan, R. (2018). *Counseling and psychotherapy theories: In context and practice skills, strategies, and techniques.* Wiley & Sons.

Sorenson, S. B., & Schut, R. A. (2018). Nonfatal gun use in intimate partner violence: A systematic review of the literature. *Trauma, Violence & Abuse, 19*(4), 431–442. https://doi.org/10.1177/1524838016668589

Substance Abuse and Mental Health Services Administration (SAMHSA). (2016). *Trauma-informed care in behavioral health services.* Office of Applied Studies, SAMHSA.

Substance Abuse and Mental Health Services Administration (SAMHSA). (2017). *Trauma-informed approach and trauma-specific interventions.* U.S. Department of Health & Human Services. https://www.samsha.gov/nctic/trauma-interventions.

Tjaden, P., & Thoennes, N. (2006). *Special report. National institute of justice and the centers for disease control and prevention: Extent, nature, and consequences of rape victimization: Findings from the national violence against women survey.* U.S. Department of Justice. https://www.ncjrs.gov/pdffiles1/nij/183781.pdf

Walker, L. (1990). A feminist therapist views the case. In D. W. Cantor (Ed.), *Women as therapists* (pp. 78–79). Spring Publishing Company.

Weaver, T. L. (2009). Impact of rape on female sexuality: Review of selected literature. *Clinical Obstetrics and Gynecology, 52*(4), 702–711. https://doi.org/10.1097/GRF.0b013e3181bf4bfb

Whiting, J. (2016). *Eight reasons women stay in abusive relationships*. Institute for Family Studies. https://family-studies.org/eight-reasons-women-stay-in-abusive-relationships-2/

Worell, J., & Johnson, N. E. (Eds.). (1997). *Shaping the future feminist psychology: Education, research, and practice*. American Psychological Association.

Wyatt, G. E., Davhana-Maselese e, M., Zhang, M., Wong, L. H., Nicholson, F., Sarkissian, A. D., Makhado, L., & Myers, H. F. (2017). A longitudinal study of the aftermath of rape among rural South African women. *Psychological Trauma: Theory, Research, Practice, and Policy*, *9* (3), 309–316. https://doi.org/10.1037/tra0000246

Wyatt, G. E., Loeb, T. B., Williams, J. K., Davis, T. D., & Zhang, M. (2012). A case study of sexual abuse and psychological correlates among an HIV-serodiscordant couple. *Couple and Family Psychology: Research and Practice*, *1* (2), 146–159. PMCID: PMC3731162. https://doi.org/10.1037/a0028773

Zinzow, H. M., Resnick, H. S., McCauley, J. L., Amstadter, A. B., Ruggiero, K. J., & Kilpatrick, D. G. (2012). Prevalence and risk of psychiatric disorders as a function of variant rape histories: Results from a national survey of women. *Social Psychiatry and Psychiatric Epidemiology*, *47*(6), 893–902. https://doi.org/10.1007/s00127-011-0397-1

Exploring the Link between Autoimmune Disorders and Pain with Sexual Activity in Ova-Having Individuals

Karen Washington and Helen Wyatt

ABSTRACT

This article proposes a connection between autoimmune disorders and pain with sexual activity in ova-having individuals. The authors focus on accumulating research from psychology data, medical data, the field of psychoneuroimmunology (PNI), and the field of sex therapy. Current research supports a connection between the mind-body bidirectionality and effects on the immune system, and effects of the mind-body bidirectionality and pain with sexual activity. Content analysis will first discuss the occurrence of autoimmune disorders in ova-having individuals from a PNI perspective followed by a discussion of the occurrence of sexual pain in ova-having individuals. Finally, the authors discuss the overlap in what is happening based upon psychoneuroimmunology and pain during sexual activity in ova-having individuals, as well as clinical implication and a call-to-action for further study of the link between autoimmune disorders and sexual pain.

Introduction

Connecting autoimmunity and painful sex in ova-having bodies can provide a framework for therapists to clinically assist the truest biopsychosocial, holistic, collaborative treatment of clients in line with "Primum non nocere," or first do no harm (American Association of Marriage and Family Therapists, 2015; American Association of Sex Educators, Counselors and Therapists, 2014). Both autoimmune disease and painful sex clinically impact clients and their ability to function.

The term *ova-having* instead of *woman, women, or female* is used because *ova-having* is more inclusive of the demographics addressed. The term includes not just women, but also non-binary and transgender individuals that have ovaries but do not identify with the term *woman, women*, or *female*. This decision is intentional, and is consistent with feminist theory. Feminist theory promotes inclusivity and social justice through the critique of traditional dominant discourse and status quo (Gurman, 2008; Roberto-Forman, 2008; Sensoy & DiAngelo, 2014).

Psychoneuroimmunology (PNI) looks at mind–body interactions and their effects on the individual, much like systems theory informs therapists to look at a client holistically. Systemic therapists consider a client's presenting problem in the context of their current life circumstances as influenced by their family of origin; current and previous relationship history; medical and mental health history; and social, culture, and religious factors (Hertlein et al., 2015), i.e. the biopsychosocial-spiritual approach (Saad et al., 2017). A feminist lens critiques the dominant culture's effects on the system and each domain within that system (Gurman, 2008; Roberto-Forman, 2008). PNI focuses on the nervous system connections starting with stress as perceived by the brain. It follows the path of that stress as it flows through the body, ending with consequences to the nervous system when stress remains suppressed, repressed, or dissociated (Maté, 2003). If all of the mitigating factors are present, stressors can result in an autoimmune disorder. Following those same pathways of stress perceived by the brain as it flows through the body oftentimes also results in pain with sex.

According to the National Institute of Health (NIH), approximately 23.5 million Americans have an autoimmune disorder (National Institute of Health, 2012). The American Autoimmune Related Disease Association (AARDA) estimates that number is actually closer to 50 million Americans, as the NIH only accounts for 24 of the 80 known autoimmune disorders (AADAR, 2018). Ova-having individuals are more frequently diagnosed with autoimmune disorders. Seventy percent of ova-having people experience chronic pain (Kiesel, 2017), while 43% reports sexual issues directly related to sexual pain (Laumann et al., 1999). Based upon these numbers and accumulated raw data, this article hypothesizes a connection between the diagnosis of autoimmune disorder and painful sex in ova-having individuals. At this time, no known research exists which connects autoimmunity to painful sex.

Research has shown that sexual dysfunction is far more prevalent in ova-having individuals than testes-having individuals, and that sexual dysfunction stems specifically from sexual pain (Laumann et al., 1999). Sexual pain occurs due to many different biological and psychological factors including inflammation from chronic stress, emotional distress, the feeling of inadequacy, and physical symptoms from illness (including, but not limited to, autoimmune disorders). Sexual pain can also stem from the natural inflammation that occurs with the menstrual cycle in ova-having bodies, which is nature's way of supporting successful reproduction. Sexual pain can be experienced by any ova-having person throughout all life stages, and therefore it is a relevant concern for medical and mental health professionals.

According to the Upsala Principles, sex is a basic human function and its expression is a basic human right (Carrera & Calderone, 2004). If sex is a basic human right and ova-having individuals deserve the right to their sexuality even with an autoimmune disorder, sexual pleasure becomes pertinent and sexual pain becomes dire to address. Desire for sexual activity often becomes diminished due to pain, pain avoidance, neurological rewiring, neuro sensitivity, pain sensitivity, and the potential impacts on the relational dynamic where the sexual activity takes place (Basson, 2012; Laursen et al., 2006). This becomes relevant to therapists because diminished normative functioning, sexual pain, and disrupted sexual activity within relational dynamics can all contribute to psychological distress (Meana et al., 2015; Wylie et al., 2015). There is also distress on the couple/partners involved, and there are many potential outcomes resulting from diminished sexual activity, such as: lack of sexual activity, inability to experience pleasure, diminished overall intimacy due to avoidance, inability to start/have a family, and relationship distress (Meana et al., 2015; Wylie et al., 2015). The systemic impacts include the internal impacts of the ova-having individual experiencing the pain, the autoimmune disorders' impacts, and the psychological distress experienced. These impacts will externalize by distressing partner(s) involved in the relationship through the diminished physical, and possibly emotional, intimacy. The distress spreads to the family systems and is perceived and re-felt by the ova-having individual, thus creating a negative feedback loop.

Psychoneuroimmunology and the system

Psychoneuroimmunology (PNI), or psychoendoneuroimmunology (PENI), is the study of mind–body interactions and their effects on the immune system (Maté, 2003; Tausk et al., 2008). The PNI is a supersystem wired together by nervous system connections with the bidirectional influence of immune function via the vagus nerve using cytokines as messenger cells (Maté, 2003; Tausk et al., 2008). The PENI is similarly, the study of the mind–body interactions with the addition of the endocrine system's impact. Systemic therapy also considers mutually influencing factors as part of the presenting problem, as they understand that no problem exists in isolation of the client or their context (Hertlein et al., 2015).

PNI and anatomy

In the brain is the prefrontal cortex, which holds the hypothalamus, the amygdala, and the anterior pituitary gland which connect to the spinal cord and the vagus nerve (Masters, 2019). The prefrontal cortex and the amygdala stores memories and interprets stimuli through lenses of past experiences, which includes the experience of emotional, physical, and mental pain (Basson, 2012; Maté, 2003). When an emotionally significant event occurs, the limbic system interprets the message and activates the hypothalamus to notify the sympathetic nervous system of a flight/fight response (Maté, 2003). Chronic activation through stress causes the prefrontal cortex and related structures to remain in a hypervigilant state (Maté, 2003). They control the rest of the body by sending messages down the spine and vagus nerve to the thymus and eventually the liver, which produces C-reactive proteins (CRP) (Lorenz et al., 2015). CRP is a marker in blood levels of inflammation, whether from acute or chronic illness (Lorenz et al., 2015).

The nervous system is made of the peripheral and central nervous systems. Within the peripheral nervous system is the autonomic nervous system, which holds the sympathetic and parasympathetic nervous systems. The sympathetic nervous system is responsible for the fight/flight/freeze response to stressors (Masters, 2019). The central nervous system and the immune system are bidirectional, and the hub of the PNI system is called the hypothalamus-pituitary-adrenal axis (HPA axis; Maté, 2003; Tausk et al., 2008). Emotional stress and certain psychological factors are the most powerful psychic triggers for activating the HPA axis' response (Maté, 2003).

Anatomy and stress

Chronic stress activates and negatively impacts the HPA axis (Basson, 2012; Tausk et al., 2008). External stress is perceived and interpreted by the hypothalamus in the prefrontal cortex (Basson, 2012; Maté, 2003). Messages about the stress are sent via corticotropin-releasing hormone (CRH) to the anterior pituitary, which releases adrenocorticotropic hormone (ACTH) (Basson, 2012). ACTH is produced in response to stress, and moves onto the adrenal glands, which produce glucocorticoids (GC). GCs released by the adrenal glands alter inflammatory and immune responses in the body (Basson, 2012).

A dysregulated immune system stemming from early emotional stress or trauma that is left unaddressed, suppressed, repressed, or dissociated cannot effectively fight off the onset of illness or disease (Maté, 2003). When the HPA axis is chronically activated, it becomes dysregulated while also dysregulates apoptosis (Basson, 2012; Maté, 2003). Dysregulated apoptosis creates an unnatural biochemical milieu in the body, which interferes with natural cell death (Maté, 2003). When cells do not die naturally, the unhealthy cells remain in the body. When the system is dysregulated, the immune system cannot always tackle all issues simultaneously (Cuevas et al., 2012; Lorenz et al., 2018b). When cells become unhealthy and do not die off, there are not always enough healthy cells to tackle and ward off disease. Thus, the immune system must prioritize which issues to tackle and with how much of its current resources to allocate (Lorenz et al., 2018b). Based upon these proven systems, when an autoimmune disorder or chronic illness is present in a dysregulated immune system, there are not enough healthy cells to fight the onset of these new issues, e.g., painful sex.

Autoimmunity and mental health

Autoimmune disorders arise when the body turns against itself, attacking the body as if it is a foreign object. The chronic features of autoimmune disorders involve the entire PNI supersystem (Maté, 2003). Mental health practitioners can holistically conceptualize and assist in the treatment of their clients through understanding this link. Furthermore, mental health practitioners use this information to assist clients in processing through stress to prevent/negate potential negative outcomes of physical and mental disorders. Though research does not show a clear connection between autoimmune disorders and gender, the pervasive hypothesis is that the absence of a Y chromosome makes one more susceptible to autoimmune disorder diagnosis. This is evidenced by a confirmation of higher incidences of autoimmune disorders in ova-having bodies (Manno, 2016).

The type of autoimmunity and its effect on ova-having persons are profound. Stress, unprocessed trauma/emotions, and autoimmune disorders can negatively impact an ova-having individual's sexual response cycle and functioning. Basson (2012) finds that the HPA axis' negative impacts include feeling sexually substandard, which exacerbates internal stress. High and/or chronic stress shows potential exacerbation in both the development and severity of endometriosis (Cuevas et al., 2012). An ova-having body's immunity is in direct opposition to their fertility; immunity levels decline to allow for conception, lest the immune system attacks the fertilized egg during implantation (Lorenz et al., 2018a; Lorenz et al., 2018b). A decline in immunity puts an ova-having person at more risk for infection or the development of a disorder that might otherwise be fought off by a fully-functioning immune system (Abrams & Miller, 2011; Lorenz et al., 2018a).

Seventy percent of ova-having people suffer from chronic pain (Keisel, 2017). Yet, ova-having persons are subjected to the "Yentl" syndrome, meaning they must prove they are as sick or in as much pain as a testes-having individual (Hoffman & Tarzian, 2001). Hoffman and Tarzian (2001) found that ova-having individuals' pain is often dismissed in the medical field because of the emotional component inherently perceived in their complaint. Testes-having persons are perceived to underreport pain; thus, their complaints are taken more seriously (Hoffman & Tarzian, 2001). Mental health practitioners utilizing a systemic assessment approach are more likely to hear a client's list of medical complaints and diagnoses at all once (Hertlein et al., 2015). This provides the mental health professional the ability to aggregate complaints into a whole picture that is often overlooked or missed by medical specialists that focus on specific complaints. While mental health practitioners are not medical professionals, they are able to refer to medical professionals to provide more holistic, client-centered, and interdisciplinary care. As mental health practitioners who identify as advocate and ally, teaching ova-having clients how to advocate for self in such circumstance while assisting with the client's potentially negative outlook on seeking help is incorporated into the treatment goals.

Pain with sexual activity and PNI

Laumann et al. (1999) studied 3,000 Americans ages 18 to 59 and found that sexual dysfunction was more prevalent for women (43%) than men of the same age group (31%), and that the marker of poor health in females was directly related to sexual pain specifically. In the United Kingdom's third annual National Survey of Sexual Attitudes and Lifestyles (NATSAL) survey of over 7,000 women, 7.5% of women reported experiencing painful sex, which was accompanied by a strong link between sexual pain and poor health and/or chronic health conditions (Mitchell et al., 2017). Sexual pain in ova-having people is an increasingly relevant issue, presenting ever more frequently in offices of not only physicians, but also therapists. Though hypothesized to be a naturally occurring evolutionary means of fostering more successful reproduction, this circular relationship sometimes becomes a feedback loop from which sexual pain occurs, particularly with the way in which female hormones naturally behave (Gadgil & Bossert, 1970; Lorenz et al., 2015; Stearns, 1976, 1989; Williams, 2018). Additionally, chronic stress further creates another type of feedback loop particular to female stress hormones in which the production of cortisol, inflammation, and ensuing sexual pain perpetuates more stress, anxiety, and depression (Brotto, 2018; Lorenz et al., 2015). The presence of a mind/body connection regarding stress level, emotional state, and state of health is clear in the existence of sexual pain in ova-having bodies, and therefore psychoneuroimmunology (PNI) becomes essential when studying and addressing sexual pain.

Studies have shown the sex differences in immune function between testes-having and ova-having people, most importantly that ova-having individuals have more active immune systems than testes-having individuals. Estrogen generally has an immunopotentiating effect when it comes to the immune response to foreign cells – for example, sperm cells – whereas testosterone tends to be immunosuppressive in nature (Lorenz et al., 2015; Siciliani, 2000).

Evolutionary theory argues that the act of fertilization has much causality with the reactivity that occurs in ova-having immune function. Natural selection creates a trade-off between immune system defense and the reproduction process involving the implantation of an embryo, which could easily be mistaken as a pathogen if the two functions occurred at once (Lorenz et al., 2015). The goal of the immune system is to distinguish foreign antibodies, adapt, and attack pathogens by neither over-nor under-working, and redirect as few resources from the reproduction mechanism as possible

(Abrams & Miller, 2011). When chronic stress is present, the repeated cell-mediated response reduces humoral immunity consisting of immunoglobulins G and A – which are both important to reproduction – and therefore the effectiveness of the immune system as a whole (Abrams & Miller, 2011).

Chronic stress, inflammation, and sexual activity

Natural selection and the ova-bodied immune response make the ova-having person a catalyst for overly active inflammation and stress response (Hamilton & Meston, 2013). When chronic, daily stress from seemingly small stressors such as maintaining mental health status (e.g., anxiety or depression), the "female tendency" toward the task of relationship management, and the societal tendency to multitask and fit as much activity into a day as possible, the female body becomes prone to problems with sexual functioning. When the hormonal reaction to psychological stress and the sympathetic nervous system were measured it was found that ova-having people who experienced high levels of stress had lower levels of genital arousal (Hamilton & Meston, 2013). Even if they were psychologically ready for sexual activity, the body has increased its allostatic load and is too busy handling the chronic stress response with its innate immune function to properly respond to sexual cues (Hamilton & Meston, 2013).

The creation and biological behavior of cortisol are the key to understanding why stress becomes so destructive to the ova-bodied immune system. The purpose of cortisol is to regulate a range of functions, including immune response and reaction to stressors. When the body is functioning well, cortisol rises quickly when we wake and tapers down over the course of the day (i.e. the cortisol awakening response) (Brotto, 2018). Estrogen tends to upregulate glucocorticoid levels in ova-having people during acute stress and the entire nervous, endocrine, and immune systems become affected due to their interconnectedness (Hamilton & Meston, 2013; Toufexis et al., 2014).

With chronic daily stress and ensuing regulation that occurs in ova-having individuals, the body remains in a state of fight-or-flight and cannot return to homeostasis. The fight-or-flight mechanism activates the sympathetic nervous system, directing blood into our major muscles that allow us to stay and fight or escape to safety. For example, when muscles are constantly tense due to the lack of change in blood flow, pelvic floor tightness (leading to sexual pain), lack of arousal, and lack of lubrication occur (Brotto, 2018). The psychosocial consequences of these biological processes which result in sexual dysfunction can cause stress, prompting the stress response cycle to never alleviate. The DSM-5 specifies the psychosocial factor of "personal distress" as an important specifier, as well as *fear* of pain with the female or ova-having identified partner being "typically unreceptive to a partner's attempts to initiate sex," thereby pathologizing the partner and causing stress due to psychosocial consequences of declining sex with their partner over an extended period of time (American Psychiatric Association, 2013; Taylor, 2015). Distress due to sexual difficulties has been greatly neglected in epidemiological research, especially regarding those who possess ovarian reproductive systems (Hendrick et al., 2015).

Though we live in a sexually motivated society where sexual activity is seen as a "normal" occurrence in young adults, sexual desire discrepancy due to pain was found to be most prevalent in younger women (Hendrick et al., 2015; Mitchell et al., 2013). The result of chronic, relentless daily stress from taking on "female tasks" such as the responsibility of ensuring healthy relationship functioning, carrying emotional labor, and performing caretaking responsibilities in families and partnerships is desire discrepancy and sexual pain. On top of this stress, Western culture now gives ova-having people an added expectation of making their mark and gaining positions of power as members of the non-dominant population in the workforce (Brotto, 2018.) As a result of this stress, ova-having persons are put into a systemic double-bind: do what is expected socially regarding success and gender *and* have sexual desire that mirrors that of our partner(s). Never mind that stress creates painful sexual experiences when an individual has an overactive immune response, which causes over-functioning of different mechanisms, which causes sexual pain in many different forms.

Neurological processing of pain

Central sensitization refers to changes within the central nervous system that make the sympathetic nervous system's response to certain harmful or potentially harmful stimuli hyperreactive and extremely sensitive (Basson, 2012; Neblett et al., 2013; Woolf, 2011). Because of the brain's inherent neuroplasticity throughout the life cycle, pain can result from the adaptation of neurons and microglia in the central nervous system's pain circuitry. Neurons can, therefore, become activated by low-threshold, mild stimuli (Basson, 2012; Woolf, 2011). It is as if pain receptors "remember" an experience (e.g., an agonizing sexual experience resulting in extreme vaginal pain) and adapt by becoming hypersensitive with a lower threshold for the pain the next time that instance occurs. This is a response of hypervigilance in an effort to help the body protect itself before the original pain threshold is crossed.

When chronic stress is present, rather than returning to homeostasis, the HPA axis continues to stay activated by the amygdala, causing the system to become maladaptive. Chronic pain can develop as a result of stress that accumulates and compounds as the brain adapts and becomes hypersensitive to stimuli (Basson, 2012).

Through a neurological lens, the mechanism of pain amongst emotional, psychological, and physical dimensions can be particularly problematic for females, given that their bodies react to infection, chronic stress, and inflammation in a hypervigilant manner due to estrogen's immunopotentiating effect (Basson, 2012; Siciliani, 2000). Research has shown that females with diagnosed sexual pain due to provoked vestibulodynia (PVD) have a ten times increased occurrence of anxiety disorder and a three times increased occurrence of depressive disorder (Basson, 2012; Khandker et al., 2011). Similarly, when researchers controlled for the previous diagnosis of anxiety or depression, females were found to be four times more likely to have PVD in later years (Basson, 2012; Khandker et al., 2011). These findings are just one example of the comorbidity between sexual pain and emotional distress supporting the linkage between autoimmunity and painful sex.

Basson (2012) conceptualized a circular loop of the effects of sexual dysfunction on overall allostatic load. As changes take place in the central nervous system, central sensitization and pain amplification occur. The brain becomes wired to reject or fear sexual stimuli at the time of sexual activity. This causes avoidance, fear, loss of sexual motivation, and stress. There are stress and emotional distress in feeling sexually substandard, undesirable, and a letdown to oneself or one's a sexual partner(s). This emotional distress and general stress around sexual activity perpetuates neurological changes and central sensitization, turning sexual stimuli into a trigger (Basson, 2012).

Connections between autoimmune disorders and pain with sexual activity

There is a gap in the literature investigating the overlap between autoimmune disorders and pain with sexual activity in ova-having bodies. This overlap is important to consider for the wholistic concern of the health and well-being of ova-having people. In examining the way in which autoimmune disorders can occur – especially in ova-having bodies – as well as the way in which pain with sexual activity can occur in the same population, there are many connections that point to a feedback loop between the immune system, cortisol production, and estrogen's effect on these functions.

The hypothalamus is important to consider because it is responsible for interpreting messages based on past experiences, leading us to end up in a hypervigilant state in chronic stress situations (Maté, 2003). The main function of the pituitary gland is to secrete hormones into the bloodstream (Masters, 2019). These hormones particularly affect the thyroid, adrenal glands, and reproductive organs. The pituitary is the connector between the HPA (which responds to stress) and the HPG (which is involved in the control of reproduction and sexual response) axes, and is also responsible for both the process which creates the conditions for autoimmune disorders to occur and the process in females through which pain with sexual activity can occur (Masters, 2019).

Both the HPA and HPG systems are activated by chronic stress. Glucocorticoids (i.e. cortisol) are produced which, in ova-having bodies, are upregulated by estrogen (Dube et al., 2009). Overall, glucocorticoids cause inflammation throughout the body, which increases the prevalence of CRP's (markers of inflammation) (Lorenz et al., 2015). When the hypothalamus over-functions and cortisol is over-produced, ova-having people are left in a hypervigilant state. As cortisol fails to taper off during the day, the potential for apoptosis is high. The body cannot move out of the fight or flight state and the body begins to attack itself (autoimmune disorders), remains inflamed (pain with sexual activity), can produce cysts (pain with sexual activity), and the brain can even rewire itself to remain in a hypervigilant state (central sensitization) (Basson, 2012; Brotto, 2018).

Aside from the internal mechanisms that create inflammation, a hypervigilant immune system, and extra-sensitive nociception, mobility is an important overlap between the presence of autoimmune disorders and pain with sexual activity. Autoimmune disorders come in many different forms, many of which create a symptom of difficulty with mobility (Zhang et al., 2018). Mobility typically associated with sexual activity, whether partnered or solo, can become difficult in many ways depending on the manifestation of the autoimmune disorder. For example, as joints swell and stiffen with rheumatoid arthritis, patients experience limited mobility with activities such as partnered and/or penetrative sex, as well as with day-to-day living (Laursen et al., 2006; Zhang et al., 2018). With Behçet's syndrome, painful sores can form on the mouth, skin, and genitals, making any sort of rubbing extremely painful (Yetki et al., 2012). The vaginal dryness and inflammation that accompany endometriosis and provoked vestibulodynia also is a symptom of autoimmune disorders which can make masturbation or penetrative sex painful (Basson, 2012; Caruso et al., 2019).

An important overlap between research in autoimmunity and research around inflammation and sexual pain is the presence of adverse childhood experiences (ACE's), identification of low socioeconomic status, and education status (Basson, 2012; Khandker et al., 2011). The 1998 NATSAL survey found that women with lower educational attainment (i.e. have not graduated from high school) have greater prominence of sexual pain and higher levels of anxiety (Laumann et al., 1999). Dube et al. (2009) found that the experience of childhood traumatic stress and maltreatment (i.e., ACE's) increased the likelihood of manifestation of and hospitalization from autoimmune disease as adults due to elevated CRP levels, compounded stress, and reductions in hippocampal, intracranial, and cerebral volumes (Dube et al., 2009).

The cyclical feedback loop of hypervigilance, hypersensitivity, and/or chronic stress leading to autoimmunity and/or central sensitization is also in a feedback loop with pain and/or emotional distress (Basson, 2012). A parallel between the factors that cause autoimmunity and the factors that are present with the occurrence of sexual pain is essential to understanding the link between them. Research in the medical and mental health fields is still ongoing regarding what specific factors create the "perfect storm" in individuals to cause a hypervigilant immune system in some people, sexual pain in others, and a combination of both autoimmune disorder and sexual pain of different manifestations. This overlap between autoimmunity and sexual pain is both relevant and necessary in helping clients and clinicians fully understand what is occurring in the body, what action can be taken in treatment, and what future research must be done to further understand the internal female system.

Clinical implications

Given that autoimmune disorders and pain with sex are prominent issues in ova-having persons, this literature provides a new option in clinical considerations when a client with the comorbid diagnosis of autoimmune disorder and sexual pain comes in for treatment. Knowing that an overlap in diagnosis exists, this article informs and encourages clinicians to investigate the comorbidity of pain with sex if the autoimmune disorder is present and vice versa. Therapists can better assist with the emotional and cognitive aspects of autoimmune disorders and pain with sex. Both diagnoses are correlated with anxiety, depression, perfectionism, and high/chronic stress levels. Whether to help heal preventively or to aid the client in emotions and stress after the diagnosis has been made, the therapist is key to aiding the client's cognitive and emotional aspects of diagnosis.

Research shows that 20% of clients state they are discussing sex with their therapist; however, 70% of clients would like to discuss sexuality problems and are not being asked by the therapist about them (Blount et al., 2017). Those numbers show a vast discrepancy in clients wanting to discuss sexual issues versus those that actually have the ability to discuss their sexual issues. Specific to sex therapy and sexual problem knowledge within the realm of family therapy, the Commission on Accreditation for Marriage and Family Therapy Education Accreditation Standards (COAMFTE, 2017) requires Foundational Curriculum Areas (FCA) for MFT training. The sole mention of human sexuality education comes within FCA6: Biopsychosocial Health & Development Across the Life Span, stating that a minimum of three credits is required to address "individual and family development, human sexuality, and biopsychosocial health across the lifespan" (COAMFTE, 2017). The amount of information to cover within FC6 is vast. All three areas – individual and family lifespan development, biopsychosocial health, and human sexuality – could by themselves be an entire degree or dissertation foci. There is much within the realm of human sexuality that an MFT can learn which would assist in a full biopsychosocial conceptualization of a client, thus three credit hours are simply not enough. In research specifically focused on AAMFT members who have been trained through those COAMFTE standards and are in practice, it was found that having high-perceived factual knowledge about sexuality did not decrease anxiety in talking to clients about sexual content to cause MFT's to initiate sexuality conversation (Harris & Hays, 2008). It was also found that unless a therapist has experience with sex education and working with sex issues in supervision, they are not likely to initiate discussions regarding the subject (Harris & Hays, 2008). This evidence speaks to the state of family therapy – though sexuality is a lifespan issue and an experience of all people to some extent, clinicians are largely unable to address sexuality issues based on lack of training, as well as therapist values and experience working with sexuality.

Feminist family therapists believe that neutrality does not exist, that gender and power dynamics are always present, and the need to amplify voices is typically marginalized (Harvey et al., 2016). Feminist theory also recognizes a sensitivity to the biological effects of the ova-having life cycle on presenting symptoms' presentation and interpersonal relationships. Additionally, the feminist lens promotes the need to understand ova-having bodies' sexuality response to prevent a perpetuation of confusion or mistaken beliefs (Salkil & Goff, 2014). Autoimmunity impacts ova-having bodies at statistically higher numbers than their counterparts (Manno, 2016). Ova-having persons also experience higher rates of chronic pain and sexual issues related to pain (Keisel, 2017; Brotto, 2018). Their voices remain unheard, or at least unattended to. Ova-having people must prove they are just as sick as their testes-having counterparts to receive less than adequate treatment (Hoffman & Tarzian, 2001). As a feminist family therapist, the gender and power dynamics upholding a system of barriers to holistic and adequate treatment must be addressed. The voices of ova-having individuals must be amplified by those in positions to provide the megaphone They need unique approaches to address the intersectionality of their gender identity, physical, and sexual health.

Medical students only average two-and-a-half hours of sexuality study per year for a four-year program (Solursh et al., 2003). These same students average a failing score on a 32-question exam about human sexuality (Warner et al., 2018). The more a medical professional specializes, the more focused their treatment is; thus, specialists may miss a holistic conceptualization of their patient. Furthermore, clinical implications for medical professionals include addressing the bias currently held against ova-having patients (Keisel, 2017; Hoffman & Tarzian, 2001). For example, that ova-having individuals are predisposed to pain sensitivity (Archey et al., 2019; Bartley & Fillingim, 2013). Current data shows a disinclination to listen to ova-having individuals, a lack of credence given to their complaints of pain, and frequent dismissal of reports of pain as exaggerated and emotional; thus, ova-having individuals are often under-diagnosed and under-treated (Keisel, 2017; Hoffman & Tarzian, 2001).

This example is one way that collaborations between medical and mental health professionals can provide better outcomes through encompassing assessments and a feminist approach to treatment. Rather than ova-having bodies working against "Yentl" syndrome, the collaborative approach acknowledges the unique experiences of ova-having individuals sexually, especially when impacted medically. With the statistically high numbers of autoimmunity and painful sex, "women's health" needs a shift in its approach to treating clients as whole humans. If therapists look at the entire person's presenting problem and all of its context, collaborating with medical professionals to adopt a similar approach means that both the autoimmunity and the subsequent sexual pain will receive appropriate attention and treatment. The mental, emotional, biological, and sexual impacts on each client can be addressed as vital parts of the whole.

Future research

Future research is needed to further explore these findings and concretize the next steps. The current findings reinforce the need for a systemic biopsychosocial conceptualization of ova-having clients, both by mental health professionals and medical professionals. Additionally, more education and communication are needed between these two fields to better assist ova-having clients. Medical family therapy is an example of a collaboration between these two systems. It provides a framework to understand how the psychophysiological and the somatic interact (Salkil & Goff, 2014). Furthermore, it provides techniques for working with both the client and the team of professionals involved in managing the physiological issue and its mental health consequences (Salkil & Goff, 2014). Virginia Satir's Humanistic Experiential therapy is another model by which the framework is built upon the mind-body connection; Satir created the assessment and intervention tool called the self-mandala to holistically conceptualize the eight aspects of self and their interactional interdependence (Satir et al., 1991). Satir et al. (1991) believed that a systemic, holistic conceptualization of a person is rooted in the positionality that one's body operates under the direct effects of that person's thoughts, feelings, and context. Even 30 years later, there seems to be a struggle to fully integrate and work from this model.

Not only is further research needed to continue exploring the link between ova-having individuals diagnosed with autoimmune disorders and pain with sex, a call to action must happen. Every layer of a client's system needs auditing, from the internal system to the multiple external systems involved in assessment and treatment. The educational systems preparing professionals that eventually treat the ova-having individuals requires audit and reorganization to provide more comprehensive education, thus enabling eventual professionals to most effectively assist in the treatment of these overlapping disorders. The systems employing the professionals treating ova-having bodies also require audit and reorganization so that the diagnoses are reached and collaboratively treated. This article focuses on one gap in both the literature and treatment of ova-having individuals, but it is far from comprehensive.

ORCID

Karen Washington http://orcid.org/0000-0002-1756-6858

References

Abrams, E. T., & Miller, E. M. (2011). The roles of the immune system in Women's reproduction: Evolutionary constraints and life history trade-offs. *American Journal of Physical Anthropology*, *146*(S53), 134–154. https://doi.org/10.1002/ajpa.21621

American Association of Marriage and Family Therapists. (2015). *Code of Ethics*. American Association of Marriage and Family Therapists. https://www.aamft.org/Legal_Ethics/Code_of_Ethics.aspx

American Association of Sex Educators, Counselors, and Therapists. (2014). *Code of ethics and conduct for AASECT certified members.*

American Autoimmune Related Diseases Association, Inc. (2018). *Autoimmune disease statistics* [Data file]. American Association of Sex Educators, Counselors, and Therapists. https://www.aarda.org/news-information/statistics/

American Psychiatric Association. (2013). *Diagnostic and statistical manual of mental disorders* (5th ed.). American Psychiatric Association.

Archey, M., Goldey, K., Crockett, E., & Boyette-Davis, J. (2019). An investigation of the effects of testosterone and behavioral expression of pain on sex/gender differences in pain perception. *Psychological Reports*, *122*(3), 826–840. https://doi.org/10.1177/0033294118781320

Bartley, E. J., & Fillingim, R. B. (2013). Sex differences in pain: A brief review of clinical and experimental findings. *British Journal of Anaesthesia*, *111*(1), 52–58. https://doi.org/10.1093/bja/aet127

Basson, R. (2012). The recurrent pain and sexual sequelae of provoked vestibulodynia: A perpetuating cycle. *Journal of Sexual Medicine*, *9*(8), 2077–2092. https://doi.org/10.1111/j.1743-6109.2012.02803.x

Blount, K. C., Booth, C., Webb, T., & Liles, R. G. (2017). *Integration of sex and sexuality into counseling programs. Ideas and Research you Can Use: VISTAS 2017.* American Counseling Association. https://www.counseling.org/docs/default-source/vistas/integration_of_sex_and_sexuality.pdf?sfvrsn=4

Brotto, L. A. (2018). *Better sex through mindfulness: How women can cultivate desire.* Greystone Books Ltd.

Carrera, M., & Calderone, M. (2004). 1980: The SIECUS/Uppsala principles basic to education for sexuality. *SEICUS Report 32*(2): 17–19.

Caruso, S., Iraci, M., Cianci, S., Vitale, S. G., Fava, V., & Cianci, A. (2019). Effects of long-term treatment with dienogest on the quality of life and sexual function of women affected by endometriosis-associated pelvic pain. *Journal of Pain Research*, *12*, 2371–2378. https://doi.org/10.2147/JPR.S207599

Commission on Accreditation for Marriage and Family Therapy Education. (2017, August). *Accreditation Standards*. Commission on Accreditation for Marriage and Family Therapy Education.

Cuevas, M., Flores, I., Thompson, K. J., Ramos-Ortolaza, D. L., Torres-Reveron, A., & Appleyard, C. B. (2012). Stress exacerbates endometriosis manifestations and inflammatory parameters in an animal model. *Reproductive Sciences*, *19*(8), 851–862. https://doi.org/10.1177/1933719112438443

Dube, S. R., Fairweather, D., Pearson, W. S., Felitti, V. J., Anda, R. F., & Croft, J. B. (2009). Cumulative childhood stress and autoimmune diseases in adults. *Psychosomatic Medicine*, *71*(2), 243. https://doi.org/10.1097/PSY.0b013e3181907888

Gadgil, M., & Bossert, W. H. (1970). Life historical consequences of natural selection. *The American Naturalist*, *104*(935), 1–24. https://doi.org/10.1086/282637

Gurman, A. S. (2008). A framework for the comparative study of couple therapy: history, models, and applications. In A. S. Gurman (Ed.), *Clinical handbook of couple therapy* (4th ed., pp. 1–26). Guilford Press.

Hamilton, L. D., & Meston, C. M. (2013). Chronic stress and sexual function in women. *The Journal of Sexual Medicine*, *10*(10), 2443–2454. https://doi.org/10.1111/jsm.12249

Harris, S. M., & Hays, K. W. (2008). Family therapist comfort with and willingness to discuss client sexuality. *Journal of Marital and Family Therapy*, *34*(2), 239–250. https://doi.org/10.1111/j.1752-0606.2008.00066.x

Harvey, R., Brown, K. S., Miller, B., Williams-Reade, J., Tyndall, L., & Murphy, M. (2016). Theory into research practice: Reflections and recommendations on collaborative feminist research. *Journal of Feminist Family Therapy*, *28*(4), 136–158. https://doi.org/10.1080/08952833.2016.1235410

Hendrick, L., Gijs, L., & Enzlin, P. (2015). Age-related prevalence rates of sexual difficulties, sexual dysfunctions, and sexual distress in heterosexual women: Results from an online survey in Flanders. *The Journal of Sexual Medicine*, *12*(2), 424–435. https://doi.org/10.1111/jsm.12725

Hertlein, K. M., Weeks, G. R., & Gambescia, N. (Eds.). (2015). *Systemic sex therapy* (2nd ed.). Routledge.

Hoffman, D. E., & Tarzian, A. J. (2001). The Girl Who Cried Pain: A bias against women in the treatment of pain. *Journal of Law, Medicine & Ethics*, *29*(4_suppl), 13–27. https://doi.org/10.1111/j.1748-720X.2001.tb00037.x

Khandker, M., Brady, S. S., Vitonis, A. F., MacLehose, R. F., Stewart, E. G., & Harlow, B. L. (2011). The influence of depression and anxiety on risk of adult onset vulvodynia. *Journal of Women's Health*, *20*(10), 1445–1451. https://doi.org/10.1089/jwh.2010.2661

Kiesel, L. (2017, October 9). *Women and Pain: Disparities in experience and treatment [Blog post]*. Harvard Medical School. https://www.health.harvard.edu/blog/women-and-pain-disparities-in-experience-and-treatment-2017100912562

Laumann, E., Paik, A., & Rosen, R. (1999). Sexual dysfunction in the united states: Prevalence and predictors. *JAMA: Journal of the American Medical Association*, *281*(6), 537–544. https://doi.org/10.1001/jama.281.6.537

Laursen, B. S., Overvad, K., Olesen, A. S., Delmar, C., & Arendt-Nielsen, L. (2006). Ongoing pain, sexual desire, and frequency of sexual intercourses in females with different chronic pain syndromes. *Sexuality and Disability*, *24*(1), 27–37. https://doi.org/10.1007/s11195-005-9001-5

Lorenz, T. K., & Heiman, J. R. (2018a). Inflammation may alter perception of sexual arousal and pleasure in healthy women. *Journal of Sexual Medicine*, *15*(6), 99–122. https://doi.org/10.1016/j.jsxm.2018.03.051

Lorenz, T. K., Heiman, J. R., & Demas, G. E. (2018b). Interactions among sexual activity, menstrual cycle phase, and immune function in healthy women. *Journal of Sex Research*, *55* (9), 1087–1095. https://doi.org/10.1080/00224499.2017.1394961

Lorenz, T. K., Worthman, C. M., & Vitzthum, V. J. (2015). Links among inflammation, sexual activity and ovulation: Evolutionary trade-offs and clinical implications. *Evolution, Medicine, and Public Health*, *2015*(1), 304–324. https://doi.org/10.1093/emph/eov029

Manno, R. (2016, April 19). *Haywire: Autoimmune Disorders in Women* [Video file]. Johns Hopkins Medicine. https://www.youtube.com/watch?v=stwo0kDz0qQ

Masters, S. (2019). *Biological foundations of human sexuality [powerpoint presentation]*. Retrieved from Canvas.

Maté, G. (2003). *When the Body Says No: The cost of hidden stress*. Scribe Publications Pty Ltd.

Meana, M., Maykut, C., & Fertel, E. (2015). Painful Intercourse: Genito-pelvic pain/penetration disorder. In K. M. Hertlein, G. R. Weeks, & N. Gambescia (Eds.), *Systemic Sex Therapy* (2nd ed., pp. 191–209). Routledge.

Mitchell, K. R., Geary, R., Graham, C. A., Datta, J., Wellings, K., Sonnenberg, P., Field, N., Nunns, D., Bancroft, J., Jones, K. G., Johnson, A. M., & Mercer, C. H. (2017). Painful sex (dyspareunia) in women: Prevalence and associated factors in a British population probability survey. *BJOG: An International Journal of Obstetrics and Gynaecology*, *124*(11), 1689–1697. https://doi.org/10.1111/1471-0528.14518

Mitchell, K. R., Mercer, C., Ploubidis, G., Jones, K., Datta, J., Field, N., Copas, A., Tanton, C., Erens, B., Sonnenberg, P., Clifton, S., Macdowall, W., Phelps, A., Johnson, A., & Wellings, K. (2013). Sexual function in Britain: Findings from the third national survey of sexual attitudes and lifestyles (Natsal-3). *Lancet*, *382*(2013), 1817–1829. https://doi.org/10.1016/S0140-6736(13)62366-1

National Institute of Environmental Health Sciences. (2012). *Autoimmune diseases* [Data file]. National Institute of Environmental Health Sciences. https://www.niehs.nih.gov/health/Matérials/autoimmune_diseases_508.pdf

Neblett, R., Cohen, H., Choi, Y., Hartzell, M., Williams, M., Mayer, T., & Gatchel, R. (2013). Establishing clinically significant values for identifying central sensitivity syndromes in an outpatient chronic pain sample. *The Journal of Pain*, *14*(5), 438–445. https://doi.org/10.1016/j.jpain.2012.11.012

Roberto-Forman, L. (2008). Transgenerational couple therapy. In A. S. Gurman (Ed.), *Clinical handbook of couple therapy* (4th ed., pp. 196–226). Guilford Press.

Saad, M., de Medeiros, R., & Mosini, A. C. (2017). Are we ready for a true biopsychosocial-spiritual model? The many meanings of "spiritual". *Medicines*, *78*(4), 1–6. https://doi.org/10.3390/medicines4040079

Salkil, S. E. B., & Goff, J. D. (2014). LMFT Exam Preparation Workbook [PowerPoint Slides].

Satir, V., Banmen, J., Gerber, J., & Gomori, M. (1991). *The Satir Model: Family therapy and beyond*. Science and Behavior Books, Inc.

Sensoy, O., & DiAngelo, R. (2014). Respect Differences? Challenging the common guidelines in social justice education. *Democracy and Education*, *22*(2), 1–10. Available at: https://democracyeducationjournal.org/home/vol22/iss2/1

Siciliani, J. (2000). *The effect of sexual activity on secretory immunoglobulin A and cortisol levels in married couples* [Doctoral dissertation]. PsycINFO. UMI number: 9996388.

Solursh, D. S., Ernst, J. L., Prisant, L. M., Mills, T. M., Solursh, L. P., Jarvis, R. G., & Salazar, W. H. (2003). The human sexuality education of physicians in North American Medical Schools. *International Journal of Impotence Research*, *15*(5), 41–45. https://doi.org/10.1038/sj.ijir.3901071

Stearns, S. C. (1976). Life-history tactics: A review of the ideas. *The Quarterly Review of Biology, 51*(1), 3–47. https://doi.org/10.1086/409052

Stearns, S. C. (1989). Trade-offs in life-history evolution. *Functional Ecology, 3*(3), 259–268. https://doi.org/10.2307/2389364

Tausk, F., Elenkov, I., & Moynihan, J. (2008). Psychoneuroimmunology. *Dermatologic Therapy, 21*(1), 22–31. https://doi.org/10.1111/j.1529-8019.2008.00166.x

Taylor, C. (2015). Female sexual dysfunction, feminist sexology, and the psychiatry of the normal. *Feminist Studies, 41*(2), 259–292. https://www-jstor-org.proxy.cc.uic.edu/stable/10.15767/feministstudies.41.2.259

Toufexis, D., Rivarola, M. A., Lara, H., & Viau, V. (2014). Stress and the reproductive axis. *Journal of Neuroendocrinology, 26*(9), 573–586. https://doi.org/10.1111/jne.12179

Warner, C., Carlson, S., Crichlow, R., & Ross, M. W. (2018). Sexual Health Knowledge of U.S. Medical Students: A national survey. *Journal of Sexual Medicine, 15*(8), 1093–1102. https://doi.org/10.1016/j.jsxm.2018.05.019

Williams, G. C. (2018). *Adaptation and natural selection: A critique of some current evolutionary thought (Vol. 61).* Princeton university press.

Woolf, C. J. (2011). Central sensitization: Implications for the diagnosis and treatment of pain. *Pain, 152*(3), S2–S15. https://doi.org/10.1016/j.pain.2010.09.030

Wylie, K. R., Markovic, D., & Hallam-Jones, R. (2015). Inhibited Arousal in Women. In K. M. Hertlein, G. R. Weeks, & N. Gambescia (Eds.), *Systemic sex therapy* (2nd ed., pp. 152–170). Routledge.

Yetki, D. O., Celik, O., Hatemi, G., & Kadioglu, P. (2012). Sexual dysfunction and depression in premenopausal women with mucocutaneous Behçet's disease. *International Journal of Rheumatic Diseases, 16*(4), 463–468. https://doi-org.proxy.cc.uic.edu/10.1111/1756-185x.12005

Zhang, Q., Zhou, C., Chen, H., Zhao, Q., Li, L., Cui, Y., & Shen, B. (2018). Rheumatoid arthritis is associated with negatively variable impacts on domains of female sexual function: Evidence from a systematic review and meta-analysis. *Psychology, Health & Medicine, 23*(1), 114–125. https://doi.org/10.1080/13548506.2017.1338738

Invisible Loss: A Delphi Approach to Develop a Term for Individuals Who Experienced Perinatal Loss

Rachel Diamond, Jessica L. Chou and Susan Bonis

ABSTRACT

The purpose of this Delphi pilot study was to 1) identify potential benefits to people who experienced perinatal loss if a term were established; 2) develop a term for people who experienced a perinatal loss because, at present, no term exists; and, 3) identify areas of consensus and contention between perinatal loss professionals and parents when considering terminology. Fifty-five participants (perinatal loss professionals, n = 33; perinatally bereaved parents, n = 22) proposed, reviewed, and rated terms through three rounds of surveys until *bereaved parent* was selected. Top terms were equally preferred between parents and professionals and, in general, participants described benefits to term development. Findings provide the perinatal loss community a first step in considering terminology.

Perinatal loss

"My loss is invisible, it's as though (my baby) never existed." – Participant

Perinatal death is a profoundly traumatic event (Diamond & Roose, 2016; Kersting & Wagner, 2012; Koopmans et al., 2013), affecting an estimated one million individuals in the United States each year (MacDorman & Kirmeyer, 2009). Perinatal death is typically associated with feelings of loss, grief, emotional numbness, and sorrow (Capitulo, 2005; Diamond & Diamond, 2017; Hutti et al., 2017; Wagstaff & Teska, 2018). A common finding in the extant perinatal grief literature is that it is not objective facts (e.g., length of pregnancy) that best comprise the significance of a perinatal loss experience nor predict grief reactions; instead, it is an individual's perception of the loss that influences their reaction (Hutti, 1992). In other words, the meaning a person attributes to the perinatal loss is a critical determinant for the psychological response (Hutti et al., 2017). While the loss may feel real and significant for the individual(s) experiencing it, family, friends, and members of the healthcare community often dismiss perinatal death as commonplace and, therefore, inconsequential (Diamond & Diamond, 2016; Markin, 2017). Further, the loss is often abstract without societal or legal means of recognition. For example, there are few socially sanctioned mourning practices for perinatal losses and, with early fetal deaths or when there is not a live birth (depending on the state) there may not be a legally recognized birth or death date/certificate to signify the existence of this significant experience. These invalidating messages about the experience has led to understanding this type of loss through the lens of disenfranchised grief (Doka, 1989). To further layer invalidation to this experience is the notable absence of a conceptual term that identifies individuals who experience this type of loss. Feminist therapists have long been tied to the perinatal loss experience, with efforts toward offering supportive services being seen for over 50 years (Layne, 2006). Accordingly, the aims of this paper are tied to the advocacy and support seen from the feminist movement. The present pilot study was conducted to begin to conceptualize a term for individuals who have experienced perinatal loss using Delphi methodology (Helmer & Rescher, 1959; Polit & Beck, 2017) with perinatal loss professionals and parents with first-hand experience. Recommendations are included for further term development.

Perinatal loss definition & experience

The concept of the perinatal period emerged in the late 1940s as researchers and clinicians became increasingly aware of the relatively large number of deaths occurring in the period before and after delivery (MacDorman & Gregory, 2015; World Health Organization, 2006). A review of literature revealed varying parameters for what constitutes a perinatal death. During gestation, the standard definition of perinatal death only captures fetal deaths at and after 20 weeks (MacDorman & Gregory, 2015; World Health Organization, 2006). While this temporal definition captures intermediate (20–27 weeks gestation); and late (28 weeks or more gestation) loss, it excludes intrauterine deaths of the fetus prior to 20 weeks gestation (e.g., miscarriages; MacDorman & Gregory, 2015). Estimates of early fetal loss range from 10–25% up to 75%, as many pregnancies end in the first trimester before a pregnancy is confirmed (Kersting & Wagner, 2012; March of Dimes, 2017). At the other end of the perinatal period, the standard definition for newborn (neonatal) deaths include deaths among live births during the first 28 completed days of life (World Health Organization, 2006).

For the purposes of the present project, we conceptualized the perinatal period as broadly as possible to include early fetal deaths because the psychosocial experience may not differ based on weeks of gestation and this gestational period is the time in which most fetal deaths occur (Hutti, 1992; Hutti et al., 2017; MacDorman & Gregory, 2015). Our conceptualization is aligned with that of perinatal loss researchers (Hill et al., 2008; Kersting & Wagner, 2012) and can also be seen within national organizations for perinatal bereavement care, such as Resolve Through Sharing (RTS) Bereavement Services (Midland & Limbo, 2004) and Share Pregnancy & Infant Loss Support, Inc (Share Pregnancy & Infant Loss Support, 2015).

In addition to unclear and varied temporal parameters of what constitutes a perinatal death, there also exists variations in terminology related to the individuals who experience perinatal loss. At present, there is no term to describe the identity of an individual who has experienced perinatal loss. This lack of an established term can be seen as recently as a 2017 special section on psychotherapy for pregnancy loss. Indeed, even within a special focus journal authored by experts in the field there is varying language used to refer to individuals who experienced perinatal loss (see Table 1). These variations are critical to note, as language facilitates communication and understanding for the people who experience the phenomenon and, consequentially, society at large.

Language is used to help organize thoughts, as well as to understand and find meaning in experience (Rosenblatt, 2016). The absence of a dedicated term creates barriers and challenges for the individual, as well as researchers and clinicians. Most losses, such as death of a spouse (i.e., widow/widower) or parents (i.e., orphan) are socially defined through specific terminology. Thus, the lack of a socially recognized term for an individual experiencing a significant event, such as perinatal loss, can further contribute to a sense of isolation and disenfranchisement. This lack of terminology coupled with societal reactions to this type of loss (e.g., minimization and avoidance), can

Table 1. Perinatal Loss Terms

Perinatal Terms Used	Article Reference
• Patients grieving the loss of a pregnancy • Women who experience a pregnancy loss • Patients who have suffered a pregnancy loss • Patients who have experienced a pregnancy loss	Markin (2017). An introduction to the special section on psychotherapy for pregnancy loss: Review of issues, clinical applications, and future research direction. *Psychotherapy, 54*(4), 367–372.
• Bereaved parents of babies who die during pregnancy or shortly after birth • Parents who have experienced a prenatal loss • Bereaved parents	O'Leary and Henke (2017). Therapeutic educational support for families pregnant after loss (PAL): A continued bond/attachment perspective. *Psychotherapy, 54*(4), 386–393.
• Clients experiencing pregnancy loss • Pregnancy loss clients • Bereaved parents	Jaffe (2017). Reproductive trauma: psychotherapy for pregnancy loss and infertility clients from a reproductive story perspective. *Psychotherapy, 54*(4), 380–385.
• Postloss parenting • Couples who have had a loss • Reproductive loss patients • Patients who have suffered reproductive losses • Parents who have suffered reproductive loss	Diamond and Diamond (2017). Parenthood after reproductive loss: How psychotherapy can help with postpartum adjustment and parent–infant attachment. *Psychotherapy, 54*(4), 373–379.
• Women who have experienced pregnancy loss	Wenzel (2017). Cognitive behavioral therapy for pregnancy loss. *Psychotherapy, 54*(4), 400–405.
• Clients (i.e., women and couples) dealing with pregnancy termination for fetal anomaly (PTFA) • PTFA clients	Leon (2017). Empathic psychotherapy for pregnancy termination for fetal anomaly. *Psychotherapy, 54*(4), 394–399.

have detrimental effect on one's ability to process and cope. To address this language gap, we proposed the development of a pilot study as a first step toward conceptualizing such a term.

Feminist lens

The feminist movement has been connected to infant loss, with the start of infant loss support groups over 50 years ago. As women's rights and voices became more prominent among society, so did support groups for women who experienced pregnancy loss (Layne, 2006). The present study was guided by a feminist lens in an effort to continue creating a platform of empowerment and voice for people who have experienced perinatal loss. Because language and the meaning behind can shape our experiences (Mize, 2003) and empower people; it is important to understand the potential benefits of identifying a preliminary term that may give language to people who have experienced perinatal loss.

Research aims

The principal aims of the present study included:

(1) Identify potential benefits to people who have experienced perinatal loss if a term were established.
(2) Develop a term for people who have experienced a perinatal loss for further exploration because, at present, no such term exists.
(3) Identify areas of consensus and contention between professionals and parents when considering terminology for persons who have experienced perinatal loss.

Study design and methods

Design

The present study was designed as a pilot study to be an important, first step in the development of a term for persons of perinatal loss. Delphi survey methodology was used to directly access perspectives of professional experts in the field of perinatal loss, as well as individuals who had personal experience with perinatal loss. Delphi methodology was originally developed to resolve dilemmas related to selecting a plan of action based on a group consensus (Helmer & Rescher, 1959). In this case, Delphi was used to find agreement on a term for individuals who experienced perinatal loss. This goal is consistent with use of the method to resolve the dilemma of "defining a foundational concept" (Jorm, 2015, p. 889). Typically, statistical procedures are used to distill information gathered from a panel of experts about a broad research question; responses are thematically analyzed and given back to participants for clarification and comment. Parents with first-hand expertise were also included on the panel creating a platform of empowerment and voice for people who have experienced a perinatal loss so as to not just rely on professionals to comprise the expert panel, as is typical of Delphi studies. Furthermore, unlike typical studies that employ Delphi methodology, the present study was not simply seeking consensus from the panel to find agreement (e.g., 75% median threshold consensus) across, for example, a list of statements (Diamond et al., 2014). Instead, our goal for using Delphi methodology was to find agreement on a single outcome – a term for individuals who have experienced a perinatal loss as the first step in conceptualizing a potential term for future use in practice settings. While we understood it was unlikely unanimous agreement could be achieved, our aim was to achieve majority agreement on a single term. To reduce the risk of significant attrition that could compromise results, we planned for the term to be selected by participants following three rounds.

Participants

Purposeful and snowball sampling were used to recruit participants which resulted in 55 participants for the panel: professionals (n = 33) and parents (n = 22). All participants were over 18, English-speaking, and within the United States. Delphi studies have demonstrated stability with panels of around 20 or more (Jorm, 2015); however, because the research team understood the possibility of attrition given the higher than typical number of rounds, a larger panel was sought. In Round 2, 42 participants responded: 28 professionals and 14 parents. In Round 3, 31 participants responded: 21 professionals and 10 parents.

Qualifications for professional experts included clinical expertise, such as certification in perinatal loss care (CPLC); professional contributions, such as related publications; and/or years and focus of experience in perinatal loss. Parent experts were identified and recruited from perinatal loss organizations in the Midwest and New England that the PI had a previous affiliation. The clinical directors of these programs managed the recruitment of parent participants so that the research team was not in direct contact until after parents expressed interest. Parents were actively involved in the perinatal loss organization (e.g., served as peer support parents) and were identified by the organization to have the following qualities: developed insight into the grieving process, resolved their grief to be able to participate in a meaningful way, and were able to provide helpful information from their own experience.

Data collection

Online responses to survey questions were collected through three rounds conducted over 6 months. Upon participants electronically indicating they had reviewed informed consent, they were directed to the Round 1 survey that gathered participant demographic information and asked open-ended questions about perinatal loss terminology. In the Round 2 survey, participants were provided each unique term generated in Round 1 and asked to rate each term. Participants utilized a visual analog scale in which they could rate each response from 0 (lowest) – 100 (highest). A comment box was additionally provided to allow for modifications and/or rationale for ratings. In the Round 3 survey, participants were presented with the five terms receiving the highest overall ratings from Round 2. In this round, participants were asked to rank order the terms from 1 (most preferred) – 5 (least preferred).

Data analysis

As is typical in Delphi research, the analysis of data in the present study required both qualitative (Round 1) and quantitative (Round 2 and 3) approaches (Skulmoski et al., 2007).Thematic analysis was used to identify codes, themes, and categories. The first-round survey responses were read and reread independently by each researcher to find meaning and develop understanding in the words participants used. Words and phrases were highlighted and reference notes were made. A table was constructed to organize the highlighted terms and phrases into categories based on emerging themes. Themes and categories were compared among the researcher team and tied to the data.

Rounds 2 and 3 involved a quantitative approach in order to determine a majority agreement on terminology and to highlight similarities and differences between participant groups (i.e., parent and professional participants). Statistical summaries of mean (M) and standard deviations (SD) of Round 2 responses were analyzed between groups and by total responses. Between-group and total responses from Round 3 were also generated into statistical summaries of percentages. Using the statistical summaries from Round 2 and 3, comparative analysis was used to assess for consensus and contention between participant groups using t-tests, chi-square test of goodness-of-fit and Freeman-Halton extension of Fisher's exact test.

Results

Descriptive data

Professional participants (n = 33) included individuals with relevant professional knowledge and experience (Baker, Lovell & Harris, 2006) in perinatal loss (See Table 2). The professional experts were multidisciplinary with the majority (57.6%) identifying as nursing professionals with varying levels of education and responsibilities coordinating perinatal loss bereavement

Table 2. Participant Demographics.

Demographics	Parent Expert		Professional Expert	
	n=22	%	n=33	%
Gender				
Male	2	9.1%	1	3.0%
Female	20	90.9%	32	97.0%
Identified Race*				
Non-Hispanic White or Euro-American	18	81.8%	33	100%
Black, Afro-Caribbean, or African American	1	4.5%	0	0.0%
Latino or Hispanic American	2	9.1%	0	0.0%
East Asian or Asian American	0	0.0%	0	0.0%
South Asian or Asian American	0	0.0%	0	0.0%
South Asian or Indian American	1	4.5%	0	0.0%
Middle Eastern or Arab American	0	0.0%	0	0.0%
Native American or Alaskan Native	0	0.0%	0	0.0%
Other	1	4.5%	0	0.0%
Current Location				
Northeast United States	6	27.3%	4	12.1%
Northwest United States	0	0.0%	1	3.0%
Southeast United States	5	22.7%	7	21.2%
Southwest United States	2	9.1%	1	3.0%
Midwest United States	9	40.9%	11	33.3%
Mid-Atlantic United States	0	0.0%	9	27.3%
Highest Educational Degree				
Certificate	1	4.5%	0	0.0%
Some College	1	4.5%	0	0.0%
Associates	2	9.1%	1	3.0%
Bachelor's	6	27.3%	12	36.4%
M. Ed	3	13.6%	0	0.0%
MSN	3	13.6%	5	15.2%
MSW	2	9.1%	2	6.1%
MBA	1	4.5%	0	0.0%
MS	2	9.1%	1	3.0%
MDiv	0	0.0%	2	6.1%
PhD	0	0.0%	9	27.3%
DNP	0	0.0%	1	3.0%
Other	1	4.5%	0	0.0%
Primary Profession				
Researcher/Scholar			4	12.1%
Nurse			19	57.6%
Therapist/Clinician			7	21.2%
Professor			2	6.1%
Minister/Chaplain			1	3.0%
Years working in Perinatal Loss Community				
2-5 Years			6	18.2%
5-10 Years			6	18.2%
10-15 Years			5	15.2%
15-20 Years			3	9.1%
20+ Years			13	39.4%
% of week working in Perinatal Loss Community				
0-10%			4	12.1%
10-20%			9	27.3%
20-40%			7	21.2%
40-60%			3	9.1%
60-80%			4	12.1%
80-100%			6	18.2%
Perinatal Loss				
Yes	22	100%	17	51.5%
No	0	0.0%	14	42.4%
Missing Data	0		2	6.1%
Perinatal Loss Experience*				
Ectopic	1	4.5%	0	0.0%
Single Miscarriage	11	50.0%	10	30.3%
Multiple Miscarriages	5	22.7%	4	12.1%
Stillbirth	8	36.4%	3	9.1%
Newborn Death	7	31.8%	1	3.0%

* percentages can exceed 100, as more than one answer is possible

programs. Years of experience and percentage of time working in the perinatal loss community varied: the majority (63.6%) had 10 or more years of experience and; notably, all professionals who reported spending 0–10% of their work week in the perinatal loss community had 5 or more years of experience. While professional experts differed from the parent experts in that they were not required to have first-hand experience with perinatal loss, 17 (51.5%) reported having experienced some type of perinatal loss.

Parent experts (n = 22) reported a range of perinatal losses, with the majority (57%) reporting more than one loss experience (See Table 2). Participants had a variety of ways in which they had participated in the perinatal loss community, with the most common being volunteer work (n = 15; 68.2%).

Delphi results

Round 1

Participants were asked to respond to two open-ended questions. The first question asked: *How would people who have experienced a perinatal loss benefit from the establishment of a common term?* The overarching theme that emerged was a perceived benefit to the establishment of a term. All 14 (100%) of the parent participants and 25 (89%) of professional participants responded that people who experienced perinatal loss would benefit from establishment of a common term. Three subthemes were identified: 1) community and connection, 2) validation of loss and 3) identification.

Community and connection

Responses from 6 (37.5%) parents and 5 (25.0%) professionals indicated an established term could benefit the perinatal loss community by promoting a sense of community and connection. This was exemplified in the words of this parent, "*sense of belonging, sense of unity, being part of a group and not alone as we often feel alone.*" A response by a professional participant supported this notion of community and support, "*[...] a common term would start to give a language to an experience that typically is not spoken of which helps alleviate isolation and shame.*"

Validation of loss

Responses from 6 (37.5%) parents and 6 (30.0%) professionals indicated an established term could validate and legitimize the loss. This was exemplified in the words of one parent who responded, "*We would finally have a word in our culture that may honor this deep loss*" and another who responded, "*it helps validate that the loss was a real loss of human life.*" Similarly, a professional responded, "*it would acknowledge the loss in a way that is currently ignored. Most commonly I hear 'Am I still a mother/father?'*"

Identification

Responses from 6 (37.5%) community and 10 (50.0%) professional participants indicated an established term could create an ability to have a means of identification that can benefit the ecological system affected by the loss: the individual, the microsystem directly interacting with the bereaved, and larger systems. The notion of identification could directly benefit individuals who experienced perinatal loss by establishing a focus on the grief process. As one professional explained, "*it would help with their identity and the processing of their grief.*" Additionally, the establishment of a term was also seen as having benefits in the microsystem in with which the bereaved individual interacts. Specifically, responses focused on improved communication of the loss with others. As one parent described, "*people wonder what to call those of us that lost a baby. We are still parents. Perhaps it would be easier on others if there was a word for it.*" This notion of support was reiterated by a professional, "*it has been my experience that people who suffer the loss of a baby struggle with the term parent. They know they are a parent, but sometimes feel that others do not see them as a 'parent' because their baby is no longer here.*" Finally, identification could affect larger systems through enhancement of funding, research, and medical opportunities by shifting the belief system and understanding of the experience for perinatally bereaved individuals. One parent noted, "*[establishment of a term] identifies us as a group – that can be studied/funded or simply acknowledged.*" A professional identified the following benefits within the medical system, "*if there was a common term that could be used in a patient's chart, then the patient may not have to explain over and over again the circumstances around the death which could create less trauma for the parent.*"

In addition to the themes discussed above, it is notable that four professional participants expressed varying opinions related to development of a term. One conveyed a need for different terms for different types of losses, "*I don't know if there is one single term that will fit for everyone.*" Three others questioned the need for any term to be established, "*I can't see how a name would unite them more than their experience of their loss already does.*"

The second question in Round 1 asked: *What terms have you heard used for people who have experienced perinatal loss?* The terms were analyzed and categorized into two groups reflective of: 1) identity as a person and 2) identify as experience (see Table 3 for complete list of responses).

Identity as a person

Language from both parents and professionals included terms related to being a parent (e.g., mother and father) either on its own or coupled with descriptors tied to the loss (e.g., bereaved, grieving, without a child, etc.). Additionally, there were unique terms provided that described the person having had this specific loss. One such example is vilomah, a word borrowed from Sanskrit meaning

Table 3. Commonly used Terms for Perinatal Loss at Present.

Identity as a Person

- Angel mother, father, parents[1,2]
- Baby loss mother, father, parents[1]
- Bereaved mother, father, parents[1,2]
- Empty arms[2]
- Grieving mother, father, parents[1,2]
- Loss mother, father, parent[1,2]
- Mother, father, parents[2]
- Mother, father, parents without a child[2]; Childless mother, father, parents[1,2]
- Nahpro[2*]
- Perinatally bereaved parents[2]
- Perinatal loss parents[2]
- Psychological parent[2]
- Reavan[2*]
- Still mother, father, parent[1]; Still a mom, dad, parent[1]
- Unemployed parent[2]
- Vilomah[2*]

Identity as Experience

[Description of experience]

- Barren; infertile; sterile [1]
- (History of) stillbirth[2]
- Lost their baby[2]
- Maternal fetal demise[2]; reproductive demise[2]
- Miscarriage [1,2]
- Multiple losses[2]

Mother, Father, Parents [description of experience]

- ... of babies born too soon[2]
- ... of a stillborn baby[2]
- ... of a baby who died as a newborn[2]
- ... with difficulty having a baby[1]
- ... with multiple losses[2]
- ... who have experienced the death of an unborn or newly born infant [2]
- ... who had a pregnancy loss[2]
- .... who lost a child/baby[2]

No terms

- *Never heard a term, just her baby died, or she lost a baby* [1]
- *I haven't heard any terms unfortunately other than she/they just lost their baby*[1]
- *I have never heard a term. They are always referred to as 'she has had a miscarriage, she has had a stillbirth, or her baby died shortly after birth'* [2]
- *In general, I have not heard terms used for persons who have experienced a perinatal loss*[2]

1 Information provided by parent participant(s)
2 Information provided by professional participant(s)
*Naphro: Meaning provided for term by participant: 'orphan' spelled backward
*Reavan: Participant provided no meaning for term
*Vilomah: Meaning provided for term by participant: means 'empty' in Sanskrit, same language we adapted widow (also empty) from

"against a natural order" – as in children should not precede their parents in death (Holloway, 2006). The terms presented here support the need for the development of a term specific to the individual and their experience with perinatal loss.

Identity as experience

In contrast, both parents and professionals provided descriptions of one's experience of perinatal loss that highlighted the lack of a unique term. As one example, one parent explicitly made note that descriptions are provided with "*nothing specific to the person*" and another parent reported that they "*never heard a term.*" The terms categorized in this group described the experience alone, not the person. That is, they were not linked to the identity of the person or, at best, made little reference to the actual person.

The final questions asked in Round 1 included: *If a common term was established for people who experienced a perinatal loss, what term would you recommend?* Twenty-three unique terms were generated. The terms and their corresponding rationale were compiled (see Table 4).

Round 2

The 23 terms generated in Round 1 were provided back to participants to review and rate. The statistical summaries of participants' scores can be found in Table 5. T-tests revealed statistically significant differences (p =.05) between parents and professionals for the term *perinatal loss mom/dad/parent* and the term *parent*, with ratings for the parent group being higher for both. Results demonstrate no statistical difference on ratings between parents and professionals for all other terms (See Table 5).

Using the combined group ratings, the top five rated terms from Round 2 included: 1) *bereaved mother/father/parents*, 2) *perinatal loss mother/father/parents*, 3) *perinatally bereaved parent*, 4) *pregnancy loss*, and 5) *referred to as the baby's mom/dad (e.g., Sara's mom)*. Additionally, participants included the following responses that were not anticipated in the original design: a) the need for different terms for different types of losses and b) no need for the establishment of a term. Therefore, relevant questions were added to Round 3.

Round 3

Round 3 involved two parts. Participants were asked to rate the top five generated terms into order of preference, then were asked to respond to two questions: 1) *Do you feel there should be different terms for different types of loss?* 2) *Do you think the establishment of a term is needed to describe a person/s who experienced perinatal loss?*

Top five rating

Bereaved parent was the highest ranked term, put in the top position by 14 (45.2%) of the 31 participants: 5 parents (50.0%) and 9 professionals (42.9%) (See Table 6 for descriptive statistics). Using the descriptive summaries from Round 3, a chi-square test of goodness-of-fit was performed. Greater than 20% of the expected counts were less than 5 and not all individual expected counts were 1 or greater (Yates et al., 1999). Therefore, categories were collapsed to compare participants who chose bereaved parent as the top-rated term as compared to choosing another term. Bereaved parent was equally preferred between parents and professionals, X(1) = .140, p = .103.

Table 4. Term Development.

	Parents	Professionals
Terms	Reason(s) Provided	Reason(s) Provided
Bereaved mother/father/parents*	• It's inclusive and doesn't designate the person with their particular experience • I saw it online and I feel like it suits the situation	• Their parenthood is real, as is their grief • It's clear and concise • It defines the relationship and the emotion
Perinatal loss mother/father/parents	• Fits most accurately- 'loss or bereaved parents' include those who lose an older child which seems in many ways like a different kind of loss	
Perinatally bereaved parent		• It defines the context, the relationship, and the timing. To reiterate a statement from the previous response, the relationship aspect (parent) depends on the meaning the experience has for the one going through it (e.g., numerous research findings indicate that "miscarriage" can mean "loss," "death of a child," or other)
Pregnancy Loss	• To me *Pregnancy Loss* seems more meaningful than Miscarriage. Miscarriage is so widely used, that I find anymore it doesn't carry the weight of the loss as *Pregnancy Loss* could potentially	
Referred to as their baby's mom/dad (e.g., Sara's mom) *		• In my experience parents are most comforted if they are referred to as their baby's mom/dad
[Different terms for different losses]	• There should be different terms for different types of perinatal loss so the parent does not have to further explain their situation (one term for a miscarriage, one term for still birth, one term for a neonatal death)- each of these terms may be related	
Vilomah	• Means 'empty' in Sanskrit, same language we adapted widow (also empty) from	
Parents		• Makes sense
Grieving mom/dad/parent		• I am unsure about a common term. I find psychotherapy patients grieving the loss of a pregnancy/baby prefer different terms. For example, some prefer to be called a parent and some do not. I supposed the term "grieving parent" is the best one I can think of but doesn't seem to really capture the experience of being a parent without a baby and again some patients do not want to be called a parent. • For a start term includes parent and a child has died – but does not include death during a pregnancy or perinatal loss
Loss mom/dad/parent	• Inclusive of gender; Parenthood is respected when so much of society minimizes that component of our loss	
Forever mom/dad/family	• That is what we are – we are forever grieving and loving our children. Nothing and no one – not a different child or time – will change it. We will forever miss them and love them. I also like that this doesn't have a religious connotation or put other "beliefs" on others as in something to do with angels.	

(*Continued*)

Table 4. (Continued).

	Parents	Professionals
Terms	Reason(s) Provided	Reason(s) Provided
Baby loss*		• People often refer to the fetus they are carrying as the baby this or the baby that (kicking, rolling, resting), so there is some common consensus that there is a baby inside. It is also more specific than pregnancy making it more real and human. Miscarriage and stillbirth describe a time limited event that is now in the past and while some of the trauma of that event may still be relevant to process what is more relevant is to be able to talk about what was lost and miscarriage and stillbirth do not really speak to this piece
Parent/Parents of an Angel		• I can only, ever, remember hearing parents who have suffered the loss of a baby saying they were Parents of an Angel. I have seen it time and time again in this community.
Something with the root word "hope"	• We always have hope	
Angel mom/dad/ parents	• Because your babies are angels in Heaven now. Inclusive to both parents, heard it time and again in the community	
Courageous mother*		• Women who suffer stillbirth or neonatal death come home after birth with no baby. They are continuously asked about their pregnancy or congratulated, only having to tell the story over and over. Those who weren't visibly pregnant yet suffer in silence–no one asks them about their baby. Instead, these mothers congratulate other mothers and listen to other people's birth stories and no one ever knows how much they hurt. Then there are those women who choose to carry a baby with a life-limiting diagnosis. In my opinion, they are the most courageous. They go about those months of pregnancy just hoping to meet their little one alive. All the while, people ask them about the baby and what the nursery looks like, etc.
Babyless parents		• It offers validation that a baby did exist and turned human beings into parents, whether their baby lived to be met or died before that time. Babyless clearly defines there is no baby to hold in their arms and to raise.
Forever loved lost		• Because they are forever lost and always loved
Something that means "torn meeting"	• The divine meeting of a new life with their parent or parents was torn or ripped apart by the death of the new life	
Psychological parent*		• Developmentally we make a psychological leap when attempting to become a parent. With a perinatal loss, the shift in identity has occurred even though there is no baby to bring home. We become psychological parents before becoming physical parents.
Fathered or Mothered	• No reason	
No term needed*		

* Term generated by individual(s) who included professional expert(s) who reported personal perinatal loss

Table 5. Results of Descriptive Statistics and T-Tests for Rating of Terms by Groups.

	Group								
	Parents			Professionals					
Terms	M	SD	n	M	SD	n	95% CI for Mean Difference	t	df
Bereaved mother/ father/ parent	65.08	28.92	13	69.12	29.06	26	-24.01, 15.93	-.41	37
Perinatal loss mother/ father/ parents	66.50	28.48	12	45.50	25.58	24	1.92, 40.08	2.24*	34
Perinatally bereaved parent	43.08	34.99	13	45.67	31.44	36	-26.51, 18.40	-.37	34
Pregnancy Loss	48.82	37.66	12	45.05	36.77	21	-24.00, 30.74	.25	31
Referred to as their baby's mom/ dad (e.g., Sara's mom)	47.64	36.27	11	36.91	32.80	22	-14.85, 36.30	.86	31
[Different terms for different losses]	34.20	35.80	10	38.56	32.30	18	-31.56, 22.85	-.33	26
Vilomah	34.08	31.08	12	40.47	34.98	19	-31.70, 18.92	-.52	29
Parents	57.30	35.26	10	28.55	29.85	20	3.61, 53.89	2.34*	28
Grieving mom/ dad/ parent	42.91	34.85	11	35.55	32.74	20	-18.35, 33.06	.59	29
Loss mom/ dad/ parent	47.73	40.77	11	32.74	30.04	23	-10.22, 40.20	1.21	32
Forever mom /dad/ family	42.82	33.17	11	36.00	33.87	24	-18.12, 31.75	.556	33
Baby loss	27.00	26.29	11	30.67	31.02	21	-26.11, 18.78	-.33	30
Parent/ Parents of an Angel	25.00	29.67	11	32.16	29.34	19	-30.02, 15.70	-.64	28
Something with the root word "hope"	26.36	30.76	11	18.79	19.34	19	-11.08, 26.24	.83	28
Angel mom/ dad/ parents	28.45	36.76	11	21.43	22.49	21	-13.98, 28.03	.68	30
Courageous mother	25.00	28.64	11	18.11	23.21	18	-13.02, 26.80	.71	27
Babyless parents	17.25	18.39	8	29.21	31.84	19	-32.24, 8.31	-1.22	22.12
Forever loved lost	23.22	36.16	9	26.76	34.94	21	-32.34, 25.26	-.25	28
Something that means "torn meeting"	26.00	32.03	9	15.42	21.99	19	-15.22, 36.38	1.03	26
Psychological parent	14.27	23.35	11	12.06	15.68	17	-12.90, 17.32	.30	26
Orphaned parent	18.63	20.77	8	20.11	25.07	19	-22.26, 19.30	-.15	25
Fathered or Mothered	16.11	32.92	9	5.56	5.93	18	-14.80, 35.92	.96	8.26
No term needed	8	15.74	6	26.62	34.77	13	-43.07, 5.84	-1.61	16.99

* $p < .05$.

Table 6. Descriptive Statistics for Preferred Term by Participant Group.

	Term				
Participant Group	Bereaved Parent	Perinatal Loss Parent	Perinatally Bereaved Parent	Pregnancy Loss	Referred to as Baby's Parent
Parent	5 (50.0%)	4 (40.0%)	1 (10.0%)	0 (0%)	0 (0%)
Professional	9 (42.9%)	2 (9.5%)	7 (33.3%)	3 (14.3%)	0 (0%)
Total	14 (45.2%)	6 (19.4%)	8 (25.8%)	3 (9.7%)	0 (0%)

Numbers indicate the number of participants who identified the respective term as their top rank. Numbers in parentheses indicate column percentages.

Different terms

In this round participants were directly asked: *Do you feel there should be different terms for different types of loss?* Participant responses were mixed: 9 (29.0%) agreed there should be different terms for different types of loss. As one participant reported, "*yes, it shows respect and honor to the specific relationship.*" Alternatively, 14 (45.2%) responded no, as the following response demonstrates: "*no, because the grief process is not defined by the type of loss, but rather how that loss affects that person.*" Additionally, 8 (25.8%) responses were categorized as unsure, as indicated with the following: "*not sure – I can see both sides – if there were different terms it could better describe the loss, but it may also make it seem that certain losses are less painful than others.*" No difference was noted in distribution of responses between parents and professionals (p = .70, Freeman-Halton extension of Fisher's exact test; Freeman & Halton, 1951).

No term

Participants were also directly asked: *Do you think the establishment of a term is needed to describe a person/s who experienced perinatal loss?* Responses were less divided: 19 (65.5%) agreed that establishment of a term is needed. One individual commented, "*we are a community of people without a set name. It's awkward enough to have to describe who we are. A term makes it more socially acceptable ... It eases the listener into a painful answer ... It also bonds those of us together who have a shared experience.*" Alternatively, 5 (17.2%) participants reported in the negative: "*No, why complicate things.*" Lastly, 5 (17.2%) responded in an unsure or ambivalent way, "*there are many terms describing persons who have lost pregnancies and infants now. Do I think that we need a specific term, not necessarily but it might be meaningful to some.*" No difference was noted in the distribution of responses between parents and professionals (p = .19, Freeman-Halton extension of Fisher's exact test; Freeman & Halton, 1951).

Discussion

The meaning a person attributes to a loss plays a critical determinant for his or her psychological response (Hutti et al., 2017). And, language plays an important role in this process (Rosenblatt, 2016). This pilot study utilized Delphi methodology with a panel of parent and professional experts as a first step in understanding and addressing the profound absence of a term in our society for parents who have experienced the death of a child, specifically during the perinatal period. This has been seen both through variant use of language by professionals (e.g., terminology in scholarly writing; Table 1) as well as within the results of the present study (e.g., participants' reports of a perceived absence of unique term(s) for individuals who experienced perinatal loss; Table 3).

The pilot study demonstrated feasibility and a need for continued efforts toward term development. Responses in the present study suggested a perceived benefit for a shared, common term being developed to connect to the identity of bereaved parents from a perinatal loss. This affirmative stance supports the framework of disenfranchised grief for perinatal loss (Doka, 1989). Round 1 themes suggest that an established term could validate and legitimize the loss in a way that is not presently done. Validation could occur both on a personal level for the parent as well as increase society's means of being able to appropriately acknowledge the legitimacy of the loss. Following three rounds the term *bereaved parent* was selected.

While this study has demonstrated potential benefits of a common term, these benefits must also be weighed with the lack of majority agreement. That is, the term *bereaved parent* was selected with 45.2% of participants ranking it as their first choice. This should be understood adjacent to the responses of participants responding in favor of 'different terms for different losses' and those questioning if any term should be established. Therefore, the fact that majority agreement could not be reached may in fact be representative of the experience of grieving perinatal loss and is important in understanding assessment needs in the follow-up study.

Limitations and future research

The decision to conduct a pilot study prior to embarking on the main research project can be difficult, be we recognized it as a necessary first step in uncovering unforeseen difficulties in the assessment and development of a term for perinatal loss (Hassan et al., 2006). Given the project's time commitment (i.e., three rounds conducted over 6 months), there was a higher than typical attrition rate. And, because demographic variables were not collected at each round it is unknown who remained in the survey across time. Participants were not required to complete the previous round(s) to answer a survey; thus, we are unable to assess selective participant characteristics vulnerable to attrition. The next study will make efforts to minimize the number of rounds to collect data and record demographic information throughout to be able to have a deeper understanding of the participant pool over time.

An additional limitation of the present study was the small and homogenous nature of the sample. A more heterogeneous sample in terms of gestational stages/types of loss, gender, race, ethnicity, and religion will allow for a deeper clinical understanding of beliefs and values as it relates to terminology. Additionally, recruitment of parents not involved in the perinatal loss community will further aid in the understanding of fit of a term with parents of varied experiences. Lastly, a larger sample in which meaningful within-groups comparisons can be made will better allow us to understand what or who accounts for variability in perspectives which may be clinically meaningful.

Conclusion

Following a perinatal loss, providers must explore the unique meanings each person attributes to the experience and how this impacts his or her thoughts, feelings, and behaviors (Markin, 2017). To this end, while we recognize the strengths in the methodology employed in this pilot study to gather the perspective from parent and professional experts in perinatal loss we must also balance this with recommendations in perinatal bereavement care to make a careful assessment of each person's perceptions of the loss. As such, we recognize the need to continue to assess the benefit of term development for perinatal loss and work toward appropriate term development. That is, while our methodological aim was to achieve majority agreement, the term *bereaved parent* was selected with only 45.2% of participants ranking it as their first choice. We understand the publication of this pilot study, while beneficial, is unlikely to produce many practical benefits; thus, we see this study as a first step in term development. The next study will be used to assess the fit and benefit of having this term developed for diverse individuals who experienced perinatal loss. The evaluation will also focus on within-group differences as it relates to important demographic characteristics (gender, ethnicity, and race, and individuals who experience perinatal loss at various gestational stages) to see how fit may differ between groups.

Acknowledgments

In conducting the present study, we would like to acknowledge and thank the tremendous efforts of the expert panel of parents and professionals in the field of perinatal loss that made this project possible*:

Allison Rogers MSN, RN, CEN, perinatal loss experience
Anonymous Parent 1
Anonymous Parent 2
Bereaved Mother/RN Care Manager
Chandra L Clark
Christine A Pinto
Clinical psychologist
Cynthia D Lovan RNC-OB
Deborah Mueller, RN, BSN, CPLC
Dezna Napier
Dvora Entin, LCSW
Elizabeth Shaeffer, BSN, RN, CPLC
Erin Bull RNC-NIC, BSN, CPLC, CHPPN
Jeannie Zuk, PhD, RN University of Colorado School of Medicine
Joni Cutshaw BSN, RNC CPLC, CCAP Franciscan Health Indianapolis
Judy Philbrook, MSN, NNP-BC; Co-Coordinator, Neonatal Advanced Practice Service; Cape Fear Valley Medical Center; Fayetteville, NC
Julie Evans, LCSW
Kathy Perko, MS, CPNP CPLC
Karen Kavanaugh, PhD, RN, FAAN; Senior Nurse Scientist, Children's Hospital of Wisconsin
Lindsey J. Wimmer, RN CPNP, CPLC
Lisa M Wuertz
Marcia Meyer Jenkins RN CPLC
Melanie Chichester, BSN, RNC-OB, CPLC
Melissa Petersen, RNC, MS, WHNP-BC
Mommyof5angels
Moshe Winograd, Ph.D
Nadiya Dolce, MSW, LCSW

Nancy Ann Ferguson
Patti Budnik; National Share Pregnancy & Infant Loss Support
Rana Limbo, PhD, RN, CPLC, FAAN
Rayna D. Markin, PhD
Rev. Beth Mosier, MDiv, BCC, CPLC
RN and professional board-certified chaplain
Rosmarie E. Roose MSN, RNC
Tammy Ruiz Ziegler RN CPLC
Theresa K. Liberatori, PhD, LCSW-C, CPLC
Vincent Kowalski
William Dolce, MBA

*Authors received express permission from participants for acknowledgments. Names appear as requested by participants.

ORCID

Rachel Diamond http://orcid.org/0000-0003-2560-6052

References

Baker, J., Lovell, K., & Harris, N. (2006). How expert are the experts? An exploration of the concept of "expert" within Delphi panel techniques. *Nurse Researcher*, *14*(1), 59–70. https://doi.org/10.7748/nr2006.10.14.1.59.c6010

Capitulo, K. L. (2005). Evidence for healing interventions with perinatal bereavement. *The MCN, American Journal of Maternal/Child Nursing*, *30*(6), 389–396. https://doi.org/10.1097/00005721-200511000-00007

Diamond, D., & Diamond, M. (2017). Parenthood after reproductive loss: how psychotherapy can help with post-partum adjustment and parent-infant attachment. *Psychotherapy*, *54*(4), 373–379. https://doi.org/10.1037/pst0000127

Diamond, D. J., & Diamond, M. O. (2016). Understanding and treating the psychosocial consequences of pregnancy loss. In A. Wenzel (Ed.), *The Oxford handbook of perinatal psychology* (pp. 487–523). Oxford University Press.

Diamond, I. R., Grant, R. C., Feldman, B. M., Pencharz, P. B., Ling, S. C., Moore, A. M., & Wales, P. W. (2014). Defining consensus: A systematic review recommends methodologic criteria for reporting of Delphi studies. *Journal of Clinical Epidemiology*, *67*(4), 401–409. https://doi.org/10.1016/j.jclinepi.2013.12.002.

Diamond, R. M., & Roose, R. E. (2016). Development and evaluation of a peer support program for parents facing perinatal loss. *Nursing for Women's Health*, *20*(2), 146–156. doi: 10.1016/j.nwh.2016.02.001

Doka, K. J. (1989). Disenfranchised loss. In K. J. Doka (Ed.), *Disenfranchised grief: Recognizing hidden sorrow* (pp. 223–240). Lexington Books D. C. Health & Co.

Freeman, G. H., & Halton, J. H. (1951). Note on exact treatment of contingency, goodness of fit and other problems of significance. *Biometrika*, *38*(1–2), 141–149. https://doi.org/10.1093/biomet/38.1-2.141

Hassan, Z. A., Schattner, P., & Mazza, D. (2006). "Doing A pilot study: Why is it essential?". *Malaysian Family Physician*, *1*(2–3), 70–73. https://www.ncbi.nlm.nih.gov/pmc/articles/PMC4453116/

Helmer, O., & Rescher, N. (1959). On the epistemology of the inexact sciences. *Management Science*, *6*(1), 25–52. doi:10.1287/mnsc.6.1.25

Hill, P. D., DeBackere, K., & Kavanaugh, K. L. (2008). The parental experience of pregnancy after perinatal loss. *Journal of Obstetric, Gynecologic, & Neonatal Nursing*, *37*(5), 525–537. https://doi.org/10.1111/j.1552-6909.2008.00275.x

Holloway, K. (2006). *Giving a name to the pain of losing a child.* https://www.npr.org/templates/story/story.php?storyId=5511147

Hutti, M. H. (1992). Parents' perceptions of the miscarriage experience. *Death Studies*, *16*(5), 401–415. https://doi.org/10 1080/07481189208252588

Hutti, M. H., Myers, J., Hall, L. A., Polivka, B. J., White, S., Hill, J., & McGrew Grisanti, M. (2017). Predicting grief intensity after recent perinatal loss. *Journal of Psychosomatic Research*, *101*, 128–134. https://doi.org/10.1016/j.jpsychores.2017.07.016

Jaffe, J. (2017). Reproductive trauma: Psychotherapy for pregnancy loss and infertility clients from a reproductive story perspective. *Psychotherapy*, *54*(4), 380–385. https://doi.org/10.1037/pst0000125

Jorm, A. F. (2015). Using the Delphi expert consensus method in mental health research. *Australian & New Zealand Journal of Psychiatry*, *49*(10), 887–897. https://doi.org/10.1177/0004867415600891

Kersting, A., & Wagner, B. (2012). Complicated grief after perinatal loss. *Dialogues in Clinical Neuroscience*, *14*(2), 187–194. https://www.ncbi.nlm.nih.gov/pmc/articles/PMC3384447/

Koopmans, L., Wilson, T., Cacciatore, J., & Flenady, V. (2013). Support for mothers, fathers and families after perinatal death. *The Cochrane Database of Systematic Reviews*, *6*, CD000452. https://doi.org/10.1002/14651858.CD000452.pub3

Layne, L. L. (2006). Pregnancy and infant loss support: A new, feminist, American patient movement? *Social Sciences and Medicine*, *62*(3), 602–613. https://doi.org/10.1016/j.socscimed.2005.06.019.

Leon, I. G. (2017). Empathic psychotherapy for pregnancy termination for fetal anomaly. *Psychotherapy*, *54*(4), 394–399. https://doi.org/10.1037/pst0000124

MacDorman, M. F., & Gregory, E. C. W. (2015). Fetal and perinatal mortality: United States, 2013. *National Vital Statistics Reports*, *6*(8), 1–24. Hyattsville, MD: National Center for Health Statistics. https://www.cdc.gov/nchs/data/nvsr/nvsr64/nvsr64_08.pdfhttps://pubmed.ncbi.nlm.nih.gov/26222771/

MacDorman, M. F., & Kirmeyer, S. (2009). The challenge of fetal mortality. *NCHS Data Brief*, *16*, 1–8. https://www.cdc.gov/nchs/data/databriefs/db16.pdf

March of Dimes. 2017. Miscarriage. Retrieved August 23, 2019, from https://www.marchofdimes.org/complications/miscarriage.aspx

Markin, R. D. (2017). An introduction to the special section on psychotherapy for pregnancy loss: Review of issues, clinical applications, and future research direction. *Psychotherapy*, *54* (4), 367–372. https://doi.org/10.1037/pst0000122

Midland, D., & Limbo, R. (2004). *RTS coordinator training manual* (5th ed.). Gundersen Lutheran Medical Foundation, Inc.

Mize, L. K. (2003). Relationships between women in families: Voices of chivalry. In L. B. Silverstein & T. J. Goodrich (Eds.), *Feminist family therapy: Empowerment in social context.* (pp. 121–133). American Psychological Association.

O'Leary, J. M., & Henke, L. (2017). Therapeutic educational support for families pregnant after loss (PAL): A continued bond/attachment perspective. *Psychotherapy*, *54*(4), 386–393. https://doi.org/10.1037/pst0000130.

Polit, D.F. & Beck, C.T. (2017). *Nursing research: Generating and assessing evidence for nursing practice* (10th ed.). Philadelphia: Wolters Kluwer Health. https://doi.org/10.1016/j.iccn.2015.01.005

Rosenblatt, P. C. (2016). *Parent grief: Narratives of loss and relationship*. Routledge.

Share Pregnancy & Infant Loss Support. (2015). *Parent's grief.* http://nationalshare.org/wp-content/uploads/2018/04/FAQs-on-GriefParents.pdf

Skulmoski, G. J., Hartman, F. T., & Krahn, J. (2007). The Delphi method for graduate research. *Journal of Information Technology Education, 6*, 1–21.

Wagstaff, J., & Teska, J. (2018). *Parental bereavement and grief.* Cinahl Information Systems.

Wenzel, A. (2017). Cognitive behavioral therapy for pregnancy loss. *Psychotherapy, 54*(4), 400–405. https://doi.org/10.1037/pst0000132

World Health Organization. (2006) . *Neonatal and perinatal mortality: Country, regional and global estimates.* WHO Library.

Yates, D., Moore, D., & McCabe, G. (1999). *The Practice of Statistics* (1st ed.). W.H. Freeman.

Index

Note: **Bold** page numbers refer to tables and *italic* page numbers refer to figures.